LARRY FORMATO
DANGEROUS WAYS

Many thanks to Robin Formato;
Patty Hagens;
Dawn Wickkiser; Deborah Seretis;
Jay V. Surgent;
and my children, Sonny, Christian,
Samantha, Nicole, Michael, Danielle;
and my sister Maria and my mother
who are always in my prayers.

Special thanks to Carson Parks and Sean Sanbeg.
Without them this book would not have been possible.

Dedicated to
Lorenzo "Red" Formato
1914 – 1975

Larry in 1966

Chapters

INTRODUCTION: THE EARLY YEARS   13

CHAPTER 1: LOOKING BACK   16

CHAPTER 2: HEATING UP   22

CHAPTER 3: BAD GUYS AND SLICK MOVES   27

CHAPTER 4: THE POSTMAN COMES JUST IN TIME   33

CHAPTER 5: THE BIG BOYS IN THE GAME   36

CHAPTER 6: THE RED ZONE   40

CHAPTER 7: DOC CAN YOU HELP ME   43

CHAPTER 8: SO YOU WANNA BE A WISE GUY   49

CHAPTER 9: BEARER IS BETTER   54

CHAPTER 10: DUMB AND DUMBER   63

CHAPTER 11: AND THE WALLS CAME TUMBLING DOWN   69

CHAPTER 12: IT'S A SMALL WORLD   74

CHAPTER 13: THE WARNING   81

CHAPTER 14: WELCOME TO CHAPTER 11   87

CHAPTER 15: THE INDIAN LEADS THE CHARGE   91

CHAPTER 16: END OF ANOTHER CHAPTER   97

CHAPTER 17: LIGHTS AND MIRRORS   105

CHAPTER 18: THE GREEK SPENDS BIG   116

CHAPTER 19: MISSING IN ACTION   138

CHAPTER 20: LITTLE DAVIE AND THE ONE-EYED COCKSUCKER   145

CHAPTER 21: THE TROUBLE WITH BLINDER ROBINSON   148

CHAPTER 22: SIT DOWN AT PALS CABIN   150

CHAPTER 23: A TURN FOR THE WORSE   153

CHAPTER 24: THE INSIDER AND A BAD HONEYMOON   160

CHAPTER 25: WORLD WIDE VENTURES, PART TWO   168

CHAPTER 26: THE WORLD STOPS SPINNING   176

CHAPTER 27: THE TROUBLE WITH EVE   181

CHAPTER 28: THE JUGGLING ACT   187

CHAPTER 29: THE CHILLING EFFECT   191

CHAPTER 30: THE TAKE DOWN   199

CHAPTER 31: THE WAY OUT   208

CHAPTER 32: THEY NEVER LET GO   224

CHAPTER 33: THE FINAL CURTAIN   229

EPILOGUE   231

"Rat"   234

Congressional Testimony   235

"I needed the protection and I needed the strength of organized crime
and they needed me… they needed me to be a money machine,
and that is just what I was, and that is what I became; a money machine."

"…this circle dominates by fear and by power.
We not only tell stockbrokers what to sell, we tell them what price
to sell the stocks for. We tell them whether to go up or whether to go down."

"…when they didn't do what they were told to do, they were scared
into doing what they were told to do. If they wanted to sell a stock for their
customers, if we didn't want them to sell,
they weren't allowed to sell."

"Take away the name white-collar crime,
because this is one of the dirtiest businesses there is.
I know from a first-hand basis that behind the suits and ties,
there are a lot of real nasty people."

"Some way or another, one form or another, organized crime
has their hand on the shoulder of someone inside
every over-the-counter brokerage firm that is making
any kind of money in the industry."

Lorenzo "Larry" Formato, Congressional Testimony, Sept 7, 1989

"…you, this morning, have leveled a blistering, scalding indictment
of the entire penny stock market…"

"Mr. Formato, this has been an extraordinary piece of testimony,
which has been delivered to our subcommittee.
We thank you very much for having the courage
to appear before us today…"

"I think that there is a ring of truth to what you are saying,
and I don't think it is lost on those who serve on this committee.
You have provided an important public service here today,
and we thank you."

Congressman Edward J. Markey, Massachusetts

INTRODUCTION: THE EARLY YEARS

I liked fighting, and fighting every day was a way of life for me. My father told me if there is more than one kid, pick up a stick and make the odds even. At seven years old, I was the only white kid still living on North 17th Street in East Orange, New Jersey. I had no fear.

As summer of 1958 came, my father wanted to take my mother to visit her brothers in California. Being the youngest of four kids, it was a tight squeeze getting all six of us into the car. However, our long trip ended one thousand miles in. I became seriously sick, so my father decided to turn around and get me home. I was almost eight years old and I had come down with rheumatic fever, and back then if you had this sickness, your life expectancy was very short. If you were lucky, you might make it to fifteen. One of the main things it does is it attack your heart.

My parents thought I was dying. My mother told me later that my father spent his nights praying in the hospital chapel. I spent two years pretty much confined to a hospital bed, and when I was finally allowed to go out, I couldn't go run and play like the rest of the kids. I kept getting sick.

My mother eventually took me to Canada to visit St. Anne's Cathedral. Like so many before us, my mother and I climbed each step on our knees praying for a miracle. I can remember looking up from the bottom of those steps, and they seemed to reach to heaven. When we reached the top, there were many crutches and braces left from people whose prayers were answered. The Lord must have listened to my mother that day, because I never had rheumatic fever or suffered any after effects from it again. My mother called it a miracle—the first of many to follow in my life.

* * *

We moved to what we called "The Country" in 1961. I was a ten-year-old tough Italian kid from the city who really didn't fit in with the rest of the kids of West Caldwell, NJ, but I loved the woods, streams, and especially the fishing ponds the Country had to offer. Best of all, I had no more fights. Life was actually becoming normal for me.

Our family somehow still seemed out of place, though. We just didn't fit in. We had the oldest car in the neighborhood. I was embarrassed to ride in it when my dad would drive me to school. Still, I was happy.

I wanted to play guitar and be like Elvis Presley, but like so many families, my parents didn't have the extra money to afford luxuries, let alone a guitar. One day my Uncle Johnny, who lived with us, took me to a music store and bought me a used guitar for $10. It was an old used acoustic Silvertone guitar from Sears & Roebuck. As time went by, I met some kids down the street that had guitars, too. I watched them play and asked them to teach me how to play some songs. I knew I wanted to be famous.

*　　*　　*

As the conflict in Vietnam buzzed through the United States, the Beatles emerged with a new kind of music. I finally got an electric guitar and formed a band with my friend, Skip Halloran. We soon recorded our first record—a song I wrote one night while waiting to go to band practice. At twelve years old, I made my first record. That was 1963.

I knew I wanted to be famous. I didn't expect what I'd be famous for.

A hooded Lorenzo Formato goes before a congressional subcommittee

CHAPTER 1: LOOKING BACK

It was September 1989. I couldn't see the TV cameras or photographers, but I knew I was heading right at them. Alphie, the head United States Marshal for the district of New York, stood right next to me.

"Larry, we have to put this hood over your head. We don't want anyone taking any pictures of your face," Alphie said. "As soon as we get you inside, we will take it off."

One of the Marshals slipped the hood over my head. With Alphie guiding me through the crowd, I soon found myself sitting in front of a Congressional Subcommittee that was investigating the role of the Mafia in the penny stock market. I was considered by the Government to be the leading expert in the penny stock market, and the only one who was also connected to the mob.

Here I was again, with all the lights on me. I was center stage, but this time I wasn't playing my guitar. I was singing. In fact, some people called it ratting.

I took the Subcommittee back to 1973.

* * *

I was working in an auto-body shop, when one day an old friend, Ray Delburry, came in with a brand new red Porsche Carrera. I asked him who he stole the car from, because I couldn't believe this guy could ever own a Porsche. He told me it was his car and that he was a stockbroker. He worked in an office in Hackensack, New Jersey, for a company called Mayflower Securities—an over-the-counter brokerage firm owned by Gene Mulvahill. He was making thousands, and he had the car to prove it.

I had no idea what a stockbroker was or what they did, but it sounded important to me. I asked him to explain what he actually did. His explanation lost me, but I could taste the thousands of dollars he said he was making. I asked him if he could take me to his office, and Ray agreed to take me. I wanted to meet his boss. He must have thought I was going to buy stock from him.

I walked into the Hackensack branch office of Mayflower Securities and sat in the lobby. I looked around and counted about twenty guys in suits and ties. Some talked on phones; others sat back in their chairs and played with their nails. I was waiting to meet the manager, Mr. John Engle. After about fifteen minutes, Ray came and got me. He led me to an office all the way in the back of the building. John Engle was a man in his early forties. A bit overweight, he had a light complexion with straight blonde hair over his ears and forehead. He wore a big gold bracelet on one wrist and a gold watch on the other. I sat in front of him with my dirty work clothes on as I watched him chain-smoke cigarettes, waiting for him to get off the phone.

"Mr. Engle, I don't know what Ray does for you, but I do know if he can do it, I can do it better. Give me a shot to prove myself to you," I told him after he hung up.

"What are you doing for work now?" he asked me.

"I work in an auto-body shop."

"Do you have any sales experience?"

"Mr. Engle, I want to make more money than you. I just need a chance."

John took a chance and hired me. He told me I needed to pass a test called the Series 7 exam, given by the Securities and Exchange Commission. I assured him I could pass the test, all the time wondering in the back of my mind just how the hell I was going to do that. Hell, I cheated my way out of high school.

I was working for Justus Buick in their auto-body shop while going to high school. It was some kind of work school program for kids that were not going forward to college or were just barely making it through school, like me. My senior year was ending, and I was given a chance to go to General Motors Training Center for auto-body work. Justus Buick was going to pay for it. It was a great opportunity for me, but I failed my history class, and I needed to pass the class to get my diploma. The only way I'd get a diploma was to go to summer school and miss going to General Motors Training Center.

The summer school teacher for history, Mr. Newman, lived behind my house, and I went to see him. I told him I wanted to go to General Motors Training Center. I looked at his car; it was an old blue Ford station wagon. The paint looked terrible. I made him an offer that if he would mark down that I was in summer school every day, I would paint his car. He told me I was trying to bribe him. He said I was crazy. I begged him to do this favor for me. I just kept pleading with him until he said it's a deal, but he wanted me to do the schoolwork at night and bring it to him. I don't recall ever doing the work, but I do know I got an A for history with perfect attendance, and Mr. Newman got his car painted.

When I walked out of Mayflower Securities that day, I was done with auto-body work forever. I quit and took a job as a security guard working nights so I could earn some money while I studied for the exam. There were three Series 7 exams, and through friends of mine I was able to get copies of the three different tests, along with the answers. I had no idea which of the three tests I would have to take, so with the help of my mother, I memorized all three sets of answers. She would read me the questions every day and quiz me.

I was dead broke and could not afford to buy a suit and shoes to wear to the office. I didn't even own a car. I borrowed everything from my father, including his shirts, ties, suit and even his shoes. Every morning I would start my journey to Hackensack from West Caldwell. I would hitchhike all the way to Interstate 80, and then I would hitchhike to the Hackensack exit and walk the rest of the way to the office. Sometimes, I would get lucky and the same people would actually pick me up. No one believed that I was actually hitchhiking to work and back every day.

I asked John Engle if I could have a key to the office. I would get there at 7:00 a.m., before anyone else would arrive, and would stay until 11:00 p.m. I was the first to get there and the last to leave. The office was open Monday through Friday, but I showed up on Saturdays and Sundays, too. With no one around listening to me make calls, I was able to fine-tune a cold call pitch without having to care about what I was saying. I was embarrassed to let anyone see me come and go. I told everyone I got dropped off and picked up. I never had any money, so when the other guys went out for lunch, I always said I wasn't hungry.

John called me into his office one day.

"I don't want to embarrass you, but I noticed you have been wearing the same suit every day and you never leave the office," he said. "How do you get here and get home every day?"

I took a chance and confided in him. I told him I hitched to work and borrowed my father's suit. John just looked at me and shook his head.

"I just can't believe it. I've never seen anything like this," John said. "Go back to your desk. I will talk to you again in a minute."

He came to my desk an hour later.

"Come and take a ride with me," John said.

He took me clothes shopping. He bought me suits, ties, shirts, and shoes. Then he gave me a blue 1970 Cadillac Coupe deVille to drive to work. He told me he has never seen anyone work as hard as I did. I would cold-call from a phone book from 7:00 a.m. until 11:00 p.m., meaning I'd call people I didn't know and try to sell them something. I was good at it; I just didn't realize how good until I went out with John that day. The calls always varied based on the clients' responses, but I would start my call by saying something like this:

"Hello, my name is Larry Formato, and what I'm doing is calling people in your area who are interested in making money through investments in the stock market. Now, may I ask you, are you currently investing in the stock market?"

John told me the clothes and car were just a small bonus, and that I opened more new accounts than anyone in the whole firm. I started out by using Ray Delburry's name, since he was a registered representative, or a stockbroker, until I could pass the test. I was opening a lot of accounts and making Ray a lot of money. I took the test and was sure I failed, but I passed on my first try. I was now legal to sell stocks and very hungry to make money.

I had a lot of clients that I got right out of the phone book. I would sell whatever stock the company was paying the biggest commissions on. I had no idea what the hell I was doing, or for that matter, what any of these companies did. I sold one thousand shares to a client of a two-dollar stock and got paid $250. So, ten thousand shares to one client, or even in a day, meant I was making $2,500 a day. The more I sold, the more I made, and I just kept selling. My first month on the books, I made $25,000. I went from hitchhiking to driving a new Cadillac.

My dad was a working alcoholic, until he couldn't work anymore. He had cirrhosis of the liver. He would call my office when he wanted to get out for a beer or a drink, and he would embarrass the hell out of me by asking for Junior, because I was a junior named after him. My family called me Junior all my life. Everyone would tease and say, "Junior, your daddy wants you." It was all in fun, though. I would leave my office to go get my dad and take him out.

"Don't worry about a thing, Pop," I remember telling my father. "I'm gonna be a millionaire."

"*Dream, dream, dream,*" he would sing back with some melody he made up, and we would both laugh.

In 1974, a new firm with a new president formed when Mayflower Securities went out of business. To be honest, nothing really changed. I never even moved my desk. All they did was take the name off the windows and replace it with the new one.

I learned how to get to the top by listening at meetings, keeping my mouth shut, and getting close to Bob Brennan, the president of the new firm— First Jersey Securities. By sitting in on meetings with guys like Brennan, I learned how to structure a stock deal to get the most for both my firm and myself. Brennan offered me my own branch offices with overrides on all of my sales people. He didn't want me to move to a different firm; he wanted to keep me happy.

Brennan flew all of his top sales people to the Bahamas on a chartered jet. It was there that I met his "big hitters" as we called them: Peter Aiello, Bart Barek, Dwyer Wedvick, and Bruce Burmell. These were crazy times. I made a hundred thousand a month with Brennan. At 24 years old, I owned two houses and a Cadillac limousine. I made easy money, and all I had to do was push First Jersey's stocks to all of my clients.

The Securities and Exchange Commission started doing a little pushing of its own. They were after Brennan and some of his top guys. I would get phone calls from my salesmen wanting to know why the SEC was contacting their clients. Everyone was getting scared.

Ray Delburry & Larry Formato
1973

CHAPTER 2: HEATING UP

Bart Barek called and asked me if I wanted to get out of First Jersey. He wanted me to start a firm with him after the first of the year. I had several meetings with him discussing how much money we were going to need and what our roles would be. I had the biggest client book, so I would handle the retail end and Bart would take care of the administrative end. I finally agreed to do it. I put up $250,000 and matched Bart dollar for dollar. In 1976, I opened Excelsior Securities with him. It was located at 60 Wall Street in New York City. Even though I was now an owner of a brokerage firm, I never stopped cold calling. Always adding to my book of clients was my security, knowing I had so many clients to reach out to. I felt good. I actually owned my first brokerage firm, and what better place to be than on Wall Street?

The SEC had subpoenaed me to give sworn testimony about First Jersey Securities and Peter Aiello. They were really after Aiello and anything they could make stick against First Jersey Securities. This was the very first time I was involved with SEC investigations. I went to see Bob Brennan and Peter Aiello for advice on how to handle the SEC.

"Don't worry. They have nothing," Brennan said.

As we were talking, the SEC paid Brennan a visit to review First Jersey Records. He called Freddy Ireman, his compliance manager, and told him to bring him a check. Brennan told the investigators to wait a minute. He then wrote out a check for one million dollars and showed it to the investigators. At first, I thought he was going to try to bribe them.

"I'm giving this to my lawyers," Brennan told them. "Go ahead. Fight me."

I believe at that time, Robert Brennan had a bigger budget than the SEC did.

The SEC subpoena asked for all my records including my client book and phone records. I showed up at Federal Plaza in New York for what was to be depositions about Peter Aiello and First Jersey Securities. When I walked in the room, there was a table with a microphone and a stenographer. Across from me were three investigators with the SEC. They were not pleased when I showed up with no records and I took the fifth to every question they asked me. I was convinced that day the SEC added my name to their list of people to go after.

Excelsior Securities was doing its first initial public offering, or IPO, called Levin Computer. We offered units at four dollars with each unit consisting of one share of common stock and two warrants convertible into common stock at $4.75 and $5. Levin Computer was a successful IPO, and after the stock opened, it continued to trade around the $4 range. As good as things were going for me in business, they were going really bad for me at home. I was having personal problems with my first wife and had to leave Excelsior Securities and the securities business. Without my buying power to support Levin Computer, the stock price fell to five cents. It was a big blow to Excelsior and to my clients, but it seemed as though everything was going to be okay at Excelsior, even without me.

*   *   *

My first wife hated that I was in bands, and her jealousy kept me from going out to perform. Music was my passion. With my first wife out of the picture and a much stronger voice, I was back to writing some good songs. I thought I would go back to music and revisit the career I left for her when I received a call from Bruce Burmell, another big hitter from First Jersey Securities. He wanted me to meet his partner, Don Messenger. They wanted to open a brokerage firm in New Jersey.

In my year away from the business, I missed the rush of doing deals. Don and Bruce gave me another reason to leave my music behind me. They didn't have any capital, so I put the money together to start the firm. I was excited to get back in the game. We started a consulting company called DLB Financial Corp. until we could either apply and get our own Broker-Dealer License or buy an existing one. DLB stood for Don, Larry, and Bruce.

What Italian kid from the streets doesn't know how to shoot pool? There's no doubt I could. Luckily, the owner of a bar I used to hustle pool in had a brother who wanted to retire from the brokerage business, and he owned a brokerage firm that we could buy. I negotiated the deal, and we purchased A.L. Williamson & Co. We opened our new offices in West Caldwell, NJ. How ironic that my high school was in West Caldwell. I wanted a completely new change, but I felt happy about my life and the new firm. I celebrated by going on a shopping spree.

I loved buying clothes, maybe because I never could when I was younger. I also loved cars and boats. With my new brokerage firm came a new wardrobe of suits, ties, shirts, and shoes. Of course, I got new jewelry, cars, a boat, and even a new girlfriend, Glenda, who my sister Maria introduced me to on my 26th birthday. Glenda was a beauty at 5'5", 110 pounds. She had long brown silky hair with a great smile and a cute, sexy little body. Life was feeling pretty good again. Maria worked for me, and believe me, she made sure I was treating Glenda right.

I was on top of the world. I had assembled a sales team that I had personally picked, and we started out with about twenty-four brokers, all hungry to make money. It was up to me to keep these guys selling all the time. I would sit and teach them how to open new accounts and how to get a client to stop whatever they were doing and listen to the next big deal to hit the stock market. Most of all, I would teach them how to make the client say yes.

Don Messenger had a friend by the name of Johnny Formicola, who was a stock promoter. Johnny was doing a deal called Piggy's Pizza in Bergen County, NJ. He needed money for the deal. Don convinced me to lend Johnny the money because he was also involved in a deal out in Kansas City called Buchman Electronics. Buchman was an over-the-counter penny stock trading in the pink sheets. Its president was Tony Antonucchi. Don and Johnny had made a commitment to Tony to raise three million dollars in a secondary offering for Buchman Electronics at $3.00 per share. Bruce could help some with the buying. He was a big producer at First Jersey, but he lost most of his clients through First Jersey deals. I was really the only one with enough buying power to do a three million dollar deal. I didn't bring in Buchman to A.L. Williamson. Buchman wasn't my deal. This was Don's deal that he needed to make good on, making it A.L. Williamson's first deal as well. I wanted it to be a good one.

I took an interest in a start-up company in Arizona. It was an electric car company headed by Bob Keebler. I really liked the idea of electric cars, and Keebler had a great story I could tell my investors to get him the money he needed. He needed seed money to keep his company going until I could do an IPO. I agreed to help him, and I raised the seed money he needed. Bruce Babbitt, the Governor of Arizona at the time, was a friend of Keebler.

Babbitt called and invited me to come to Arizona to play golf with him. I didn't know how to play golf, but I figured, "How hard could it be?" I had my sister Patty, who was now working for me as a secretary, call a client of mine who owned a golf range so I could go for a couple of quick lessons on how to hit the ball. Just a few days before leaving, I started to notice some activity in Levin Computer. The stock had started moving up slowly. I thought this was strange because I had most of the stock in my customers' accounts. I called Bart Barek, my ex-partner at Excelsior Securities. He made me an offer of two dollars for all the stock and warrants I could get my hands on. Bart Barek knew something and he was not going to share it with me. I knew something too—there was going to be a big stock play with Levin Computer.

I called all my clients and bought all their units from them at two dollars. I then stripped the warrants, which means to separate them as a unit. I converted all the warrants into common stock by paying the conversion price set on the warrants when the IPO was first completed. I started selling the shares into the market, and I found no resistance to my selling. I knew there was a big deal going down.

The day I left for Arizona, Levin Computer announced it struck a deal to supply the casinos in New Jersey with computers. The stock was flying and so was I—on a plane to Arizona. When I left New Jersey, it was 78 degrees. When I landed in Phoenix, it was 115 degrees. I was dying. I wanted to be on the phone knowing what was going on with Levin Computer, so when I got to the first hole, I told the governor I had to go back. It was just too hot for me. I went back to the clubhouse and went straight to the payphone. I sold out of my whole position of Levin Computer, netting myself a profit of about one million dollars.

Bob Keebler, Larry Formato, Bruce Babbitt & Ralph Watkins

CHAPTER 3: BAD GUYS AND SLICK MOVES

It's somewhat strange how you meet people, and sometimes it's easy to mistake what type of a person you're meeting. John Tobin fits into this category.

Tobin came to our firm to do some carpentry work. We got to talking, and he wanted to invest ten thousand dollars without losing it. I had him put the money directly into A.L. Williamson and guaranteed him a profit. What I didn't know about John at the time was that he was a Vietnam Vet with many kills under his belt. He was also a big pot smuggler.

Tobin was a tough guy and we became good friends. I was reading a book about a guy named Mack Bolin who was after the Mob for killing his wife. This guy Mack Bolin was a low-key guy and he traveled in a van he called his battlewagon. Well this character reminded me so much of John Tobin that I started calling John Tobin, "Mack." He even drove a van that I called his "battlewagon." If you met John Tobin, or Joe Bags as his underworld buddies knew him, you would never suspect him of being a stone cold killer.

Johnny Formicola had a guy around him called Big Jim. He was a high school coach and one of Johnny's investors. I heard through the grapevine that he was also a connected guy. Although I only met him once during this time, I knew I didn't like him. I heard he and Don Messenger had problems with each other over money.

I recruited another big hitter by the name of John Patten. I never liked John Patten, but he and Don became good friends. I brought in a money guy from New York, Richard Lyle Cannon. I really liked this guy. He drove an old Rolls Royce, and I had just purchased a 1951 Bentley. We would talk about people and old cars, and he always had great stories to tell me.

The new year was coming; 1978 had been a good year. Richard Lyle Cannon, on my recommendation, invested fifty thousand dollars in our firm, and Don Messenger and John Patten started doing deals with him behind my back. When I found out about it, I told them I wanted them to buy me out. I sold my fifty percent of A.L. Williamson to Don Messenger and John Patten.

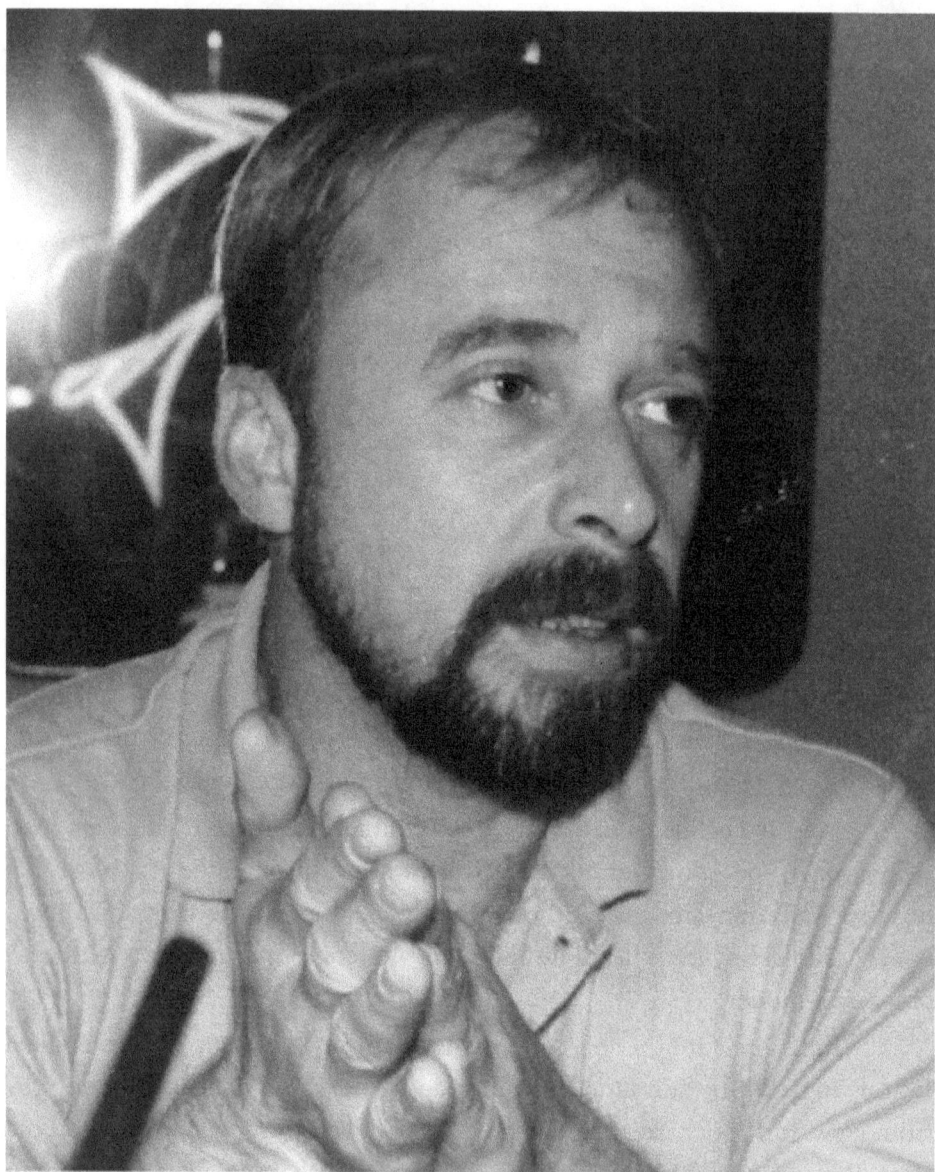

John Tobin

I opened a Financial Consulting Firm, keeping the name of the company that I started with D.L.B. Financial Corp. Dwyer Q. Wedvick was one of the best salesmen I have ever known. After First Jersey Securities went out of business, Dwyer went to work for Peter Aiello. Dwyer was Peter's top producer. I became friends with Dwyer after meeting him in the Bahamas with some of the other big hitters from First Jersey Securities.

Dwyer called me and told me Peter Aiello wanted to talk. I told Dwyer to put him on the phone. Peter pitched me on taking over a Member Firm—a brokerage firm with a seat on the New York Stock Exchange. Peter wanted me to be his partner. I told him to meet with me to go over the details of the takeover.

I met with Peter and Norman Rothstein, a stock promoter and friend of Peter's. The deal that they offered me was pretty simple. The name of the Firm was Ross Stebbins. I didn't need to put up any money for my share in the company. Peter needed me to sell the stock that he and Norman were getting from the owner of a public company, and my investment would be my retail buying that I would bring to the table. In other words, my clients would be buying this stock. The stock was trading around one dollar, and they wanted to move the stock up to ten dollars.

It was another energy company. I would handle the sales force, and we would retail all the stock that Peter and Norman had received out to the public. I would get a piece of the firm and split the commission on the stock. It was a generous offer to me, and I figured I would earn, not counting the money from the brokerage firm, somewhere around a half a million dollars. I checked out the firm and I decided I would take the offer.

I have had partners before this deal, and I understood the word partner, but with Peter Aiello, he wanted to be the boss. I stopped working for other people a long time ago. Peter and I had many disagreements on how to handle our Sales Reps, and he was becoming very bossy towards me. I really wasn't getting along that well with him. It may have been an ego problem between us. I'm not sure, but I backed out of the deal shortly after starting with Ross Stebbins. My name never showed on any paperwork that I was an owner, or going to be an owner of Ross Stebbins, so it was easy for me to walk away. Peter was pissed at me for quitting.

"You're your own fucking man and so am I," I told him. "I don't take fucking orders from anyone, and I don't work for you."

I never received one penny from the sales I generated, and I had no desire to talk with Peter Aiello again.

A few months later, I was talking to Dwyer Wedvick from my office in Parsippany, NJ. I told Dwyer I was working on a new deal in New Jersey. It was a Gas-Ahol Company (Gas-Ahol is a mixture of gasoline and alcohol) they were involved with the purchasing of the old Rheingold Beer Brewery in Orange, NJ. I also told him I was thinking of opening another brokerage firm. Dwyer wanted to leave Peter Aiello and come to work for me, but he was afraid of how Peter would react to the news. Top Producers are the life of a firm, and Peter wasn't going be happy about me stealing Dwyer from him. I knew I was going to have a problem with Peter, but I needed Dwyer for my new firm. I figured Peter would eventually get over it.

The Gas-Ahol deal was starting to look exciting and was getting some attention from the newspapers in New Jersey. I knew this would help me to raise the seed money that was needed to get the deal off the ground. I had problems with some of the guys that were working for that company. They seemed a little too desperate and put pressure on me for money. I really didn't trust them. I just didn't have a good feeling about them.

They wanted me to come with a fifty thousand dollar certified check to show I was serious about the deal. I was not ready to give these guys fifty thousand dollars, and I have a rule about not putting my own money into a deal. I knew this could be a good deal, but they wanted to see the money to know I was real. I told them I would get a certified check from my bank for the fifty grand, but I would not turn it over to them. I would show them a certified check made out to their company to prove they were dealing with a real guy.

I wrote a check to their company for fifty dollars and I had it certified. I wrote the check with all the letters and numbers spaced apart, including the date, so when the teller looked at the check she would think that is just the way I write. The teller stamped CERTIFIED across the check, and then I wrote the word "thousand" between the words fifty and dollars. I also added zeros to change it from $50 to $50,000. Now I had a fifty thousand dollar certified check made out to the company, and I only paid fifty dollars for it. When I flashed that check, I knew I was in the deal to stay.

When Dwyer left Peter's company to come to work for me, Peter's reaction was a lot worse than what I expected. He called my office and told my secretary, my sister Maria, he was going to send people to my office to kill me and everyone else in the office. John Tobin was now working with me every day doing deals and supplying seed money for our deals from his friends in the pot business. He wanted to go see Peter.

I called my cousin, John "Big John" Formato. John made friends with some Wise Guys in Jersey and was an intimidating guy himself. I told him what was happening, and he said he was going to call Peter. Peter set a meeting for the next day to be held at Peter's office in New York. I felt very confident that my cousin John and John Tobin would scare the hell out of Aiello and straighten this all out. The following day, I couldn't help but wonder what the expression on Aiello's face looked like when Big John told him if he ever calls my office and threatens anyone again, he is going to come and throw him out the window.

It was 4:00 p.m. when they came back to my office. Big John was visibly upset. He told me he needed to get to Newark to meet someone and get permission to use a name. Aiello called a guy named Johnny Fats, who turned out to be his brother in law. Fats came on really strong with Big John and said he was with the Chin. He told Big John he better be in Little Italy the next day for a sit down, and he better show up. Big John told me Aiello was a connected guy and that the Chin is a Boss. A fucking Boss. Here I was thinking Aiello was gonna to be worried when my guys showed up, and instead, Aiello had me worried now.

Tobin wanted to go and just take them all out. Tobin would have thought nothing of going into the city late at night and setting bombs every few houses. He would have blown a whole city block away, along with Fats and all his guys, but you just don't do that with Wise Guys. You don't even show up with a gun at a sit down. Big John couldn't reach out to anyone that day. They would be going to a sit down with no one to back them up from the Wise Guy world. He had no choice but to show up the next day.

I rode with them into the city that morning and waited around the block from the meeting place. Without talking to me, it was decided that if I would pay Aiello thirty thousand dollars for taking Dwyer away from him, there would be no more threatening phone calls, and all would be forgiven. I was pissed to hear that I had to pay that kind of money, but I was very relieved that we were all not going to be killed. Tobin still wanted to whack them all. Me, I felt we got off easy. I mean, what the fuck? The Chin? We're not talking a Captain here. We're talking a Boss.

With Dwyer now in my camp, I began putting together a sales team for the brokerage firm I was planning on opening. My offices in Parsippany soon became too small, so I relocated the operations to new offices in Wayne, NJ. In

January of 1979, I placed an ad in the Wall Street Journal to buy a brokerage firm. It wasn't too long before I received a call from a man in Philadelphia, PA. He was looking to get out of the business, and I purchased his brokerage firm—Royer Securities. I moved the Royer Securities main office from Philadelphia, PA to Wayne, NJ.

"Big John" Formato

CHAPTER 4: THE POSTMAN COMES JUST IN TIME

Sandy Wallach was one of the biggest car dealers on Jerome Avenue in New York. He was a good friend of mine. He was the guy I went to when I wanted a car. Sandy called me and told me he just got in a Rolls Royce Silver Shadow II. I told Sandy to deliver the car to me. I wanted it. Just two months before that, I bought a Stretched Lincoln Continental Limousine. My Dad died in 1975, and in 1978, my Mom remarried. Along with the marriage came my stepbrother, Rick, who I hired as my chauffeur. I was criticized by a lot of people for the way I would spend money, especially on cars, but I always believed that money goes to money. When I had no money, I couldn't borrow five dollars. It was like I smelled or something. No one wanted anything to do with me, but when I had money, everyone wanted to be close to me. People would just offer their money up to me. I would always say, "You've got to look the part to act the part."

There is a magazine in NJ called the Want AD Press. I would buy it every week just to see the cars that were advertised for sale. There was a 1965 Buick Riviera advertised for sale, and I called about it. The guy who owned the car told me it was a one-owner, and it just needed some paint work, but other than that it was in excellent condition. I made an appointment to meet him halfway and see the car.

My stepbrother Rick drove me to see the car. I loved it, and I bought it. Mark Sherman, the owner of the car, needed a ride back to where he lived. Mark rode home with me in my limo. On the way to his house, he told me he worked for the post office. I have always taught all my sales people that everyone you meet is a potential new client. It could be at a baseball game or the person sitting next you. Maybe even behind you or in front of you. Anyone could be a client—even the postman sitting next to me.

Mark Sherman asked me what I do for a living. I told him I owned a stock brokerage firm. I told him I make markets in certain stocks, for short-term gains for my clients. He asked me how much money he would need to invest. I told you should never invest what you can't afford to lose. I always loved that line.

"What if I gave you fifty thousand dollars to start with? Would that be enough?" Mark asked me.

This guy just sold me some old car because it used too much gas, I thought. He lives in an apartment building and works for the post office. He cannot be for real.

"Most of the clients I handle usually start out with $250,000," I told him, "but because I'm buying your car and you're a good guy, I will personally handle your account."

I never believed for a second this guy was real. I just went along with him. By now, it was funny, and I could see Rick in the mirror making faces listening to me talk to Mark about making pennies into dollars. I really had him going—almost as much as he had me and Rick going.

"If you write me a check for fifty grand, I will show you how the inside of the stock market operates," I said.

"When we get to my apartment, I'll write the check," Mark said.

Mark's apartment had an old recliner and an old TV in the living room. That was it.

This guy is just plain crazy, I thought.

"Who should I write the check out to?" Mark asked me.

"If you don't mind, just write it out to me," I said.

I was sure this was one check that would never clear. My stepbrother kept making faces behind Mark's back, making motions like he was crazy. Several times, I all but laughed in Mark's face. Mark said he'd like to visit my offices. Then, he said something that convinced me that he was totally nuts.

"You know, kid, I like you. You must be a pretty smart guy. Why don't I just write you a check for a hundred grand now, and when I see you in your office, I might give you a few hundred more," Mark said.

So, here I am in this guy's apartment. He doesn't know me for more than one hour, and he wants to write a personal check made out to me for one hundred thousand dollars. I had some strange things happen to me, but would you believe a guy who worked in a post office and lived in a dumpy apartment offered me almost half a million dollars?

I called his bluff. I told him to come to my office in the beginning of the week, and after the check clears, we could talk about some of my deals I may want to put him in. There was no way I thought that check would be good. Rick and I laughed all the way back to the postman/millionaire's car.

Mark Sherman, a postman from Westfield, New Jersey, was real, and his check was good. Mark Sherman became my go-to guy. When I needed big money, he was my guy. Mark's father was an executive for a big insurance company. His family was very wealthy. His father, before he died, gave Mark and his brother portfolios of all Blue Chip Stocks and Bonds. His father made the two of them millionaires.

When I met Mark Sherman, he was a timid, almost introverted, kinda guy. Mark could have lived anywhere he wanted to. He could have the finest of things, but instead he lived the life of a pauper. He told me he thought what I did was exciting. He liked all the action. Mark wanted to get closer to me and take a bigger role in some of my deals. Here was a guy who became so obsessed with making money that he would think of nothing else except making money.

He would call me and say, "What do you think about this deal?" or "What do you think about that deal?" He was always coming up with some crazy ideas on making money. I really got to like Mark as time went on. It wasn't just the money. I really felt bad for him, because he was alone and he would never spend a penny. I would tell him, go buy yourself a new car or some clothes. His answer was always the same: "I'll think about it." Mark Sherman liked me so much he turned his entire portfolio over to me.

CHAPTER 5: THE BIG BOYS IN THE GAME

Malcolm Cannon, who was freelancing as a public relations man, was actually just another stock promoter. He would bring deals to me every so often. It was Malcolm who brought me the Popeye's Chicken deal. Royer Securities made good money as a co-underwriter and as part of that selling group for that IPO. Royer Securities was starting to build a name for itself on the street.

A.L. Williamson, however, wasn't doing so well. They had capital problems, and Don Messenger and John Patten split up. Don took on a new partner, Grover McConnell. John Patten opened his own brokerage firm, Patten Securities.

Don asked me if I would be interested in taking over his sales force and the A.L. Williamson offices in West Caldwell, NJ. Don's plan was for Royer Securities to buy some of the stocks that A.L. Williamson had been buried in. This would free up some capital for Williamson and allow them to stay in business. Royer Securities would retail the stocks through its clientele base. In effect, it would cost me nothing to take over the Williamson operation.

The biggest stock promoters in the industry were calling me to do deals because I had the buying power, and I could sustain the market on a stock. Malcolm came to see me, and he told me Arnold Kimmis and Tommy Quinn (two of the most powerful penny stock promoters in the world) wanted to meet me. They made an offer to fly me and Malcolm to Las Vegas. Peter Aiello called me; he asked me if I was going to Vegas. He told me Tommy Quinn invited him out there too.

Peter wanted to do business with these guys. It would be a feather in his cap if they thought he was instrumental in bringing me on board. Peter was anxious to bury the hatchet and to get involved with me because I had built such a strong retail firm. I had a tremendous amount of buying power. He wanted to meet for dinner in Vegas to talk about making some money together. Malcolm and I arrived in Vegas about 4:00 p.m. It looked like a Who's Who in the brokerage business. I went to my suite to take a shower and change before meeting anyone. The message light on the phone in my suite was blinking. I checked with the front desk and there was a message to call Tommy Quinn in his room when I arrived.

Tommy Quinn was a guy in his early fifties. He looked a little like Paul Newman, with graying hair, and you could tell he took care of himself. He was in good shape for his age. He also was a disbarred lawyer who turned stock promoter for the Wise Guys. He was protected by Matty the Horse, a Captain in the Genovese crime family. Everyone knew he was connected. I called Tommy, and he wanted to know if I would like to join him for dinner. I was a little surprised when he asked me if I thought Malcolm would mind if he didn't come with me. He was smart and he wanted a private conversation. That way, there could be no witnesses to what was being said.

Tommy Quinn was all business, no small talk, and straight to the point of why he paid for me to come to Vegas. El Dorado Gold was the deal. Royer Securities would be the Underwriter for the IPO. Tommy would send me a list of clients who were to get the stock, and how many shares they were going to buy. These clients were only to buy EL Dorado Gold, and nothing else. I would get paid the Underwriter's fee, even though they were Tommy's clients buying the stock. The idea was to put all Tommy's people in the stock at the initial offering price, and I, of course, would be allotted shares to put some of my close people (family and friends) in too. All these people are called insiders. When the deal opened and started trading, the first ones in were the first ones out. That's where my retail force came into play. I would supply the buying to cover the selling. So the stock wouldn't go down until all of our people were out of the stock at a profit. After that, we would let the other Market Makers get in the game. We would then sell into their buying.

The IPO price was set at a dime. We would open the stock at fifty cents and move it to a dollar, based on the buying. All the insiders were out between fifty cents and a dollar, and everyone in the deal makes money. Well, that was a no brainier for me. I was all in on that deal.

Tommy also talked to me about making markets for him and his partner on other stocks they had an interest in. He told me I could get some free shares, and if not free, then certainly very cheap. Tommy made a point of telling me that he and his partner could make me a lot of money, but if I tried to screw them by back dooring the stock, there would be serious repercussions. (Back dooring is having another firm selling the stock so it doesn't look like it is you doing the selling.) I wanted to play his game, and I was making my debut into the major league of penny stocks with the biggest guys in the business.

A lot of guys go to Vegas for business, broads, and gambling. Me, as soon as I finished my business, I was outta there. Peter Aiello tracked me down before I boarded my plane to go home. He had an oil and gas deal that he needed retail help in—Centurion Oil and Gas. Peter wanted to move the stock from two dollars to six dollars per share. He had one hundred thousand shares that could be bought for two dollars. He said if I do the buying to move the stock up and support it at the six-dollar price, he would split the profit with me on the one hundred thousand shares. I agreed to do it.

When I got back to my office, I had my trader start making a market in Centurion Oil and Gas. I started moving the stock up. Through my buying, we took the stock to six dollars, as I agreed with Peter. After expenses, I figured Peter owed me four hundred thousand dollars. Peter was saying someone screwed him, and he didn't have the money. I told him this is something he is going to have to straighten out soon. I really wanted to tell him to go fuck himself and that he better have my money, but I learned my lesson about fucking around with this guy. He was connected—he had the Chin.

Arnold Kimmis was known only as Charlie to brokers and people in the business. I was one of the few people who knew his real name. I went to Florida to meet with him. I was excited because this man was a legend. He wheeled millions of dollars and controlled many brokerage firms. Kimmis owned a beautiful condo on the top floor in the Jockey Club. Kimmis' bodyguards greeted me at the door. His place was huge. It was like a palace, decorated with the best things money could buy. He had a game room with a regulation-size billiard table and about 30 arcade games.

Kimmis came out of a room in a black and gold smoking jacket. He looked like Jack Palance. His features were bold and his hair was black with a tinge of grey on the sides. He looked like money. A really beautiful woman accompanied him. He invited me into another room. He had his maid make us some coffee. There was a man there with watches and other jewelry on a table for Kimmis to buy. I just about fell over when the guy pulled out diamonds, not one smaller than one carat. I had never seen that many diamonds at one time.

Arnold Kimmis was all about money, and I was there because we were making money together. Things were going well. They were so well in fact, that

Kimmis told me he was going to put four more deals like EL Dorado Gold through my firm.

I had a great time with Kimmis listening to how he was doing his deals and hearing him on the phone talking to people. I was in awe. As I was leaving that day, Kimmis gave me an envelope with one million dollars in Bearer Bonds. It was my share of the side profits we had made together over the last two months, making 1980 look like another good year. I was 29 years old and holding a million dollars, and I was on my way back to Royer Securities where I held the world in my hands.

CHAPTER 6: THE RED ZONE

"Do you remember a friend of Johnny Formicola's named Big Jim?" Don Messenger asked me on the phone one morning.

"Yeah, I think so," I said. "He's the high school football coach who moonlights as a bookie and a strong arm guy."

They didn't call him Big Jim for no reason. He was about 6'4, 250 pounds, and balding. He had always worn sweat pants and sneakers with a baggy shirt and a thick gold rope chain around his neck.

"Yeah, well, I have a big problem with him over money."

"You are always having problems with that guy over money."

"We owe Big Jim twenty thousand dollars."

"We?" I asked him, outraged. "Who's we, Tonto?"

"Listen, Big Jim is putting in a claim from the Buchman Electronics deal we did a few years ago."

"Have Big Jim call me."

I wanted to find out for myself what Big Jim was talking about. He showed up at my office unannounced and wanted to see me. I had my secretary show him in. Big Jim wasted no time with small talk. He really came on like some tough guy demanding twenty thousand dollars. I only met this guy like one time before this, and here he is, in my office, telling me I owed him twenty grand from, like, three years ago.

Don Messenger and his buddy, Johnny Formicola, supposedly promised him the money from A.L. Williamson if he brought in buying on the Buchman Electronics deal. I mean, this guy was playing it up with me, telling me that because I owned a part of A.L. Williamson, I was responsible to pay him. I told him I didn't know what the hell he was talking about and that I had no knowledge of any such deal, not to mention I did most of the buying in Buchman. He told me if I didn't pay him by the end of the week, then he was going to start charging vig (vig is a word that Wise Guys use for interest). I told him I would get back to him.

After he left, I called my cousin, Big John. I told him about this guy, and he said he would take me to see someone who could help me with Big Jim. I met John in the morning and we drove to Orange, NJ. John took me to a drycleaners. We went inside and walked behind the counter into a back room where someone sat waiting for us. His name was Daniel Cecere, but people knew him as "Red." Red was about seventy years old—a little guy about five-foot-five. He had slicked back red hair and a coffee cake face. John introduced me to Red, and Red got really pissed off at John.

"I told you never bring any legitimate guys around here," Red said, pointing his finger at John and staring right through him.

Red then turned to me, lighting up a Kent 100 and inhaling deeply.

"What's your problem?" Red asked.

I tried to explain but he cut me off.

"Who the fuck is this Big Jim?" he asked me. "Where's he from? Do you owe him the money?"

"I don't owe him anything," I said. "This guy is just trying to extort some money out of me."

"Next time he calls or comes to see you, you tell him to go fuck himself," Red said. "Tell him, 'You're with me.'"

Red shook my hand.

"It was nice meeting you. If he gives you anymore problems, you tell John," Red said. "And remember," he emphasized, "make sure you tell him to go fuck himself."

I was walking out of there wondering what the fuck just happened. What the fuck am I doing? Should I really tell Big Jim to go fuck himself? I mean, that really takes balls to say that to a guy like him. I felt like this could be even more trouble for me, but I felt strongly that Red would not give me bad advice.

"Who was that guy?" I asked John as we left the drycleaners.

"He's a big, big man," John said. "Red is the toughest man I know, and he's one hell of a guy. He's a made guy. He's the real deal. He comes from the old days of prohibition, and he was part of the Original New Jersey Mob. He started as a bootlegger and worked his way up."

"What do you mean he worked his way up? So, I have nothing to worry about? Are you sure?"

"Do you realize that he just gave you permission to use his name? Do you realize how strong that is? What that means?"

"No, I really don't," I admitted.

"It means no one can ever fuck with you."

I still wasn't sure what that really meant.

I had a confidence I didn't have before. When Big Jim called, I told him, I went to see a friend of mine from Orange, and my friend said to tell you to go fuck yourself. I wasn't going to mention Red's name over the phone, and I guess Big Jim was smart enough not to ask. Word travels fast in the Wise Guy world, and when someone started making inquiries in Orange about me, they got the word I was with Red. I was now connected.

I had a contact at the Engelhard Mint, and I purchased a very rare solid gold coin. I met with my cousin John and asked him to give the coin to Red for helping me with the Big Jim problem. That was the last time I ever heard from Big Jim, and almost a year had passed before I talked to Red again.

CHAPTER 7: DOC CAN YOU HELP ME

I was driving to my offices on Bloomfield Avenue in West Caldwell. I stopped at the dry cleaner's in a shopping center, and I noticed a large space for rent. I had the idea to move my offices from the office complex we were in to this space in the shopping center. It was there that I built a show place.

From the custom made desk and furniture to the plush carpeting, it dripped with money. Stock symbols scrolled across the front window for all the people to see. Out front, there was a lineup of cars, from my Rolls Royce to a Mercedes Benz alongside expensive sports cars and limousines. Royer Securities was all about money, and that's the image people perceived. There was nothing like it in New Jersey. It was like a mini casino, except you would gamble on stocks instead of cards or dice.

I learned from Bob Brennan to always treat my sales people well. My private office was all glass. I could see out into my bullpen—the area where my sales people sat. Sometimes, on a Friday afternoon, I would send my secretary to the bank to get one hundred dollar bills. Depending on what mood I was in, or how good of a week we had, I would tape anywhere from five thousand to thirty thousand dollars to my office windows. I would then challenge my sales people to out-sell me for one hour. The one who could out-sell me got to keep the money. I never let anyone beat me, but who ever came in second place was always the money winner. During that selling frenzy, my sales people would sell so much stock in that hour that it never really cost me anything. In fact, most of the time, I made money doing it.

I just had my Cadillac Convertible restored, and one of my sales people loved it. I gave him fifty thousand shares of a one-dollar stock I had in inventory. I then offered him $250 for every thousand shares he sold. If he sold all fifty thousand shares in less than one week, I would give him the Cadillac Convertible as a bonus on top of his commissions. This kid sold the whole position out in one day, and he got the car. I would give my sales people anything they asked me for as long as they were selling stock. If they were not producing, there was always someone else to take their seat.

I never liked recruiting from other brokerage firms. Sales people who already had their Series 7 license were already used up or spoiled. I wanted new people right off the street. It didn't matter to me what they did before, as long as they were hungry, greedy, and had no conscience. If they were good and could open new accounts, they stayed. If not, right out the door they went. The first thing I would make them do was make a list of all their family, friends, and anyone else they thought might buy stock from them. After they did that, then I would make everyone cold call straight from the phone books. I would give referrals to the people who were opening up accounts. If you opened up ten accounts, I would give you two existing clients of Royer. To the ones who were not opening accounts, I would give them the line, "Maybe you should try another profession."

I was kidding with Dwyer Wedvick one day. I bet him a thousand dollars that I could go to a doctor's office and come out of there with an account. The bet was on. I made several appointments with psychiatrists. I told them I was suffering from guilt because people thought I was some kind of Wall Street wizard and that all my stock deals always make money. But I never had enough room in my deals for all my accounts, and some of my clients got angry when they can't get in on a new deal of mine. So I felt guilty that I couldn't get them all in. I was three for three. Out of the three psychiatrists I went to see, they all promised me that they would help me to get past these feelings of guilt that were causing me so much anxiety. All I had to do was say, "Doc, if you can help me, I'll let you in on all my deals." Needless to say, Dwyer lost the bet. I was a thousand dollars richer.

Dwyer now had a new way to get big clients. Dwyer pulled this routine on a psychiatrist in Connecticut, Dr. Phillip Katz. I have met some greedy guys in my time, but Dr. Katz is right on the top of the list. I owned a big home on the top of a mountain in Roxbury, NJ. In the front were two big brick pillars with security cameras on top of them. Engraved in the pillars were my initials. There were big iron gates preventing unwanted guests from coming up the long driveway. In the back of this California style ranch was a huge heated in-ground swimming pool, and beyond the pool, about fifty yards, were evergreen trees. I had them trimmed so when you walked through them, it was like walking through a winding tunnel. I spent close to two hundred thousand dollars just on the landscaping.

I helped Dwyer land his big fish. Dwyer invited Katz to come to NJ. He wanted to get Katz to see our firm's operation and meet the President of Royer Securities. I took Katz to my racket ball club in my limo for lunch. Before we drove away, I made sure he got a good look at my Rolls Royce. I think I said something like, "We could take my Rolls, but we will be more comfortable in the limo."

After lunch, we took a ride to my home. I had just spent a little over a hundred thousand remodeling my basement. It had a sauna and a big Jacuzzi with a tunnel leading to the pool. We sat in the Jacuzzi and talked about the market and how much money he could make. After dinner, we took a swim. Dwyer and I landed that big fish. Dwyer was going to get help with his anxiety, and for his trouble, Dr. Katz gave Royer Securities a million dollar account. I can't tell you how many doctors my sales people pulled that routine on. It was like the flood gates opened, and doctors were moving their accounts from Oppenheimer, Merrill Lynch, Shearson, and other big board firms to Royer Securities.

Daniel "Red" Cecere

Larry and his Rolls Royce

Larry and Jose,
(Jose got the Cadillac Convertible as a bonus.)

CHAPTER 8: SO YOU WANNA BE A WISE GUY

I learned a lot from those early years at Mayflower Securities and First Jersey Securities. Now, eight years later in 1981, I was rich, young, and considered by many to be the smartest guy in the penny stock game. I had no partners, and I owned the most successful over-the-counter stock brokerage firm in the country.

One morning, I remember being really busy when my cousin, Big John, came to see me. I was a little annoyed and short with him.

"John, I wish you would have called me to tell me you were coming," I said. "I really don't have any fucking time right now."

"Well my man, this is one time that you have to make time," Big John said. "There's someone outside who wants to talk to you."

"Well, tell him to come in, but I don't have a lot of time right now."

"The guy won't fucking come in. You have to go out. He said, 'If you like doing what the fuck you do every day, you better come outside now.'"

"This better be fucking important," I said, giving Big John a look. "Who the fuck is out there? And why the fuck can't they come in?"

I went to the door, pushing it open as hard as I could—just to show whoever was out there how mad I was. When I saw who was out there, I did a Jackie Gleason imitation—humina, humina, humina.

Holy shit. It was him. Red stepped out of the car.

"Let's take a walk," he said.

I just about shit my pants. Here was the Wise Guy, the fucking gangster, who saved my ass with Big Jim, and now we're walking in a shopping center together.

He wrapped his arm around mine and pulled me closer to him as we walked.

"I've been keeping a close watch on you," Red told me. "I've watched some of your deals and the people you're doing them with. I can help you with some people, like Tommy Quinn's guys."

I wondered how he knew about Tommy Quinn, and I was sure he was referring to Matty the Horse.

"You're a smart kid," Red continued. "You keep your nose clean. People like you. Now these people you do business with will fear you too. You'll have all of my protection. No one will fuck with you, and if they do, then I take care of it. That's my job.

"You have money, but you don't have power. With me, you'll have more money and all the power you could ever dream of. You will own all of these jerk-offs."

I knew with Red's power behind me, I could take over all the penny stock deals. We could be huge. I knew that everyone who wanted a deal done would need to come through me, or they would deal with Red.

"Think about it," Red said. "I'll be in touch in a couple of days."

It was pretty clear to me Red was making his move.

"I'm only gonna say this once. You're getting bigger. There are people taking notice of what you've done. Some guys may want to move in on you. They'll try to take and take from you, but with me, I will be your partner. I will make sure no jerk-offs come around. It won't take long for everyone to know you own the Street.

Red was sharp. He was even referring to Wall Street now as the Street, and we will share it together.

"Think about it."

Think about it. That's what the man said. Do I really want to be partners with the Wise Guys? Is that what I'm supposed to think about? I did think about it quite a bit. I mean, how could you not think about it? I heard stories about people getting mixed up with the mob. Once they get you, they don't let go.

I thought about what Red said about the power I could have and all the control it could bring me on Wall Street. Oh yeah, I thought about it. I had a lot of questions for Red, and I anxiously awaited his phone call. I was on some ego trip back then. Could you blame me? I wasn't even thirty and I was a millionaire. I owned houses, cars, and jewelry. I had a great business, and now I'm going into a partnership with the Wise Guys. With Red's help, I would own the whole over-the-counter penny stock market. We would get paid from everyone wanting to do business, or else.

A couple of days later, my secretary told me someone was on the phone. She said they wouldn't give their name to her.

"I'm supposed to tell you it's your friend," She said.

My heart started racing. I knew it was Red. I answered the phone.

"Do you know who this is?" Red asked me.

"Yes," I said.

"Meet me in Pine Brook in a half hour at the new Italian restaurant, Bella Vita. I'm already waiting, so leave now."

The phone went dead.

Leave now. I never just jump. What did I know back then? I finished some things around the office, and then I left. I walked in and Red looked at his watch. I told Red I was busy and had to finish a few things before leaving. I could tell he wasn't happy that it took me so long to get there, but he never said anything else about it. I sat down at his table, and we both ordered coffee.

"So, how's the business going?" Red asked, pulling a Kent 100 from its pack and lighting it. "Anyone giving you any trouble? Anyone owe you anything?"

"Things are going good," I said. "The only guy that owes me money right now is Peter Aiello."

Red took a sip of his coffee.

"Who's Peter Aiello?" he asked.

"There's nothing we can do about him. He's with the Chin."

I was so naïve back then that I didn't even know the Chin was the Boss of the Genovese crime family—the same family Red belonged to and the same family I was a proposed member of.

"How do you know that name?" Red asked, putting his coffee down.

I told Red the story of when I took Dwyer Wedvick from Peter a few years ago. I told him about Johnny Fats and the sit down on Mulberry Street in New York.

"How much money does Peter owe you?" Red asked.

"I did a deal with Peter. I figure he owes me about four hundred thousand dollars," I said. "But Peter said he got screwed and didn't have the money to pay me."

Red never said another word about Peter.

"You need to listen to me now," he said. "You need to pay attention to the things I tell you. You better not fucking lie to me—ever. I want to know what deals you're doing ahead of time, because if anyone wants to make a beef, I can say I knew about the deal."

I thought Red was a cool guy. I liked the way he talked to me. He was super intelligent, and I could tell he liked me too.

"Well, I don't know what can be talked about. Is there such a thing as a bad question?" I asked him.

"You can ask me anything," Red said. "How else are you going to know if you don't ask?"

"I don't want to be disrespectful, but you're an older guy. What do I do if something happens to you? I trust you, but I don't know these other people."

"They're all the same, including you now. If something were to happen to me, someone else will take my place. My crew is made up of mostly older guys like me—real nice fellas. The strength comes straight from the top. The Boss has the strength, and everyone under him shares it. That's why it's a family. So even if you are a low-level guy in the family, you have the strength of the whole family, straight from the Boss on down."

Including you now, I thought. That's what he said. Holy fuck, I think he just said I'm in.

Red was a high-ranking member in the Genovese Crime Family. He had a reputation, and even Wise Guys feared him. If Red wanted you dead, you were dead. Red just finished doing ten years for extorting some guy named Saperstein. Saperstein was trading options overseas and Red backed him with some money. He tried to screw Red out of the money. A guy in the crew, an enforcer for Red named Lenny Macalusso, caught up with Saperstein. It was in a hotel in NYC. He held him out the window by his feet. That was his first warning for Saperstein to pay what he owed Red. Eventually, Saperstein went to the cops. He filed charges against Red. Red was convicted and sent to jail, and Saperstein died of rat poisoning.

After that day, Red would call, and I would go to meet him. The first few meetings were at different places. I was always late. I remember this one time, Red looked at his watch when I walked in. He was pissed. I learned quickly why people feared him.

"Don't you ever keep me fucking waiting again, do you understand me?" Red warned.

Red was serious, and I knew it. He had had it with my excuses and the "I'm a busy guy" story. We agreed that Pals Cabin in West Orange would be our regular meeting place unless Red changed it.

Red started schooling me about Wise Guys. We would spend hours together talking, all the time I was learning more and more about how they work and how they think. He taught me what I could do and what I couldn't do. I listened very carefully to everything Red was telling me. I was learning how to be a Wise Guy. I was being schooled by the best.

I was Red's guy. He was grooming me, and he was going to make sure I could do no wrong. I was like a son to Red, and Red was like a father to me. I loved Red, and I loved our meetings. Red would talk to me and tell me stories about himself and people he knew. Stories about real life gangsters and some of the things they did.

One story in particular scared the crap out of me. I'll never forget it. It was about a guy that ratted on some of Red's friends. For revenge, Red and another man kidnapped this guy. They took him to an old house in the basement and beat the shit out of him. Then they tied him to a table and ripped his shirt open.

"This is what we do to rats," Red told the guy.

They had a big live rat that they didn't feed. It was hungry and they scared it. They picked the rat up and put it on the guy's stomach. They taped a bowl over the rat and put heat on the bowl. As the bowl got hotter, the scared rat had one way to escape—to chew his way out.

I never asked Red what happened to that guy. I just came to my own conclusions. Red told me he was going to start to introduce me around to some of "our friends." He wanted people to get to know me. He let everyone know I was to be treated with respect. I was now in the crew, and Red told me that he was going to move me up fast.

"We need a guy like you," Red told me. "I never want you to get in trouble, and you have to stay legitimate. That means stay clean, and make sure you don't get fucked up. "

With my friend Red as my sponsor, I was becoming a Wise Guy.

CHAPTER 9: BEARER IS BETTER

The deals were getting bigger, and the profits were too. Morton Christianson was from Utah. He had a mining company, but it wasn't trading at the time. He needed a brokerage firm to file a 15c2-11 with the SEC. He wanted to get the stock in the mining company to trade in the pink sheets. I met with Morton and Abe Glass. Abe was a stock promoter working for Morton. I told them I would help them get their company trading. My fee would be heavy. I wanted half of all the free trading stock they had, and I wanted a fifty thousand dollar consulting fee up front.

Royer was making markets in about thirty penny stocks at the time. This stock was going to be easy for me, because Morton, Abe, and Royer closely held all the shares. I could make the market (the price of the stock) anything I wanted it to be. Abe told me this was his last deal because he had lung cancer. He wanted a big score so his wife would have something when he was gone.

They were planning to spend a lot of money on promotion for the company. They thought they could generate enough buying in their company so they could sell all of their shares. Abe never made it long enough to finish the deal. He died shortly after we started making a market in the stock. Right when Abe died, Morton Christianson got into trouble for something else unrelated to what we were doing and went into hiding. So, I wound up with all the shares in a worthless mining company that Royer was making a market in.

Sandy Long was a lady that I had purchased some homes from. We were kind of like friends. She asked me if I would teach her son the securities business. Kenny Long, a nice kid, did a little too much coke, but he would do anything I asked him to do.

I was looking for a way to take some cash out of my company. I didn't want to report it to the IRS. Kenny's grandfather lived in Connecticut. He was in his ninety's. I knew the IRS would never bother someone that old. By the time they caught up with him, he would be long dead. Kenny's grandfather was perfect for what I needed to do. I devised a plan to have Kenny go see his grandfather. He would bring the shares of this worthless mining company with him. Kenny would then have his grandfather open an account at Merrill Lynch using these shares.

The way stocks trade in the pink sheets is very simple: The trading

A Special Report on Loan Swindle

Venture

June 1981

$1.75

The Magazine for Entrepreneurs

How to Make Partnerships Work

New Businesses: Live Music Clubs,
Speech Recognition

New This Month:
The Active Investor,
Venture Strategies

Building
Million-Dollar
Homes on
Speculation

Stefan Bittenbinder
$3 Million-Home Builder

55

New Issues
Using Regional Underwriters

Pressed to raise public capital, many young companies are
learning to love regional brokers and their best-efforts offerings

By Jerry Buckley

As the new issues boom continues, many entrepreneurs planning to take their companies public have discovered that their search for an underwriter need not go beyond their own backyard.

Although the trend is not a new one, dozens of regional broker-dealers around the country are playing a major role in taking companies public. And while some entrepreneurs lament being turned down

Larry Formato of Rover Securities: bringing Wall St. to West Caldwell

by the likes of Hambrecht & Quist and Kidder, Peabody & Co., others are discovering that there are advantages to be had with a small, regional underwriter. "It's the boutique approach that makes regional underwriters attractive," says an executive at National Assn. of Securities Dealers. "The smaller firm is more likely to pay closer attention to the client," the executive adds.

During 1980, regional broker-dealers accounted for 59 of the total 237 new issues offerings. Those offerings represented $703 million of the total $1.4 million raised in new issues, according to *Going Public: The IPO Reporter*, prepared by Howard & Co., Philadelphia.

Perhaps the most important thing a national underwriter can bring to a new issue is credibility. When a nationally known investment banker or securities firm underwrites a new issue, on a "firm-commitment" basis, it agrees to purchase all the shares offered by the company, guaranteeing the entrepreneur the proceeds of the offering. Frequently, however, smaller regional broker-dealers are neither willing nor able to meet net capital requirements imposed by the SEC and cannot assume the risk in selling out an issue for a small, local company. As a result, many of the smaller stock issues are handled on a "best-efforts" basis.

In a best-efforts offering, an underwriter sells shares of a company's stock to subscribers and places the money he receives in an escrow account until the targeted amount of capital is raised. When checks covering the minimum amount have cleared, the funds are released to the company, less commissions. If the target isn't reached by a deadline, the offering ends and subscribers are returned their money.

While there are several appealing advantages of the best-efforts offering for the underwriter, there are a few drawbacks for the entrepreneur. For one thing, the issue usually does not sell out nearly as quickly as a "firm-commitment" underwriting, which means a delay until the company receives the capital it needs.

But frequently the best-efforts offering can work to the advantage of both entrepreneur and broker-dealer.

"I would have loved a firm commitment, but that wasn't possible," says John Moran, 41, who raised $2 million last August in a best-efforts offering that only took a few days to complete. Moran says he began scouting around Denver for an underwriter a few years ago to finance his startup oil and gas exploration firm, American Frontier Exploration. At one brokerage firm, Moran met Darryl Gammill, a securities analyst who wanted to start his own brokerage.

The two men kept in touch and, after Gammill founded G.S. Omni in Sept., 1979, began working out the details of the American Frontier offering, Omni's first. While Moran says he could probably have found other, established firms to

take his business public on a best-efforts basis, he wanted to stick with Gammill. "I knew that the success of his firm depended in large part on what he did with his first offering." Omni sold 16 million shares at 20¢ a share in 1 million 10-share units, lining up most of the 1,100 shareholders in advance to speed the sale.

For an entrepreneur in search of an underwriter, Gammill advises, "Look for someone who knows your industry. Look for one that doesn't have a backlog of underwritings so that yours doesn't end up on the back burner. Also look for an underwriter who, when you ask and say you want to raise $6 million, says, 'Sure, come right down and sign a letter of agreement.' That indicates that the underwriter is not doing what the investor would want him to do, namely, check out the company."

Finally, Gammill says, an entrepreneur should be sure the underwriter has an adequate staff to handle the offering. He says a back-office support staff, while the most glamorous aspect of the underwriting, can be crucial to determining success or failure of the new issue.

In addition to the administrative functions a broker-dealer has to handle as underwriter, there is the more difficult job of maintaining interest in a stock after the offering has been completed. Unlike the national wire-houses, which have dozens of analysts following companies within an industry on a daily basis, smaller regional firms frequently can devote the resources necessary to keep a firm in the public eye by distributing frequent research reports.

Many brokerage retailers who resisted the underwriting business two years ago, when the new issues boom was beginning, are now actively underwriting public offerings. One of them, American Western Securities, a Denver brokerage firm, took three firms public in 1979. Last year, it was the lead underwriter for six new issues and already has eight new offerings on its calendar so far this year.

"Everybody is getting on the bandwagon," says Karen Hazeltine, a spokeswoman for American Western, a firm which handles mostly technology and oil and gas exploration issues.

American Western recently took part

'I would have loved a firm commitment, but that wasn't possible,' says Moran, who raised $2 million in a best-efforts offering

lic Energy Dynamics International, a Boulder, Colo.-based manufacturer of heating and electrical equipment, raising $2.336 million and selling 4,675,000 at 50¢ each. The offering, which began Feb. 24, did not reach the minimum goal until March 23.

Like many other regional broker-dealers, American Western charges standard 10% commission for acting as lead underwriter.

Drawn to the public capital markets by high interest rates that often bar small and new firms from borrowing, the spate of tiny firms hoping to float public offerings has fueled the underwriting business around the country. Royer Securities, West Caldwell, N.J., is another brokerage firm with major plans for new issues underwriting.

Since Royer was bought in 1979 by Larry Formato, a 30-year-old former sales manager for a New York brokerage firm, it has handled one new issue, put in motion two others, and plans to underwrite 10 to 15 more in the next year.

"We have our own niche here," says Formato. "There's plenty to go around." Royer has 10 registered brokers and expects to increase the staff soon.

Royer's first new issue underwriting since Formato moved the firm from Philadelphia to Northern New Jersey is Cartrak Systems, a Norwalk, Conn., used-car locating service for auto dealers. Cartrak, founded two-and-a-half years ago by John G. Arbour, a 51-year-old former principal of a regional brokerage firm, hoped at presstime to raise a minimum of $400,000. Arbour says he would have liked a major underwriter to do a firm-commitment offering, but is happy with Royer. "We came to the conclusion that no big firm would touch such

a small offering, particularly for a start-up," he says.

In Arizona, where there aren't nearly as many broker-dealers as in Denver, or New York's metropolitan area, Anthony Investments in Phoenix is planning to help young sunbelt firms raise capital. Anthony Silverman, who owns the firm, moved from Minneapolis 10 years ago after 10 years as a broker in Minnesota.

Silverman predicts Phoenix will become one of the leading centers of new issues offerings in the coming years and he too cites the economy as one main reason. "How are companies going to get financing," he asks, "go to a bank and borrow at 22% interest? What company can pay that rate of return?" In the next few months, Anthony Investments hopes to take public 10 companies, including medical products companies, an energy concern, and three gold mines.

While he is waiting for the gold mines to beat a path to his door, Silverman is spending his time now helping some slightly more prosaic companies raise money. At presstime, Silverman's firm was slated to handle an offering for Procom Systems, a maker of computer systems to raise about $500,000. ∎

Filing To Go Public

These companies have filed with the Securities & Exchange Commission for their first public offering.

Source: Going Public—The IPO Reporter (1528 Walnut St., Suite 802D, Philadelphia, Pa. 19102)

Filing Date	Company	Business	Price Per Share/ Total Offering	Latest Year Revenues/ Net Earnings (Loss)	Underwriter
2/9/81	Communications International Ltd., dba Telemail, Salt Lake City, Utah	Package pickup and delivery service	$3.5/$2,025,000	$383,706/$44,592	Andie Securities Corp. New York, N.Y.
2/10/81	Wallfor Telecommunications Corp., Plainview, N.Y.	Marketing and engineering consulting services	$2.50/$1,750,000	$296,561/$93,152	Kruger, Wunderlich & Co. Cedarhurst, N.Y.
2/17/81	Cyber Diagnostics Inc. Denver, Colo.	Markets a system to test lung functions	$1/$3,300,000	$364,400/($460,403)	John Muir & Co. New York, N.Y.
2/18/81	Centrex Laboratories Portland, Me.	Manufactures medical diagnostic tests	$9.25/$4,625,000	$2,537,797/$273,362	Rooney, Pace Inc. New York, N.Y.
2/23/81	MTI Inc. Chaska, Minn.	Manufactures custom-designed optoelectronic components	$9.50/$1,125,000	$6,545,623/$666,316	Dain Bosworth Inc. Minneapolis, Minn.
2/24/81	Photovoltaics Inc. Miami, Fla.	Will design and install photovoltaic systems	75¢/$375,000	None/($13,000)	Offered by company
2/27/81	Dimola Micro Systems Cupertino, Calif.	Manufactures disk drives and micro computers	$1.25/$12,000,000	$38,200,672/$934,821	Montgomery Securities San Francisco, Calif.
2/27/81	Gasonics Geophysical Co. Midland, Tex.	Acquisition and processing of seismic data	$13/$6,305,000	$11,186,000/$1,841,000	Rotan Mosle Inc. Houston, Tex.
2/27/81	FFA Cable Systems Inc. Boston, Mass.	Manufactures specialized cables and cable assemblies	$12/$6,026,880	$39,633,780/$1,690,486	Warburg Paribas Becker Inc. New York, N.Y.
3/3/81	Interferon Sciences Inc. New Brunswick, N.J.	Produces interferon	$10/$10,000,000	None/None	Oxford Securities New York, N.Y.
3/3/81	Interton Data Systems Corp. Farmington, N.Y.	Manufactures disk storage for computers	$25/$12,500,000	$13,591,353/$3,203,100	Bear, Stearns & Co. New York, N.Y.

57

room gets the pink sheets—adequately named after the color paper they're printed on. The name of the company, the name of the brokerage firm, and the brokerage firm's phone number that's making the market are printed in alphabetical order. Also, there is no price listed for buying or selling. So if you want a price on a stock in the pink sheets, you have to be a brokerage firm. You have to actually look the stock up in the pink sheets and call the market makers for a quote. The bid is what you are willing to pay for the stock, and the offer is what you are willing to sell the stock for if you are the market maker.

As a market maker, if you want the stock, you become the high bidder. If you want to sell the stock, you become the low offer. A market maker has a bid price and an offer price, and the difference between the bid and the offer is called the spread. The broker gets his commission from the spread.

I had my trader at Royer make the market for the mining company. He was told to give a quote of three dollars offer and zero bid. However, when Merrill Lynch called for a quote on that stock, they were told just the opposite—a three-dollar bid with no offer.

My plan was going to work. I was going to sell all of this worthless stock to my own company for three dollars per share. Royer Securities was going to buy every share from Merrill Lynch. Kenny's grandfather would get the check from Merrill Lynch and cash it. Kenny would bring me back the cash. I would have all the cash, tax-free. Royer bought one hundred thousand shares of this stock for three dollars per share.

Kenny had a hell of a hard time getting the bank to cash that check. He told the bank he was calling his lawyers, so he asked them to dial the number. I knew the call would be coming. The number they dialed was to my private line. I pretended to be a lawyer.

"As unusual as it may seem for someone to want that much cash," I told the banker, "it is not against the law. My client would be happy to fill out any tax forms that are required. It is very illegal for you not to cash the check, so I hope we don't need to go any further with this matter. And please don't keep my client waiting any longer than he needs to. He's an older man."

The bank needed time to order the money. They didn't keep that much in their safe. In no time at all, Kenny was on a plane home with the cash. He was thirty thousand dollars richer for his trouble. I got all that cash out of Royer without it being traced back to me. Now Royer had one hundred thousand shares of a worthless three-dollar stock in their trading account. I put a five-dollar price on the stock and told my brokers it was a new deal. There was a one-dollar spread on the stock, so I gave them a one-dollar commission on every share they sold. The market was made at four dollars bid, five dollars offer. In a couple of days, Royer's clients owned all the shares at five dollars, and Royer netted one hundred thousand dollars.

I could see the cars in the shopping center from where I sat in my office at Royer Securities. I noticed a Limousine pulling up. Malcolm Cannon told me we had an appointment with a guy from the west coast on some time-share deal. I guessed this was the guy in the Limo. I liked his style already.

David Wellington looked like a west coast guy. He was tall and slender with blondish colored hair. His deal was called Data Force. It was a very cool deal. Data Force owned, or at least said they owned, timeshared hotels in the Cayman Islands and other resort places around the world. I looked up Data Force in the pink sheets. I was amazed at all the brokerage firms making a market in Data Force, especially all the big board firms. It is almost impossible to get a firm like Merrill Lynch or Shearson to make a market in a penny stock. There were over twenty companies making a market for Data Force. The stock was trading around two bucks.

What made this stock so cool was that David Wellington had ten million shares of free trading stock in bearer form. This means anyone who held the certificates in their possession owned them, making them payable to the bearer. I had never seen stock issued in bearer form before, and I questioned Wellington on how he got away with doing that. He said he had set up Data Force as a Foreign Corporation, and that all the shares landed off shore, making it legal to issue them that way. I didn't know if he was right or wrong, but it sounded pretty damn good to me.

"I want you in my camp," Wellington told me.

"I might do business with you, but I don't join camps anymore," I said.

"Listen, I want Royer to take the lead in making a market for Data Force."

"How'd you get all of the big board firms to make a market in the stock?"

"I made a deal with a guy by the name of Pete Gattini," Wellington explained. "Pete was making the market at Oppenhiemer for Data Force. He got the other big board firms to come into the deal."

Malcolm was hot for the Data Force deal. I liked it too.

Wellington invited me into the city for dinner, but I passed. I told him I had other plans. I didn't want him to think that I would jump all over this deal so easily. I asked Wellington how long he would be in town for, and I suggested we get back together before he leaves. Wellington told me he had ten million shares in bearer form. I believed I could get half of them from Wellington if I played my cards right.

Wellington called me the next day. He wanted to test the waters with me. He asked me if I could do him a favor.

"I want you to buy one hundred and fifty thousand shares of Data Force from Pete Gattini at one and three-quarters," Wellington said.

"That's some fucking favor," I said.

"I'll buy it back the next day from you at two."

I was going to put up almost three hundred thousand dollars for this guy, and we haven't even made a deal yet.

"That's a big favor," I told him. "It's going to cost you. Don't take kindness for weakness, David. I don't want to get fucked. If you don't take the stock back by 1:00 p.m., I'm going to hit the street with it, and I'll hold you responsible for any of my losses."

Hit the street, bang the bids, or whatever you want to call it means to sell the whole position, pushing the price down.

"I'll be in to see you before one," he assured me. "I'm a man of my word."

The next day, he called me right around 10:00 a.m. and asked if he could stop by. I told him I would be waiting for him. It was around noon when he showed up with some people. One of them was Lisa Loring, a soap opera actress, and she was stunning. I liked her, and Wellington hooked us up. He was smiling and happy. He asked me if we could talk privately, so I went into another office with him.

"How would you like a couple million dollars?" Wellington asked.

"That would be nice," I said. "Is it a present?"

Wellington handed me one million shares of Data Force—two million bucks, at least. But to Wellington, it was just paper.

"This is your payment upfront if you take the lead and trade my stock," he stated.

I looked at him. I knew it was now or never. It was time for me to make my play for the five million shares.

"Wow, David, one million shares," I said, as humble and meek sounding as I could. "Is this my payment, upfront for taking the lead in your company?

"David, do you take me for a jerk-off?" I said, strengthening my voice. "Do you really think you can buy me with just a million shares when you have ten million?"

I threw the million shares down on a desk.

"Take your fucking stock and get the fuck out," I told him, pulling open the door.

"Larry, I didn't mean it that way. How much do you want?" Wellington said, taken aback.

"I want to be partners in the stock. I want five million shares."

"How do I know I can trust you? What if I give you the stock and you sell it? What if you don't do what you say you will do?"

"Hey look," I told him, "yesterday you asked me to do you a fucking favor. You asked me to buy one hundred and fifty thousand shares for you. On your word, I did it. And now I'm giving you my word. If I say I will do something, it will get done. I will do my part."

Wellington looked at me.

"You've got a deal," he said, shaking my hand with both of his.

David Wellington gave me five million shares of Data Force in bearer form. I put four million shares into my trading account. I showed it as a capital contribution from me. This was done for accounting purposes. I had a special place for the other one million shares.

I was still having my daily meetings with Red. I told him about the Data Force deal and David Wellington. I gave Red one million shares. I explained to him that they were in bearer form. He could give them to anyone he wanted to. I asked him not to sell more than fifty thousand shares a day into the market. I knew the market could absorb that much, but I didn't think it could take much more selling than that.

Red was really happy with our relationship. We were all making money. I called all the market makers in Data Force. I let them know that I, not Royer, had a personal interest in the Data Force deal. I wanted them to know not to try to fuck with me on this stock. If anyone tried to fuck with my market, then they were going to get fucked. That was the word I put on the street. Traders on the street knew of me, and they knew better not to fuck with me.

I pretty much had my way trading Data Force. David was after me to fly out to see him in Newport Beach, CA. He wanted to do some business there with me. I flew into John Wayne Airport in Orange County, California to meet my new partner, David Wellington.

David's house in Newport Beach was beautiful. It sat high on top of a mountain with a spectacular view. The outside was white stucco and the inside was all hard wood flooring and Spanish tiles. All of the walls were white and covered with expensive art. A white baby grand piano with a beautiful chandelier hanging over it sat in the center of the room as you entered the home.

I sat in the kitchen of this magnificent home. I watched David as he played chess against an electronic chess game while he was on the phone doing trades. The guy was really good. I liked chess too. I couldn't wait to get back home just to buy one of those new electronic games for myself. God, back then, I think they were a couple grand.

I was doing big trades for David in his personal account that he opened at Royer. On any given day, I would buy or sell for him one hundred to two hundred thousand shares of Data Force. Royer would always make a quarter on either side of the trade. What that means is, if he sold one share for one dollar, then twenty-five cents of that was Royer's commission. The same applied when he bought stock. Royer was making twenty-five thousand a trade.

Pete Gattini wanted to meet with me. I discussed meeting him with David. I needed to know how much Pete Gattini knew, if anything, about my deal with Wellington. I also wanted to know what deals David made with him. David assured me that Gattini just wanted to be part of the team. I figured it sure doesn't hurt to have Oppenhiemer in the stock. So, I decided I would meet Gattini just as soon as I returned home.

I flew with David to Las Vegas. We met with some other brokers there and worked a deal with them to buy stock in Data Force. Wellington was smooth, and between the two of us, we got them to buy a big position in Data Force. After we made the deal, Wellington gave them five thousand dollars in chips to gamble with. One of the guys said that he lived in Vegas, but he doesn't gamble.

"Well, then you have to give the chips back," I joked.

The guy was actually handing them back to Wellington when I told him I was only kidding. I pointed to the cashier's window and told him to go cash them in.

Wellington wanted to do some gambling. He ordered fifty thousand dollars in chips to be brought to the black jack table. He gave me twenty-five thousand, and we played for about three hours. We both lost all of the money. It was fast, easy money, and it spent fast.

The thought of having stock certificates in bearer form was just incredible. I mean, there were bearer bonds, but never bearer stocks. David Wellington, with my help, had pulled off a great stock deal, and everyone was buying into it.

CHAPTER 10: DUMB AND DUMBER

The summer of 1981 was great. Arnold Kimmis and Tommy Quinn were still doing deals with me. Royer Securities was the brokerage firm everyone wanted to do business with. Royer was the lead market maker for Data Force. Royer was still trading an average of one hundred to two hundred thousand shares a day.

I had my meeting with Pete Gattini. I learned that he was not an employee of Oppenheimer. He was at Oppenheimer trading for his own account. Gattini was a guy in his late thirty's—a nice enough kind of guy. He had some complaints about David Wellington. He was worried he might get burned. Gattini told me he had accounts at Oppenheimer in nominee names for Wellington. He wanted to know if Wellington paid for all of his trades with me. I told him that so far, Wellington has done everything he said he was going to do with me. Gattini had some guys he owed some favors to, and he needed some cheap stock. He wanted to know if I could sell him some. I told him I didn't have any cheap stock, and that my average cost of Data Force was about one and three quarters. I showed Gattini some of my other deals to see if he had any interest. Gattini had balls. He said he would like to buy me out of Royer. I told him he wasn't in my league. He said he had friends that were in the same league as me, and he wanted me to meet them. I declined. I told him I wasn't interested in selling.

One afternoon, I was talking to Dwyer in the front of our offices. I looked out into the parking lot and noticed a girl getting out of a car. She was wearing a dress, and she had great legs.

"I'll bet you a hundred bucks I can get her to go out with me," I told Dwyer.

The bet was on. I waited until she got a little closer, and I walked outside followed by Dwyer and a couple of the other sales guys. I called out to her, to catch her attention. I threw more lines at her than a first mate on a fishing boat. She was really nice, and God, she was beautiful.

"Do you have a job?" I asked her.

"No, but I'm looking for one," she said.

"Would you like one?"

She was laughing. I was really having fun with her, and all the guys were chiming in too.

"What do you do?" she asked me. "What would I have to do?"

"I want to make you a stockbroker," I said. "Do you want to go for a ride in my Rolls Royce?"

I had her.

I followed her into an ice cream store. It was her mother's birthday, and she was buying a birthday cake for her.

"Are you serious about a job?" she asked me.

"It's not a job. It's a career," I said. "Come into my office and let me show you around. If you want to make a lot of money, then come to work for me."

Her name was Robin. I didn't care about the bet anymore. I was going to make her mine. I was in love from the first time I looked at her. Soon after she started working for me, I invited her to dinner.

I took her in my limousine to my racket ball club where we played a game together. We went to a seafood restaurant and held hands as we came home later that night. I joked with her about her sweaty hands. We talked about a TV show called Heart to Heart. I told her that sitting in the back of this limo with her made me feel like Jonathan Heart, and that we were just like the Hearts in that TV show. I wanted her to know that life could be really great for us if we were together. I dropped her at her car, and she kissed me on my cheek. I was in love.

Things around the office were getting pretty crazy. We were making bigger trades for David Wellington. There was a firm in Salt Lake City that sold to Royer Securities four hundred thousand shares of Data Force. The trade was at two dollars per share. It was a trade that Wellington had asked me to do for him. He told me this firm needed to move some stock out of their trading account. It was the end of the month, and they needed to clean out some inventory for regulation purposes. I told Wellington we had enough of Data Force already. He promised me he would get them to buy back the four hundred thousand shares, and another four hundred thousand shares, if I would do the trade.

Mitchell Schreiber was a member of the New York Stock Exchange. They were also the firm that cleared all the trades for Royer Securities. Royer had about twelve million dollars in cash in their trading account, and they had another thirty million in stocks. Some of the stock in Royer's trading account was the original four million shares I had received from Wellington in Data Force. Wellington had asked me to sell big blocks of Data Force to four or five firms out on the West Coast. I was relieved, because I was freeing up a lot of inventory.

Sometimes, if you know who a broker is clearing through, you can go straight to his clearing firm with a trade. If that happens, the clearing firm calls and asks if you know the trade and if it is a good trade. Once in a while, a trader will not recognize a trade and he will "DK" it, meaning, "Don't know."

We got several trades from the firm in Salt Lake City that we bought that stock from. I didn't know the trades, so I rejected them.

"Do you know anything about these trades?" I asked Wellington over the phone.

"They have Royer confused with Gattini," he said. "They were supposed to sell it to him. Let me call you right back. I'll call them."

If I didn't get the right answer from Wellington when he called back, I wasn't going to fuck around. I was going to unload my whole position of Data Force smartly without bringing the price down too much and call it quits with Wellington.

"Alright, go ahead and sell them more stock in Data Force," he said. "Everything is okay."

I put through another four hundred thousand shares at over two dollars a share. Then Gattini called me.

"Do you know of anything going on with Data Force?" he asked. "There seems to be a mix up with a bunch of trades."

"I think everything is being straightened out," I told him.

"Well something isn't right here."

"I don't know who's dumber, you or that asshole in Salt Lake City. I don't have time for this bullshit. Go and talk to Wellington."

I was flying to Denver for a few days to work on another deal. I was buying out another brokerage firm. The firm had thirty branch offices around the country. Once I owned that firm, I would have enough retail power to do a ten, fifteen, or a twenty million dollar IPO.

"I wish you weren't going out of town," Wellington said. "There are a lot of unresolved trades."

"Don't worry, Dwyer will be around," I assured him. "Anything you need done, I'll make sure Dwyer does it for you."

I called Dwyer and told him if David Wellington calls while I'm gone, do whatever trades he wants done.

The owner of the firm in Salt Lake was furious that I DK'ed the trades. They were threatening to go to the SEC.

"Listen, jerk-off, go to whoever the fuck you want to go to. It was your trader who fucked up," I reminded him. "He was supposed to sell it to Oppenheimer, not to me. Go and straighten it out with David Wellington."

The following day, I was on a flight to Denver to buy the brokerage firm. This was going to cement my future in the securities business. While I was flying, I was unable to be reached for six hours. Wellington was on the phone with Dwyer. He had Dwyer buy almost thirty million shares of Data Force from different brokers around the country. Wellington was dumping his whole position in Data Force and then some. Royer Securities, as per Dwyer, was buying it. When I landed, I went straight to the phone booths as I always did when I traveled. I called the office just to check in. I talked to Dwyer and asked him how things were going.

"It's the busiest day we've ever had," he said.

"Why were we so busy?" I asked.

"I've been doing a lot of buying for David Wellington."

My stomach started to tighten.

"How much buying did we do?

Dwyer took a deep breath. The words seemed to take forever to come out of his mouth.

"Thirty million shares."

It was like an echo in my ears.

"I'll call you right back."

I dialed Wellington's house as fast as I could. His houseboy answered and said he was out of town and had no idea when he would be back. My heart was coming out of my chest. I left word for him to leave a number where I could reach him and that it was extremely important. I called Dwyer back.

"How could you be so fucking stupid?" I asked him, irate and dumbfounded. "How could you buy that much stock? What if he doesn't buy it back from us? How are we going to pay for it?"

"You told me to do whatever he wanted me to do," he said, fumbling with his words.

I went straight to the ticket counter and got the next flight back to New Jersey. That was the longest flight I ever took. I kept going over in my mind all the things that could go wrong if Wellington didn't make good on any of the trades. Yes, Dwyer was dumb. I was even dumber to tell him to listen to David Wellington. I knew Wellington would never make good on the trades. I knew he beat me. I had to act quickly to survive the financial disaster this would cost Royer Securities, as well as myself.

When I landed in Newark, my limousine was waiting for me. I couldn't wait to get in the car to use my car phone. I dialed Wellington first. I knew he wouldn't answer my call, but I had to try anyway. I called my office after my unsuccessful attempt to reach Wellington. I talked to Dwyer, who broke down how much money we needed to come up with to make all of the trades in Data Force good. Mitchell Schreiber, our clearing firm, was threatening to sell out the position of Data Force if we didn't come up with the money by the next day. I knew if Mitchell Schreiber hit the street with all of that stock, they would drive the price of Data Force down to pennies.

I called Pete Gattini and told him I had a big problem. I asked him if he heard from Wellington. I needed to talk to him, or we were going to have a huge problem with Data Force. Gattini was worried. He had a big position in the stock. He had put most of his friends and relatives in Data Force. He asked me if he could come out to my office. I wasn't sure if he was worried that I might think he had something to do with Wellington fucking me, or if he just wanted to see if he could help.

Eighty million dollars. That's a lot of money in anybody's bank account. Mitchell Schreiber wasn't going to get caught out there for that much money. Royer Securities was in big trouble, and I was too. There was no way I could come up with that much money. The writing was on the wall. Now it was just a question of how we would handle the sale of the stock. How much of the company could be saved, if any.

I must have called Wellington's house two hundred times and no answer. I really didn't want to tip my hand to Gattini. I didn't want to let him know just how bad Wellington had beaten my firm. I didn't want Gattini to panic and start selling ahead of me.

I called Mitchell Schreiber and spoke to the president of the firm. I asked him to work with me and let me handle the selling of the Data Force shares if I couldn't come up with the money by ten o'clock the next morning. I wanted to feed it into the market one hundred thousand shares at a time. Once the other market makers found out Royer Securities was selling, they would all drop their prices.

I had to find other ways to sell off this big position. I didn't want to burn another firm like Wellington burned mine. I just had to be careful once the selling started. It would only be fifteen minutes, if that, before the stock of Data Force would be pennies.

Larry at Royer Securities

CHAPTER 11: AND THE WALLS CAME TUMBLING DOWN

Stock Brokerage Firms, like banks and insurance companies, have rules and regulations. They have regulatory agencies they have to answer to. A stock brokerage firm has to comply with the rules and regulations of the Securities and Exchange Commission (SEC). They also have to comply with the National Association of Securities Dealers (NASD).

The SEC has a net capital requirement for all brokerage firms. Net capital is the amount of money the company has after all of its expenses, including furniture, rent, phones, and salary, are factored in. The minimum amount of money a brokerage firm can have is thirty thousand dollars. If a brokerage firm falls under that amount of money, after deducting all its expenses including its trading account, it is required to report immediately to the SEC and halt all trading activity.

I knew Royer Securities was out of net capital. I also knew I needed to buy time. I needed time to sell off the position of Data Force. Those were my thoughts as I fell asleep that night.

My home phone rang, waking me up from a deep sleep. It was about three o'clock in the morning. David Wellington was on the phone. He told me he was going to help me out with the problem that was created in my trading account.

"How could you fuck me this badly?" I asked him through clenched teeth.

"Larry, it's all a game," he said. "Sometimes you win, sometimes you lose."

"Well I'm not going to lose. If you want to keep living, you better make this shit right in the morning."

"Come on, Larry. You don't scare me. I mean, who do you think you are? God? I'll do my best to try to help you in the morning. There are other deals and millions we can make together."

"Yeah, David, but there's only one Royer Securities."

"Data Force is going to make an announcement right before the opening of the market. That should bring some buying into the stock. I'm meeting with my lawyers in the morning to handle the SEC and to try to keep Data Force trading. We'll try to have some damage control if you should get sold out of all the Data Force trades. Let's just hope this announcement will help out. I'll call you tomorrow."

"Wait, what the fuck do you mean you'll call me tomorrow? Do you realize you have effectively put me out of business? You have to take care of this first fucking thing in the morning."

All I wanted to do was get my hands on Wellington, but I had to be smart about it.

"Where are you now?" I asked.

"I'm back in Newport Beach," he said.

"David, I'm not going to get fucked like this. I have friends that will find you."

Wellington laughed at me.

"This isn't about friends, Larry. It's all about the money. Your friends don't scare me."

With that, he hung up the phone.

I was up and out of bed, calling the airport. I wanted to catch the first flight to Newport Beach, California. I boarded a TWA Jumbo Jet at 6:15 a.m. to go see Wellington. I called Dwyer and told him that if anyone called for me to tell them I wasn't feeling well. Tell them I would be in around noon. I didn't want anyone to know I was on my way to California. It was better if people thought I was close by.

I told Dwyer to call Mitchell Schreiber and try to hold them off for a couple of hours by telling them about the announcement Data Force was going to make. Wellington put out the announcement right at ten o'clock in the morning. As per my orders, Dwyer started selling the Data Force Stock that David Wellington buried us with. Pete Gattini and some of the other big board firms bought into our selling. It was a good thing they did, too. I think Wellington had told Gattini that he should be buying all the stock he could get. Who knows what Wellington did, but he tricked them into doing the buying. I knew, in my heart of hearts, that by the end of the day, without some miracle, Royer Securities would be put out of business. Anyone who bought Data Force was going to lose their money. These guys were bigger fools than we were. It took them quite a while to figure out that this was one big sell off. When they did figure it out, it was too late. They had already bought a ton of stock. I was going to be wherever David Wellington was. I was going to collect for what he did to me.

I landed in Orange County Airport right at 8:45 a.m. Pacific Time. I took a cab straight to Wellington's house. He was not there. I then went to his office, where his assistant and his lawyer were waiting for word from the SEC to see if they were going to stop trading on Data Force. His lawyer was typical California LA type. He had a Rolls Royce that looked almost like mine, and he was very flashy.

"This is one big mess we got ourselves into," Wellington's lawyer said. "Data Force is down to seventy-five cents from three dollars at the opening of the market this morning."

"Yeah, well it's even a bigger mess for my firm," I said. "What the fuck is David doing? Where is he?"

"He's out trying to get some buying to come into the stock. I think he flew to LA, but I'm not sure."

I knew he was covering for Wellington. I mean, what the hell? That was his job. I called my office. Dwyer told me that Mitchell Schreiber let all the stock go shortly after the announcement, and that we still don't know how much money we owe them. He told me we had twelve million in cash and maybe another thirty million in stocks in our trading account. We were going to take a big loss, but we still might come out of this with something.

I told Dwyer that Wellington ducked out on me, he was nowhere to be found, and that I'd be on the next flight home. Data Force was now down to twenty-five cents. Dwyer called me in a panic at Wellington's office.

"Gattini is here in the office. He just showed up with two other guys," Dwyer said.

"Put Gattini on the phone," I told him.

Gattini was calling me a motherfucker before he even had the phone to his ear.

"I'll be here waiting for you when you get back," Gattini threatened.

"I'm on my way back to the office," I told him. "I'll be there as fast as I can."

Gattini must have talked to Wellington, because he knew I was in California. He was acting like he was Al Capone on the phone, with motherfucker this and you cocksucker that.

"We'll straighten this out when I get back," I told him calmly. "Please wait."

I almost sounded as if I was really scared of this asshole.

"I'm not fucking going anywhere, even if I have to stay here all fucking night."

I was so fucking mad. Gattini had no idea what I was all about or what I was going to do to him for calling me a motherfucker. Gattini, and a lot of people like him, are what I call "telephone tough guys." These other guys he had with him were in for a fucking lesson too.

September 8, 1981, the stock market closed with Data Force sitting at ten cents a share. Royer Securities notified the SEC that it was voluntarily suspending trading because it was out of net capital. My limousine driver picked me up that night at Newark Airport. John Tobin (Mack Bolan) and two of his friends were waiting for me. Dwyer was with them as well.

I wanted Dwyer to give me an update of where we stood after the selling off of the Data Force stock. Gattini and his two friends were waiting for me at a bar in West Orange. I really couldn't wait to get to him. He had the fucking balls to call me a motherfucker. I lost almost fifty million dollars, and I was pissed. I figured by having John Tobin and his two friends there with me, we would send Gattini, and his tough guy attitude, back to New York in a body cast.

Dwyer informed me that, to best he could figure, we lost every dollar we had. We might owe maybe twenty or thirty thousand dollars. Dwyer couldn't be sure until he looked at all the trades. Actually, I was happy with that news. These trades started out like we might owe a few million dollars. If that was the case, our bonding company would get involved, and there would be a major investigation into the trading of Data Force. I didn't have clean hands in this deal. I took payments from David Wellington to trade Data Force stock. What the hell was I going to do when the bonding company started asking questions? Tell on myself? David Wellington knew that would never happen. Wellington knew he had beaten me, and it was a perfect game. Checkmate. David Wellington was going to get away with it—for now.

My limousine driver pulled right up to the front door of the bar. Inside the bar, I would handle Mr. Pete (telephone tough guy) Gattini and his friends. I knew the owners of the bar and the bouncers too. As soon as I walked in the door, I told one of the bouncers to make sure no one calls the cops. I warned him that someone was going to get their ass kicked, and to keep his people out of it.

I spotted Gattini talking to some girls at a table towards the back of the bar. I walked up to him, and before he could say one word, I hit him as hard as I could in the face. He fell backwards over a bar stool, and I grabbed a chair and started hitting him with it. I wasn't looking at what was taking place around me. I was too intent on beating Gattini to a pulp. I never heard the girls screaming, or noticed that the band had stopped playing. I was told one of Gattini's friends tried to grab me. He got his head split open, and was kicked half to death by John Tobin's friends. The other guy didn't do anything—he just stood there.

"We gotta get out of here," John Tobin said, pulling me off of Gattini.

I was tired and out of breath, and as we were walking towards the door, everyone moved quickly out of our way. I had Gattini's blood all over me. We all got back in the limousine, and I told my driver to get us the fuck out of there. As we were driving down the street, we saw a couple of police cars and an ambulance speeding towards the bar. Gattini came onto me like a tough guy, but he was a pussy. I showed him who the tough guy really was. He had some cuts and broken ribs, and his friend needed a few stitches. As far as I was concerned, they should have gotten a lot worse.

I spent the next few days trying to save my pride and Royer Securities. Dwyer was pretty close with his estimation of our losses. When all the smoke cleared, Royer Securities owed Mitchell Schreiber ten thousand dollars. Thirty-six million dollars in stocks and twelve million dollars in cash…it was all gone. David Wellington caused the total collapse of Royer Securities in just one day. He was very slick, and in my mind, very dead if and when I ever caught up with him.

I used up all of my remaining cash over the next two months trying to keep my doors open and to get Royer in a position to start trading again. I rented a small little office on Route 46 in Dover, New Jersey, as a backup office. I was thinking that if everything went bad and I couldn't save Royer Securities, I would work from there.

In November of 1981, I rented three 24-foot U-Haul trucks and moved my beautiful offices of Royer Securities in the middle of the night. I felt like a thief robbing my own company. Hell, I even took the plush carpeting off the floors. As I was pulling out of the parking lot, I turned my head back for one last look. There it was, just as if everything was still the same. It was forty feet long and six feet high. Royer Securities, Inc. That sign that lit up the night sky. It was my dynasty, and just like Jericho, David Wellington single-handedly tore the walls of my great company down.

CHAPTER 12: IT'S A SMALL WORLD

I remember it being really cold out this particular night. As I pulled up to Morty Burger's house, I could see Morty walking towards me with his two collie dogs. I thought to myself, there must be a better way than being out in this cold, walking those dogs. Morty also had his office in his house. I was not there for a social visit. I was looking for advice to see what I should be doing about all my losses and any SEC problems I might have arising out of Data Force. I liked Morty. He was a very cool guy most of the time, but he tried to be cool all of the time. Morty had blondish-red hair when he dyed the gray out of it. His hair was very curly. He may have even had a perm, and he kept it long in the back. He chain-smoked Tareyton Cigarettes, and he always had a glass of scotch on his desk. Morty was into music, and so was I. That, I believe, was our common ground.

After about an hour or so of talking music and general bullshit, we discussed Data Force. He felt I had nothing to worry about since I lost more money than anyone else. He then told me about a friend/client of his, Michael Gardner, who was a stock promoter. He was throwing a due diligence party for a company he was promoting. Morty wanted me to go with him, just to take a look at the company. After Morty assured me one more time that I had nothing to worry about with Data Force, I arranged to meet him the following week in New York City where the party was being held.

The party started at 4:30 p.m. right after the stock market closed. It was a perfect time to get stockbrokers together. I pulled up in my Rolls Royce to the address Morty had given me. It was a brownstone on the East Side of the city. I went inside and looked for Morty. He was talking to a heavyset balding guy on crutches. We must have seen each other at the same time. As I looked towards Morty, he stopped his conversation and began to motion for me to come to where he was standing.

Morty introduced me to the guy on the crutches, Michael Gardner. I could tell by looking at him that not only was he unhealthy physically, but he was also unhealthy in his pockets. I don't know how I know these things. I just do. Maybe it was because he was wearing an old style suit. The one shoe he was wearing wasn't polished, and his other foot and leg were in a cast. He was talking about the good ol' days—yeah, I was positive Michael Gardner was broke.

I was curious about the deal he was doing, and of course, I needed to make some money myself. I didn't think this deal could be too bad if Morty was somehow involved with it. Michael Gardner wanted me to meet some of the people he was involved with. As he was making the introductions, I recognized an old friend, Donald Sheppard. I had met Don way back in 1977 when he was doing a stock deal called Slender Wrap for his daughter's company. Don's daughter, Cheryl, was a knock out back then, and I almost did his deal just to go out with her.

"What the hell are you doing in New York?" I asked Don.

"I just moved back here from West Virginia," he said. "I was involved in a mining deal, so I decided it was best to get out of town."

The mining deal Don was working on went bad. They fudged their financials, and according to him, the feds were getting too close for comfort.

"So, you like this deal?" I asked Don.

"I think it's a winner," Don said. "I like working with Michael Gardner. He's trying to arrange for some private financing for this company."

"How much leverage do you have with him? What does this company do?"

"Dr. Sapse would be a better man to explain the company."

After a few drinks and some small talk, I listened to a presentation given by Dr. Sapse. The name of the company was Interferon Pharmaceutical, and the company claimed to have nothing short of a cure for cancer. I liked this deal. It had a lot of sizzle. I always believed you sell the sizzle, not the steak.

The party was nice. Dr. Sapse gave a great presentation, but with all of the people that were there, not one person reached for their checkbook. I made a commitment to raise fifty thousand dollars to start with. I wanted to sit down and restructure the deal.

Later that week, I met with my friend, Red. I told him all about the meeting in New York and that I was thinking about trying to do the Interferon Pharmaceutical deal. Red was still very upset over Royer Securities. He assured me he had people looking for Wellington.

Red asked me to do something for him. He told me about a guy in

Orange, New Jersey they called "The Greek." This guy owed a lot of money from gambling debts. Gyp De Carlo was a Wise Guy from New Jersey. He and Red were partners in a book making and loan sharking operation. It seems this guy, the Greek, was a degenerate gambler and owed Gyp a lot of money. It so happened, that Gyp De Carlo died suddenly from a heart attack.

The Greek, who thought he could out smart and lie his way out of the money he owed, went to see Red. He told Red that he visited with Gyp the night he died. He said he paid him in full for the bad debts. There were only two people who could say whether or not that actually did happen, and one of them was dead.

Red wanted me to meet this Greek to feel him out. He wanted me find out if there was any way we could make some money with The Greek. The Greek had some public companies. My job would be to see if we could get any money away from him. I told Red I would find a way to introduce myself to this guy. If he had any money, and if there was a way to get it, I would gladly relieve him of it.

As things sometimes go in this world, I met with Donald Sheppard and Michael Gardner one night at Gardner's apartment. It was in the lower east side of the city. I knew I was right about Gardner when I met him. He had a small apartment with a desk, a chair, and a couch. He was hardly living the life of a big time stock promoter. He had a big bowl on his desk. It was filled with Cocaine. In my life, I never used drugs. Being in music and working high profile deals, I never got involved with drugs and now, here was this guy, Michael Gardner, tooting away right in front of me. The way I looked at it, it was his house, and his life, so why should I care?

Michael was trying to make a comeback in the stock game. Some guys that weren't happy with his last stock deal threw him out a twelve-story window. The only thing that saved his life was that the building he was in was right next to another building. He was so fat he actually got wedged between the two buildings. He broke his pelvis, hips, and legs. He was in a full-body cast for some time and was only now starting to get mobile.

I was in a position again where I knew I was needed. I believed that Michael Gardner would go along with anything I wanted to do. I thought the best way to do the Interferon deal was to put Interferon Pharmaceutical into a public shell—a company that went public and either stopped trading or has little or no assets. We would pump the price of the stock up and sell off all the

George "The Greek" Livieratos

free trading stock that we controlled. Don Sheppard said he knew a guy that had a few shells, and he would set up a meeting as soon as possible. Michael Gardner agreed with me that this was the best and quickest way to do the Interferon deal.

I just about fell over when I asked Don who the guy was that had the shells.

"George Livieratos," he said. "George the Greek."

My mind was spinning with thoughts of my conversation with Red earlier in the day.

"From Orange?" I asked Don, still not believing what I just heard. "Is he from Orange? Make the appointment."

I wanted to meet the Greek. Don set it up. I went in my limousine to pick up Gardner. On the way to Orange, we picked up Don Sheppard. We went into a building on Main Street, Orange, NJ. The offices were called Embassy Realty, and George "The Greek" Livieratos was the owner.

I felt dirty from the second I walked in there. The offices were a real mess. Then I saw him. Oh my God. This guy looked like he just stepped out of 1930. He had on a black suit with wide white pin stripes and big wide lapels on his jacket. He was wearing a black shirt and a white tie, but best of all, he was wearing a big white hat with a black band around the brim. He was right out of the old gangster movies. He really looked funny and stupid. I had everything to do not to laugh in his face.

The Greek gave Don a big hug and Don introduced us. The Greek invited us into his conference room downstairs. I would later refer to that room as "the dungeon." It was dark, damp, and dirty. I didn't want to be there, but I had two really good reasons to be there—Interferon Pharmaceutical, and Red Cecere.

The Greek had a public company called Innovation International. I told him we wanted to buy it from him. I wanted him to think we were going to give him some cash, but my plan was to keep him in the deal with us. I wanted to get him to give us his free trading stock so we could buy his company with no money. I just wanted to sell off the Greek's stock and let him keep some of the money.

The Greek had his accountant, Rick Louongo, in the meeting with us. Rick was all for getting some money and running with it, but I wet the Greek's appetite by telling him about the deal. The Greek wanted in the deal. In no time at all, he was offering me his company for free. He would do anything just to work with us.

"I'm going to be your partner," the Greek said.

"I have no partners," I told him.

"All my life, I've waited for a guy like you—a guy who knew what he was doing in stocks."

"I do not take on partners. I don't need you in this deal. I would rather just give you your money, and you go your way and we go ours."

"Would you mind if I talk to the Greek privately?" Louongo asked.

"Not at all," I said.

Louongo and the Greek got up and left the room. I turned to Gardner.

"Tell the Greek you really would like to have him in the deal," I told Gardner, "Make the deal."

We were playing good guy, bad guy.

The Greek and Louongo came back into the room. The Greek insisted on staying in the deal.

"No way," I said.

"Let him stay in the deal," Gardner said. "We can all work together."

The Greek was as stupid as he looked. He fell for it. We did the deal, and we got his company for free. When we left his office, I told Gardner that when the Greek was wide-awake at his brightest moment and I was fast asleep in my deepest sleep, I was still sharper than he was.

We were all back in the game. This was the first time I was acting as a stock promoter. Dr. Sapse was out in Los Angeles. We needed to meet with him to conclude the deal. I was running low on money for the first time since 1973, and here I was, nine years later, rebuilding my life. Between the plane tickets, hotels, rental cars, and dinners, I was going broke.

The Greek joined us in LA. He was amazed with Dr. Sapse. I felt like I was at a freak show. The doctor was shooting everyone up with this Interferon. I refused to take a shot, and the doctor didn't like that. I said no to his miracle drug. I felt it served no purpose for me to be injected with it. The Greek didn't disappoint me. He showed up with the big hat and an old funny looking suit. He was really embarrassing to be around. He took his shot like a real man. Everyone was eager to have this miracle drug in their veins—except me. I knew I was going to have to put up with the Greek for some time to come. We had to finish this deal and sell his stock in the newly reorganized company. This was how we were all going to get paid.

When I returned from California, I met with Red and informed him that the deal was done. He could now put the arm on the Greek by telling him I was his friend. Red and I laughed, talking about the story with Don Sheppard and how I ran into him at the due diligence party. How later, Don told me that the guy who owned the public shell was George the Greek. I mean, what are the chances of that happening? I bet the Greek said the same thing. I would have loved to be a fly on the wall when Red showed up at the Greek's office and told him I was with him.

"The Greek was offering me more of his end of the deal than I was going to ask for," Red told me.

He must have shit his pants when Red told him he knew me.

"Why didn't you tell me you and Red are friends?" the Greek asked me over the phone. "It's a small world. He's been my partner for years. Now I really feel good about you. I know we're going to make a lot of money together. I want to meet with you as soon as you can."

In his mind, everyone was the Greek's partner. He should wish he were Red's partner.

"I'll meet with you as soon as I can free up some time," I told him.

When people asked me how we all got into the same deal, I stole the line from the Greek. It's a small world.

CHAPTER 13: THE WARNING

My office in Dover, New Jersey, was very small and overcrowded. The brokers that worked for me at Royer Securities were calling and stopping by. They wanted to know if I was going to reopen Royer. It was time for me to face the fact that Royer Securities was never going to reopen. I knew it wasn't fair to keep these guys waiting. With great reluctance, I said my goodbyes to the people that worked for me at Royer Securities.

I asked myself a million times why I just didn't open another brokerage firm. I think I was bothered by all the complaints about Data Force. It would have been easy for me to do. I mean, it's not like I haven't done it before. It would have cost me probably less than one hundred thousand dollars to open a new firm, but this Data Force thing really bothered me.

Dwyer Wedvick was still worried about the SEC. He became a bartender in East Rutherford, New Jersey. I have never to this day heard from him. I believe he thought I would blame him for the destruction of my company.

My girlfriend, Robin, stayed with me. She was the only one left from Royer Securities that was still a part of my life. I was just about out of money now and I didn't know how I was going to survive. I had to wait until my share of the money from the Interferon deal come through.

I was talking with Morty Burger, and he made a crazy suggestion to me—something I would never have thought of. He told me I should go see Michael Gardner and maybe go into business with him. I was clueless as to what Morty was talking about. He pretty much had to spell it out for me. Morty was talking about me financing Gardner in a cocaine deal. I thought to myself, what the hell. I needed to make some money really badly. I heard how fast you could make money in the drug business. Why not? I'll do it.

I never looked at it in the beginning as if I would be a drug dealer. Gardner told me we needed at least fifty thousand dollars to get started. I called a friend of mine, Marc Bateman, who was an attorney. He also did a lot of high-interest private mortgages. I told him I needed fifty grand, and I would put up my house. I needed the money right away to do the deal with Gardner. Three days later, Marc Bateman had the money for me. I converted it to cash and delivered it to Michael Gardner. I went to his apartment in NYC. Michael put together a shopping list, and we sent my girlfriend Robin right down the street to buy everything that was needed to cut the cocaine and to also buy vials to put it in.

This was kinda cool. I had never in my life been involved in anything like this before. I was spending more and more time at Gardner's apartment. I even took my guitar and amp there. I would play and sing as Gardner packaged the blow for our customers. It sure didn't take long for people to know I was in a new game. I had a new circle of friends and also some old ones too. Kenny Long, the kid who got his grandfather to sell all my worthless stock, became one of my best customers. My cousin Ralph was getting into the game too. I never did any of the drugs, but I might as well have. I was losing track of time and reality. Maybe I just didn't want to think about what happened to me at Royer Securities.

I was now carrying a .357 magnum nickel-plated Python Revolver. I had a shoulder holster for it. I would wear it everywhere. To this day, I don't know what the fuck I was thinking about. I think I might have lost my mind for a while. I went from a stockbroker to a fully-fledged, gun totin' drug dealer, and worse than that, I didn't really think there was that much wrong with doing it. All the drugs, and money, were kept at Gardner's apartment. If I wasn't there to keep an eye on him, Robin was there. Michael was using more and more cocaine. Fuck, he could consume more of that shit than anyone.

I got a call from George "The Greek" Livieratos. He had arranged a meeting with his accountant, Rick Louongo. Rick had a deal. It was a nightclub restaurant in Whippany, New Jersey called Moon Rise. It was right on Route 10 right where Route 287 intersects. It was a great location, and I was very familiar with the place when it was called "Damaio's."

The fellas that owned the place were in a big fight with Damaio. It seems that Damaio was taking them to court to regain possession of the club for non-payment of the monthly note. They weren't trying to make any money off the deal. They just didn't want to give it back to Damaio.

Louongo said the only way to stop the State Court action was to file a petition for protection in the Federal Bankruptcy Court. I thought this was just too simple, but it sounded like it would really be fun to try. The Greek wanted in. he wanted to be my partner in the club, but he had no money. Of course, I didn't need him, but I didn't want him to kill the deal with Louongo.

"We will all be happy if the plan works and we actually do buy the place," I told him.

Morty Burger gave me the name of an attorney in New Jersey. He could help me put the deal together and get the bankruptcy filed. His name was Jay V. Surgent. I called Red.

"We're going into the nightclub business," I said.

"Are you sure that's a good idea?" Red asked.

"We don't have much to lose, and if it all works out, we would all have a lot to gain."

I arranged for all the principals for the corporation of Moon Rise to meet at Jay Surgent's office in Clifton, New Jersey the following day. There was no time to waste if we were going to file the bankruptcy in Federal Court, which would put a stop to all state court actions.

I arrived at Jay Surgent's office first. I had some time to explain to him what I was doing. Jay was my kinda guy. He was tall with a good build. His hair was kinda long but not too long—just right for the times. He wore thousand dollar suits and shirts with French cuffs. I knew I could talk to him straight up, and he would get it. Jay was a get-it-done kinda guy—no fucking around. When I told him I was buying this club for five hundred dollars, he nearly fell on the floor. Jay called his partner in to meet me. I told him what I needed him to do for me. Jay's partner, Frank Passcralla, handled liquor license applications. The liquor license in New Jersey back in 1982 was worth almost three hundred thousand dollars. He was very familiar with the state law requirements. Jay and Frank both flipped out when I told them I was buying this club and putting it straight into bankruptcy. They were really cracking up over the idea.

"We would need to file a Chapter Eleven, and that would stop Damaio in his tracks," Frank said.

"Larry, are you going to keep the same name? What are you going to call the place?" Jay asked me. Rubbing his hands together up to his mouth and laughing his ass off.

I thought about it for a minute and started laughing.

"Come on, tell us what's so funny," Jay said.

I stopped laughing.

"Let's call it Chapter 11."

These two guys, my new lawyers, never encountered a guy like me before. They thought I was a little crazy. They were having a blast working with me. The principals of Moon Rise, Jimmy Hagen and Bobby Stewart, along with their friend known only as "Turk," arrived at Jay's office. We all sat down to do the transfer of stock in the cooperation.

"No one will ever believe that I purchased this place for five hundred dollars," I said.

Everyone in the room was laughing and rolling their eyes. I signed all the papers and wrote my check for the five hundred dollars. I was now officially in the nightclub business.

Jay filed the proper papers in the Federal Bankruptcy Court in Newark, New Jersey. Jay and Frank didn't mess around. Frank did my liquor license. They were two young, aggressive lawyers, and they were my heroes. Jay and I really hit it off, and I knew I could always count on him. They knew exactly what they were doing, and they dropped everything to get this all done for me. Armed with a copy of the filing, I went to the nightclub to see what kind of condition it was in. The front doors were locked and chained together. I had no patience to sit and wait for a locksmith. I had one of my people smash the front glass door so we could go inside. Timing is everything, and just as my guy was breaking the front door, a car pulls up, screeching its tires. A little old man jumps out of the car and starts yelling.

"What the fuck are you guys doing?"

"Hey, who the fuck are you?" I asked.

"My name's Tony Damaio. I own this place."

"Well my name is Larry Formato, and I'm the new owner of this place."

The police came just as I said that. Damaio was screaming and cursing. He wanted the police to arrest me for trespassing and vandalism. I explained to the police that I was the new owner.

"This is a civil matter, and in fact, if anyone is trespassing, it's Mr. Damaio," I said.

I showed the police the court papers. They called into their station and found out I was right. They asked Damaio to leave. Man, was he pissed off.

"You'll be hearing from my lawyer," Damaio yelled to me as he left.

I went inside. The club was wrecked. It was totally destroyed. I would need to redo the whole inside. I wasn't too worried about the cost to fix it up. I would call in a lot of favors with people who owed me. I also had the money at Michael Gardner's apartment. I went into the kitchen area, and let me tell you, there were rats as big as cats running all over the place. I had great ideas for the club. I was going to make it the hottest nightclub in New Jersey.

I went to see Gardner and told him I was going to pull out some of my profits from our business. I needed it for the club, and he didn't seem to have any problem with that.

"I'll probably need some of the money in a week or so," I said.

I was staying at Gardner's apartment over the weekend, and my cousin Big John showed up.

"Red wants to see you right away," he told me. "You are to go alone."

What the fuck did I do wrong? I knew something was really wrong. Red never, as long as I have known him, sent anyone to look for me. Red made Big John go to New York to get me and personally drive me to West Orange, New Jersey to meet with him. I must have asked Big John a million times what was wrong. He swore to me he didn't know. I was really worried when we got to the meeting place. Red wanted to speak to me alone. He looked upset. I couldn't read him.

"What's wrong?" I asked him.

"This conversation stays between us," Red replied.

"Red, anything you tell me stays between us. I never repeat anything."

"What's the procedure for selling the bearer Data Force stock?"

I was shocked.

"You should have sold that a long time ago. It's worthless now."

"Someone very close to me is a stockbroker. He worked for Merrill Lynch. I think he beat me for the money on the sale of the Data Force stock. I don't really want to believe it, but it's true. "

I felt really bad for Red.

"Lenny Macalusso is back from a short vacation in the state prison. He's going to come and see you," he said.

Red wanted him to help out with the club. Lenny was the guy who held Saperstein out of the window in New York. He would be taking over Red's book making and loan sharking operation under Red's command. Red wanted me to try to get along with Lenny, and should I have any problems, I should come to him right away.

"Can you believe I got fucked like this?" Red said.

He must have wanted to vent.

"Don't you ever try to fuck me," he continued.

"Red, with all due respect, I'm hurt that you would even think that," I said.

"Yeah I know you are, but don't ever fuck me."

With that, he gave me a hug. I found out later that Red was supposed to split that money with Joe "the Indian" Polverino. Red was on the hook for all of that money. Red just wasn't himself. He asked about the Greek and the deals we were doing with him. I told him I was waiting for the Interferon deal so we could all have some money. Then, Red asked me again about the Data Force stock, almost as if he forgot we just talked about it.

"Are you feeling alright, Red?" I asked. This was starting to feel a little strange.

"Yeah, I'm okay," he said. "I don't want you to lie to me. I need you to tell me the truth."

"Come on, Red. What's this all about? What's wrong?"

"What the fuck are you doing in New York at that jerk-off's apartment?"

I felt a little sick from the question. I didn't tell Red I went into business with Gardner or that I was selling cocaine. I knew I should have told him, and I don't know why I didn't. I told Red what I had been up to.

"By rights, I'm supposed to kill you right now," Red said. "It's forbidden in our family to buy or sell drugs. Never do this again. Don't mention this to anyone in our family. The long jail terms and the trouble drugs bring make it forbidden. Only the Lucchese family has been sanctioned to sell drugs. Anyone else caught selling drugs will be killed."

"Never go back there again," Red warned.

"I have a lot of my personal things in that apartment," I said.

"Send someone to get your stuff out of there."

I was now worried I had broke a rule I didn't even know existed, and it could get me whacked. With one last warning about selling drugs from Red, I left with Big John.

"Are you alright, my man?" Big John asked me.

"Let's go get a drink," I said.

I spent the rest of the day in the Double C Bar in Orange, NJ with John thinking about everything Red said to me.

CHAPTER 14: WELCOME TO CHAPTER 11

I closed my office in Dover and concentrated on opening the nightclub. Everyone was talking about it. I paid only five hundred dollars for the club and its liquor license. All of a sudden, there were old partners from Moon Rise that no one told me about. I mean, these guys were coming out of the woodwork, each one with a different story of how much money they invested with Jimmy and Bobby and what they were promised.

One in particular, Eddie Beck, was a real class A, number-one asshole. I didn't like this guy, not even a little bit. He talked like some tough guy, but to my knowledge, he wasn't around anybody.

Turk was a real big help to me. He would let me know who the good and bad guys were. He had built a few clubs for Bobby and Jimmy, and he knew what he was doing. He hooked me up, and told me where to go for the sound system. We also wanted to have a light show. Turk picked up all the neon lights for the ceiling and wired them in for me. We worked day and night fixing the club. You would be amazed how many people wanted to volunteer to help when you're opening a nightclub. We had people helping clean the kitchen, the floors, and the carpeting. I put in a huge dance floor right between two circular bars. All of the walls were mirrored, and so were the bars. The carpeting was a deep red, and the ceiling was all black. There were little pin lights on the stairs going to the seating and dining area.

Ronny Testa and Snake were going to be my DJ's. Snake wired up the sound system to the lighting. We had the best sound and lights around. There wasn't a nightclub in New Jersey that could host a sound and light show the way Chapter 11 could.

I wanted to open the club for New Year's Eve, but I felt the opening wouldn't go over well because it was too close to the holiday. I figured everyone already made their plans for New Year's. I waited and set the opening for the second week in January. One early afternoon, I was fixing something in the back of the club and Turk came to get me. Eddie Beck was at the door with two other guys, and Turk wanted to know if he should let them in. I told him I would handle it.

When I went up front, I didn't recognize the guys in the lobby with Beck.

Larry and Lenny Macalusso

"I'm sorry, but we're not open yet," I told them.

"What's your name?" asked one of the guys with Beck.

"Larry Formato," I said, knowing he already knew the answer. "I'm the owner."

"No, Eddie is the owner."

"With all due respect, I don't know you. Maybe you should leave me your name. There are some nice people associated with this place now, if you understand what I'm saying. I'll have someone get back to you, because right now, it doesn't matter who you are. You're not coming in here."

"My name's Sal Vitalli. I'm from Wayne. I respect the way you handle yourself. Tell Red to contact me."

Now, I'm thinking to myself, If he knows Red, why the fuck didn't he get in touch with him? The rules are, if you're anybody, to make an appointment or reach out through mutual friends. If you know the person is connected, it's considered very disrespectful to just show up. Sal was out of line, and I'm glad I didn't let him in.

Red came to the club shortly after Sal left. We stopped meeting at Pals Cabin in West Orange when I took over the club. I told Red about this guy, Sal.

"Fuck him," Red said. "Who the fuck does he think he is? He knows how to reach me. He's a fucking jerk-off anyway."

Lenny Macalusso stopped in to see Red. I guess he knew Red would be at the club. Lenny was a big guy and looked like he was in good shape. His big nose looked like it had been broken a couple of times, and he had huge hands. It was easy to see why Red recruited Lenny as an enforcer. Now Lenny had his own people who were doing the enforcing for him like Andy the Blade. Andy was Lenny's shadow. Wherever Lenny went, Andy was there too. Wise Guys like to travel with at least one other person.

Red always traveled with a guy named Brooklyn, a real nice old guy that had been around since dirt. Lenny was a real sharp dresser with your typical Wise Guy look—dress slacks, a collared shirt, and a sport jacket. Lenny always had a big smile on his face, and as I got to know him, he was on the surface a really nice guy. Just about everyone liked Lenny, except for the people he was beating up really bad or killing.

I think Red must have had a talk with Lenny about me before we met each other, because it seemed as though Lenny was trying really hard to get me to like him. Red, Lenny, and I sat down at a table in the club, and Red told me to repeat to Lenny what happened earlier with Eddie Beck and Sal Vitalli. Red told Lenny to go and see Sal.

"You tell that motherfucker he has no claim on this club, and Eddie is gonna have a big problem if he tries to start any trouble," Red said.

Lenny wanted to go smack Eddie just for principle, but I knew Red wasn't going to let him do it, not over something this petty. Red always said that Lenny had a quick temper and his hands would get him in trouble someday. Lenny and I got along really well, and we became good friends.

The remodeling of the club was going along really well, and it seemed everyone was getting involved. Even my sister, Patty, and John Tobin were there to help get the kitchen ready to open. Lenny's girlfriend, Donna, and her sister, Patty Delisanti, were helping out too. We were all excited as the opening day drew closer.

Everything was all set to go. We even had a hookup for the liquor. Eddie Russo, the salesman for the liquor, was a friend of Lenny's, and he arranged to stock the club for me with no up-front money.

Michael Gardner never came through with the money I had invested with him in the cocaine business. I couldn't go to Red to ask him to get it back for me. Red gave me orders not to ever go back to Gardner's place again. All I could do for the most part was call him on the phone and make a few threats to him, but I was pointing an unloaded gun. I was just about out of money, Michael Gardner had all of my money at this point, and it seemed like an endless stream of bills needed to be paid before opening day at Chapter 11.

CHAPTER 15: THE INDIAN LEADS THE CHARGE

I was working at the club late one night with Robin, who was helping and keeping me company. We slept at the Howard Johnson hotel that night, which was right next door to the club. The following morning, the phone in my room rang. It was Red, and he wanted to meet me at the club right away.

I walked to the club from the hotel since the parking lots were right next to each other. When I walked into the club, Red was talking to a guy I never met before. He was a stocky guy about 5'7" with dark hair. He looked somewhere between sixty-five and seventy years old, close to Red's age. His voice was a deep baritone and had a very strong Jersey accent.

"Joe, this is my partner, Larry," Red said, motioning towards me.

"It's nice to meet you," I said.

"So you're the guy that's gonna make us all millions," Joe said. "Red thinks you're a pretty smart kid, and you know how to handle yourself too—like you did with those cocksuckers Sal Vitalli and that other jerk-off, Eddie."

Wise Guys very rarely use last names. They almost always have some kind of nickname, and this Wise Guy went by "Joe the Indian."

I don't think I was there for more than two minutes.

"Let's get going," Red said. "We're going to take a ride."

I didn't ask where we were going. I just followed them to the parking lot. Red drove a black Oldsmobile Toronado, and I have to say, I was really relieved when Red handed me the keys as we walked towards the car. He wanted me to drive. Before I had the keys, the thought actually occurred to me that maybe I was really going for a one-way ride.

"Which way are we heading?" I asked Red as I settled into the driver's seat.

"We're going to New York City," he said. "We're going to pay a visit to an old friend of yours."

When Red told me we were going to see Peter Aiello, I think I almost crashed the car.

"But he's with that guy from New York—you know who I mean," I said.

I learned from Red never to mention names in front of anyone. Then

Joe the Indian spoke up.

"I went to see the Chin," Joe the Indian said. "The Chin told me to go choke that fucking guy for using his name. He said he doesn't even know who Peter Aiello is. And Johnny Fats, Peter's brother-in-law? He's a nobody. He's around some people, but that's it."

I was sure Red forgot all about Aiello. I mean, it was a long time ago. I told him that story, but Wise Guys never forget.

Holy fuck. My head was spinning. I had learned a lot from Red over the months during all of our meetings, and I knew this was going to be the real deal—not like before when Big John and John Tobin went to meet Johnny Fats. I never met Joe the Indian before that day, but I knew of him. I knew that he was a Captain, or a Skipper as some people call them, in the Genovese Crime Family—the family the Chin was the Boss of and the same family Red inducted me into.

We drove into New York City going through the Holland Tunnel, and coming out of the tunnel, some guy almost hit our car. Joe the Indian went nuts, motherfucking this guy and telling him to get out of his car. Lucky for the guy, he kept going and didn't say anything.

Red told me about a time when they were in a car with a Skipper years ago and some kid, who was only seventeen, cut them off. The Skipper jumped out of his car and went after the kid, and the kid knocked the Skipper right on his ass. Well, they got the kid's license plate number and tracked him down. The Skipper had the kid whacked for punching him out.

We parked our car in a parking lot and walked the two blocks to the building on Broad Street where Aiello's office was. I could not help but notice how these two older Wise Guys carried themselves. It was in their stride; they just walked cool, like they owned the sidewalks. Looking back, there was a movie made in 1986 with Kirk Douglas and Burt Lancaster called Tough Guys. These guys reminded me so much of that movie, and I would bet anything that Red and Joe were two of the toughest guys alive.

Red told me not to say anything unless he or Joe asked me a question. Aiello's secretary, Barbara, was sitting up front in the reception area when we walked in. I asked her to tell Peter we were here to see him. He came out to greet us and he could tell just looking at Red and Joe what was about to take place. Seriously, you just had to look at these guys and you knew.

We followed Aiello to an office down a long hall. Before we sat down, Joe the Indian turned to Peter.

"You better get that fucking Johnny Fats down here now," he said.

When Aiello heard that, he turned white. Joe's voice went right through him. Aiello smoked Pall Mall non-filters, and he was puffing on it so much I thought the damn cigarette was going to burn his lips. Aiello paged Barbara to come into his office, and then told her to go find Fats right away. Much to my surprise, Joe the Indian didn't say much more after that. He was waiting for Fats.

"You're a tough guy, huh?" Red asked Aiello.

"No, I'm not a tough guy," Aiello said.

"But you like to call people up and tell them you're gonna kill everyone in their office, right? Maybe I should kill you right now."

Peter didn't say a word. He just looked shocked that someone was talking to him like that.

"You have five more minutes to find Fats," Joe the Indian told Aiello, nodding towards the clock.

"Please, let me see what Barbara is doing," Aiello pleaded. "Can I go to the front?"

"You've got five minutes."

Peter quickly left the room. Joe and Red started talking to each other.

"What a fucking jerk-off he is," Red said.

"We should fuck him up if Fats doesn't show," Joe said.

"Let's fuck him up either way."

How tough are these guys? I wondered. I'm telling you, they were close to seventy and acting like they were twenty.

"I reached Fats," Aiello said, coming back into the office. "He should be here shortly. Do you want anything to eat or drink while we wait?"

We all declined his offer as he started to chain-smoke, lighting one after another. No one spoke a word while we waited. There was no doubt in my mind that Aiello was dying a thousand deaths with every minute that passed.

Johnny Fats finally showed up. He was tall and skinny—they should have called him String Bean. When he walked into Aiello's office, Red and Joe stood up. I think Fats thought Joe was going to shake his hand, but Joe slapped Fats right across the face and started yelling. Aiello jumped up. I think he got so scared he didn't know what to do. I think he was going to run, but Red wasn't having it.

"Sit the fuck down," Red warned.

"You better find someone to speak on your behalf, or you're going to die, right here," Joe told Fats.

Fats asked to use the phone and started making calls. After speaking to someone, they asked him who we were. They wanted him to call from a phone booth with a name. Wow, now it was coming down to mentioning names. I felt like a spectator at a championship-boxing match, knowing the knockout punch was coming.

Fats hung up the phone.

"What name can I give?" Fats asked.

I held my breath in anticipation, waiting for the answer to come.

"You tell them 'Joe the Indian."

I was so excited at this point, I almost felt like laughing when I saw Fats' reaction.

"Can I be excused to make the call from a phone booth?" Fats asked.

Red and Joe let him go, but warned him to get his fucking ass right back, so we went back to waiting for Fats. When he returned, he said two guys were on their way, and they wanted to meet downstairs in a local deli.

We all left Aiello's office together, and for the most part, everyone was quiet—until the elevator doors closed.

"What the fuck kind of trouble did you get me into?" Fats asked Aiello. "I should fucking kill you."

Red punched Fats right in the face.

"Shut the fuck up, tough guy," Red said.

The old, small deli had a narrow isle leading to the few tables and booths in the back. I walked ahead of everyone to the tables and sat facing forwards. Red and Joe sat on the same side of the table as me. Fats and Aiello sat with their backs to the door, facing us.

"Where do you wanna take these two mutts?" Joe asked Red, fucking with them while we waited.

Aiello's hands were visibly shaking now as he tried to light a cigarette.

Three guys, I'm guessing in their early thirties, came in and greeted Joe, Red, and me. They shook our hands and kissed us on the cheek. One of the guys, whose name was also Joe, apologized to the Indian and said he was sorry for any problems or misunderstandings.

"Are you willing to take responsibility for these two mutts?" the Indian asked him, jerking his thumb towards Fats and Aiello.

"No fucking way," the other Joe said.

"You fucking guys better get your Skipper down here, because by rights, you can't even talk to me about this. You don't have the stripes."

There was a phone booth in the deli, and one of the guys was desperately trying to get someone on the Indian's level to come down there. Wise Guys are funny. They normally don't react too much or do anything unless there's an end in it for them. If you're an Earner, making money for them, then they will show up for you, but if it's a bullshit thing and they aren't making money with you, then forget about it.

Aiello was almost an afterthought at this point. The Indian was running the show now, and Fats was worried about his future, if he had one at all. Three hours later, their Skipper, Tommy Stubbs, showed up. He came in greeting Joe and Red with big hugs and kisses. It was clear to everyone that they knew each other.

"I'm so sorry you had to wait this long for me," Stubbs told the Indian. "When I got the call, I was all the way out in Long Island."

"I hate that fucking drive out there," the Indian said. "I saw our friend in Florida last week when I was in Miami. He's doing pretty fucking good."

I had no idea who Joe was talking about, but it was clear that Stubbs did.

"But these jerk-offs have a big problem," Stubbs said. "What's up? What the fuck happened?"

"Aiello owes Larry a lot of money," the Indian said. "He even had the balls to call Larry's office and threaten his sister."

Stubbs glared at Aiello. In the Wise Guy world, you never threaten family members or go to someone's house.

"What are we talking about here?" Stubbs asked the Indian. "How much fucking money is owed?"

"It would take about five hundred thousand to square everything up. And just so you know, Fats used our friend's name to some of Larry's guys like he had a fucking license to just say it. You know who I mean? The guy with the chin."

Stubbs never said a word to Aiello or Fats, but he turned to the other guy named Joe.

"Who the fuck does this piece of shit think he is? And you have this asshole around you, embarrassing me like this. Aiello has to pay the money, and Fats will be held responsible. It's up to Fats to make sure Aiello pays," Stubbs said.

The sweat poured down Aiello's face.

"Please, I need some time," Aiello said, panicked. "I don't have the money right now."

The Indian turned to me.

"What do you want to do, Larry?" he asked me.

This was the first time I was asked to speak since we got to Peter's office. I knew whatever I said here would either get me respect from Red, the Indian, and Stubbs, or I was going to sound like an asshole.

"Since we're not all animals here, let's let Peter give up thirty thousand dollars now," I said. I wanted that thirty thousand worse than the half a million, because that's what Aiello made me pay when Dwyer came to work for me. "Peter can make payments of fifty grand per month 'till it's paid. I think that would be fair to everyone here."

Stubbs turned to Aiello and Fats for the first time.

"If I ever hear that you used that name again, or anyone else's name, I'll personally kill you two. You understand me?" he said, shaking his finger at them.

"Yes. Yes, I'm really sorry," Fats said.

"I'll have the thirty thousand in cash tomorrow morning, and I'll bring it to wherever you want me to bring it," Aiello told me.

"Call Larry's sister and apologize for acting like a fucking jerk-off," Red told Aiello.

Fats and Aiello were both saying, "I'm sorry," to everyone there. The sit down ended with hugs and kisses from everyone except Johnny Fats and Peter Aiello. A kiss is a way of showing respect, and no one at the meeting had any respect for Aiello or Fats.

It was looking like my money problems were going to be over. With the thirty grand from Aiello, I would now have enough money to finish the things I needed to do at the club to be ready to open on time. I also knew those fifty g's a month would get split up between Red, Joe, and me. Red kept his word with me about taking care of the problems, and I felt good because I knew he was there one hundred percent for me.

CHAPTER 16: END OF ANOTHER CHAPTER

It was the second Friday in January, and at 9:00 p.m., Chapter 11 opened its doors. Red and Lenny had all of their friends there. It was like the whole Wise Guy world in New Jersey was at Chapter 11 for opening night. George the Greek showed up in his same attire: a ridiculous pin stripe suit, black shirt, white tie, and, of course, a big fucking white hat with a black band.

The line to get into the club was literally out the door and out of our parking lot, stretching past the Howard Johnson Hotel. There were three girls to every guy. This was one of the things that made Chapter 11 so popular.

I had the idea not to have barstools at any of the bars, because I wanted the people standing and dancing. It made them drink faster, and the lines of people waiting for drinks were five deep all around the bars. The music was blasting, and our huge dance floor was packed. All the lights and strobes reflecting in the mirrors gave the club a look like no other club ever had. The excitement was everywhere, everyone was having a great time, and Chapter 11 was an instant success.

Sunday night was my favorite night at Chapter 11. It was "Oldies Night," and for me, it was especially cool because I got to sing with a lot of my old friends in the music business like the Drifters, Freddie Parris and the Five Satins, the Teen Agers, and, of course, the Duprees.

The nightclub part of the business was better than the restaurant part, so I decided I would close Chapter 11 during the day, do away with lunch and dinner, and open the nightclub Wednesday through Sunday.

After I filed the bankruptcy, there were hearings held in federal court in New Jersey. We made a big hit with everyone in bankruptcy court when a couple of my employees showed up with Chapter 11 t-shirts on.

Although filing a bankruptcy is supposed to stop all state court proceedings, Damaio managed to get a hearing in the Morris County Superior Court. It was an action brought against Jimmy and Bobby for illegally transferring the corporation and its assets to me. If Damaio was successful in his attempt to show this as an illegal transfer of ownership and assets, then the federal bankruptcy petition I filed would be thrown out.

I was subpoenaed to testify at the hearing, and in my opinion, this was just a bunch of bullshit. Eddie Beck was there and he testified that he was an owner of the corporation, and that he never received his stock because it was never issued to him. He claimed to have put twenty-five thousand dollars into Moon Rise for his share of twenty-five percent of the company. Beck had a side deal going with Damaio that if he was successful in court, then he and Damaio would become partners of the club. I had my ace attorney, Jay V. Surgent, there that day. I would always tell people his name was Urgent with an "S," and we know what the symbol S stands for.

Beck's testimony went nowhere. Jay hammered him. Beck couldn't prove any of his claims, including proof that he put up any money at all. I was finally called to take the stand after being sworn in. Damaio's lawyer started his questioning with some non-intrusive questions like my full name and address.

"How did you come to know Jimmy and Bobby?" Damaio's lawyer asked.

"Someone in the real estate business introduced me to them," I said.

"How long have you known them?"

"I met with them the day before I bought the company."

"And how much money did you pay for the controlling shares of the company, including all assets of Moon Rise?"

"Five hundred dollars."

"Would you repeat that?" the judge asked.

The whole courtroom broke out in laughter.

"Five hundred dollars," I repeated.

"Mr. Formato, why would people you don't even know sell you something of a much greater value for only five hundred dollars?" the judge asked.

"I can't answer for their actions. I only know that is what I offered, and they accepted my offer."

"Do you have a private deal with Jimmy and Bobby to pay them money?" Damaio's lawyer asked.

"No, I do not."

"Why don't you ask him about all his Mafia friends?" shouted someone in the courtroom.

With that, Jay Surgent stood up.

"Your Honor, Mr. Formato is a business man," he said. "He has never been convicted of a crime in his life. He made a perfectly legal transaction, and just because some people are mad because he paid so little, let's not forget that

Mr. Formato has put over fifty thousand dollars in renovations into the business with the full knowledge and approval of the Federal Bankruptcy Court. I think Mr. Formato has explained himself quite clearly here today, and he does not need to sit here and be accused of any wrong doing."

I was dismissed from the stand, and the judge took a recess for a few minutes to make his decision. The judge ruled the transaction to be legal, and dismissed the complaint against Jimmy and Bobby. It seemed as though the drama would never end between me, Damaio, and that fucker, Eddie Beck.

I was looking for something to build up my Thursday nights, so I decided I would put in a male revue. It started at 5:00 p.m. and went until 11:00 p.m. with no men allowed in the club with the exception of club employees. I'm not one to do anything in a small way, so our male revue hosted forty top male dancers. I lost all my respect for women after seeing how they reacted to these guys dancing and teasing them. The married women were the worst. We had a great time with this, and women would actually tackle my waiters and try to rip their clothes off. We would do crazy things like have a banana-eating contest, judged on how well they ate it instead of how fast. Words just can't describe some of these women and their talents.

Our friends would beg us to let them into the club to see these hot, horny babes. We had a back room in the club used by staff only, and it was like a revolving door. It was nothing for people to get laid or blown two to three times on a Thursday night.

The best part of Thursday night for me came at eleven o'clock. That's when we made most of our money. When we opened the doors for guys to come in, they were like dogs in heat. If you didn't get laid on a Thursday night, you had something wrong with you. Thursday night turned into my biggest night at the club.

The club closed at 2:00 a.m., and we would stop pouring drinks at 12:45 p.m. It took us that long to get everyone out of the club by closing, and that was pushing it. We would always allow some girls and some of our friends to stay after hours. The bartenders would make pitchers of kamikazes, and we would party until six or seven in the morning.

We had a dress code at Chapter 11, and one night, just as we opened, I was walking past the entrance of the club. I overheard my manager, Matt, arguing with a customer. I very seldom interfered with this type of thing, but the guy was cursing up a storm. I went to see what was going on.

It seems Matt stopped this guy because he had work boots and work overalls on. Matt wouldn't let him in because of our dress code.

"Why don't you go home, get changed, and come back," I told the guy.

"Fuck you," he responded.

"Even if we let you in with those clothes on, we're still not going to serve you. I can't serve someone who's clearly drunk."

The guy continued cursing, not only at me but at the people coming into the club as well.

"I'm with the Gambino family," he said. "I'll have all you motherfuckers killed."

"I don't give a fuck who you're with," I said. "I'm going to give you a choice. You see these two big guys here? They want to bust your ass, so you can stand here for the next sixty seconds and curse all you want, but after that, these guys are gonna drag you outside and beat your ass. You can leave on your own or get your ass busted."

As I walked away, I told my bouncers not to hurt him and to just throw him out. The guy cursed at everyone for sixty seconds, and then my guys dragged him out the door.

I was in my office when Lenny came in, and I was laughing as I told him about the drunk guy. As I was talking about him, he called my office phone.

"Dog" is slang some guys use for a gun, because a dog barks. This fucking guy was on the phone still cursing, saying he's with the Gambino's, and that he's coming back with his dog to kill us.

"Come on, tough guy," I taunted, "come on down."

I hung up the phone with him and didn't really give it much more thought. We were starting to get packed. About an hour later, Lenny and I hear a big commotion. The music stopped playing and people were screaming.

We go running out to see what was going on, and here was this fucking guy in my club with the biggest Doberman Pincher I have ever seen with a spiked collar around its neck. I looked at Lenny, and he looked at me. We did the only thing you could do in that situation: we turned around and went back to our office.

Here we were: two tough guys hiding from a dog. This guy and his dog actually held the customers in the club at bay. The police finally arrived, and they managed to get this nutcase out of the club. I was told by one of my bouncers that the police had brought their dog with them too. Now Lenny and I were brave again, so we went out to see what the cops were doing.

The front of the club was grassy and about half the size of a football field. Lenny didn't want to talk to the cops. I was the owner, so I had to talk to them. I walked across the grass to where the police were standing, and they have this guy sitting in his car with his dog. They told me they were going to let him go home.

"Are you fucking crazy? This guy could have caused a riot in there and could have gotten some people killed. You can't let him go," I said.

After hearing me say that, the guy opened the car door and told the dog to get me. My front door to the club looked like it was ten miles away. I know I could have outrun O.J. Simpson to the front door that night. I just about got in the door before closing it on the dog's head.

The police arrested the guy and his dog. They charged him with starting a riot and with terroristic acts. For days after that occurred, the guy would call the club and beg us to drop the charges. It seems the charges were very serious, and if he was found guilty, the guy would serve some jail time. We were never the kind to go to the cops to settle things, so I had my manager Matt go to the police and drop the charges.

The cops were pissed off that we dropped the charges, and they started busting our balls by parking right down the road. When we closed at night, they would pull our customers over for a D.U.I. check.

Joe Patero, a semiretired Boss living in Florida, contacted Red and asked for a meeting at the request of Sal Vitalli. Red told me that normally anything to do with Sal he would pay no attention to, but Joe Patero was a very respected man and a good friend of his. Patero didn't come to New Jersey just to meet with us, but since he was in Jersey, he told Sal he would see what he could do to help him.

Joe Patero was a well-groomed older man with white hair and a small framed body. He had a lot of class—not your usual Wise Guy. He was very well spoken and looked more like a retired banker than a Wise Guy. Joe was very nice to me, and said he had heard some very good things about me. He asked Red if there was any room for his guy, Vitalli, to earn any money from the club. Red told Joe that there was nothing he could do, and that Sal was trying to make a claim on something that he should have stayed away from. Red said that if it was true that they invested money with the old owners, then their beef was with them.

I knew Red had scored all the points he needed to after saying that and Joe agreed. I'm finally getting rid of that fucking Eddie Beck, I thought.

The club was not only an attraction for the Wise Guys. It was also getting a lot of attention from the New Jersey State Police and the Federal

Tobacco and Alcohol Agency. The male revue night was growing every week, and I guess the state police figured that would be the best night to stage a raid. That's exactly what they did.

They came into the Club with search warrants and seized all my books and records. I couldn't imagine that they could think I would be so foolish as to try anything illegal while I was in Federal Bankruptcy Court. I was pretty much ordered to be at the state trooper barracks the following Tuesday morning for questioning. Jay Surgent filed a motion with the Federal Bankruptcy Court to get all our records back from the state troopers.

I showed up at the Trooper barracks on time without my lawyers. We all felt this would be the best approach since I did nothing wrong at Chapter 11. The meeting was very informal. I was asked some questions about my background and where I grew up. I was waiting for the shoe to fall about Red or Lenny. They approached it in a different manner; they asked me if I knew why they had raided the Club.

"I have no idea," I said.

They asked me who Joe the Indian was.

"I have no idea," I repeated.

They wouldn't let up about Joe the Indian. They showed me a picture of the Indian with me and Red and asked again.

"Are you going to tell us you don't know who he is?" one of the troopers asked.

"I don't really know that guy," I said. "He came in one day with my Uncle Red."

They just about fell off their chairs.

"Red Cecere is your uncle?" the trooper asked.

"Well, he's like an uncle," I said. "You guys know I'm Italian. In Italian families, close friends of the family are sometimes referred to as Uncle. My father and Red were very close friends, and I've called him Uncle Red all my life."

I told them Red was coming to the club and bringing me business because he knew I needed all the help I could get. I think I busted their balloon with the Uncle Red story, and it actually turned out to be a good reason why Red was always with me and in the club. The state police returned all my records after making copies of everything, and they never bothered me again while I owned Chapter 11.

I was always big on security at Chapter 11. Like most clubs, you are always going to have some fights break out, and my bouncers were trained to get to the fight quick and get the people who were fighting out of the club. I had a rule with my bouncers; if I was walking through the club, they were to watch me. Should I raise my hand in the air, that meant there was trouble and to get to me fast.

One night, I was walking across the dance floor, and I spotted a guy leaning against the railing lighting a joint. I went up to him and I asked him very nicely to please put the joint out. I told him I owned the club and I could lose my liquor license if I allowed him to smoke a joint in my club. He looked at me and kept smoking it.

"I don't want to have you thrown out of the club, but if you don't put that out you will leave me no choice," I said.

This guy was about 6'5" and weighted about 250 pounds. I raised my hand in the air and told the guy I wasn't going to ask him again.

"Fuck you," he said.

I put my other hand in the air and started waiving it. I knew that I was about to have a fight with this big asshole. I gave one more attempt to try to get the attention of my bouncers—both hands in the air waiving. After doing that for what seemed like days, I figured I looked like a fool.

I punched this guy as hard as I could in the mouth, and it was like I hit a wall. I didn't even faze him. We were fighting for about the longest thirty seconds of my life when my bouncers came to my rescue.

Later that night, I held a meeting with my bouncers to find out what went wrong. What the hell were they doing not paying attention to me? The answer was so funny that all I could do was laugh.

They thought I was dancing.

All the fun and partying came to a screeching halt with just one phone call. Brooklyn called to tell me Red had a stroke, but he was alive and in the hospital. Robin was with me, and we jumped on my motorcycle and raced to the hospital to see Red. The stroke did its damage to my dear friend, and Red was left unable to speak or walk. I was devastated. My real father died years ago, and now I felt like I was losing another father. He was like my father and my best friend; he was everything to me.

Joe the Indian wasted no time moving in and taking over Red's business. I was Red's guy, and in ways, I felt resentment from some of the other guys. This really came to light when Brooklyn was sent to give me a message to continue to do the right thing. It was not a threatening message. I think some people may have been worried that since Red was out of the picture, I might not want to continue working for the Family anymore. Joe the Indian inherited me and Lenny along with the rest of Red's crew.

I met several times with Joe and Lenny at Joe's son's video rental store in Bloomfield, New Jersey. We discussed Chapter 11, and Joe thought it would be a good idea if Lenny started coming there full time to help me run the place. I personally couldn't have cared less, but I could see the move coming. It was as if they thought they might get cheated out of something, so Lenny was put there to keep an eye on things.

I started to lose interest in Chapter 11, and George the Greek kept bugging me to get involved with him on a partnership with a public company. The Interferon deal closed without me. I stepped away from it because of Michael Gardner, but I still earned twenty-five thousand from it. I met with the Indian and told him I was thinking about going back to doing deals in the stock market again. He was really happy to hear that, because that's where I always made all my money. I talked about the Greek and asked the Indian how he wanted me to handle him.

"Let's try to do something we can all earn with," the Indian said. "You just let him know you are running things."

There were problems brewing at the bankruptcy court. Damaio was bringing another action and was challenging my plan of reorganization.

"Let them have the fucking place," I told the Indian and Lenny. "Let's close it down. We built a name with it. We can always do it again."

The Indian agreed with me. Lenny wasn't sure. He loved Chapter 11. It made him feel important, especially when Wise Guys from other families would visit the club. He was always ready to party with those guys, but he couldn't go against Joe. I met with the Greek and laid out my plans for the company and my rules. I let the Greek know up front.

"It's going to be my way or no way at all," I said.

"Larry, I know you will make millions for all of us," the Greek said. "I would do anything to be your partner."

"Then the first thing you're gonna do is get rid of that fucking hat and buy some new suits."

October 10, 1982, I took one last drink and gathered my belongings from Chapter 11. There were no more weekly meetings with my friend, Red. I walked out, locking the door behind me.

CHAPTER 17: LIGHTS AND MIRRORS

The ride from my house in Roxbury, New Jersey to Orange, New Jersey was about a forty-five minute drive. I thought to myself, why the hell would I want to go to Orange every fucking day, and fight the traffic each way? I parked my car on Main Street in front of Embassy Rental, the real estate company George Livieratos owned. This rat hole was going to be my new office and the corporate head quarters for World Wide Ventures, Corp.

George Livieratos got his wish. He was going to be my partner, and I was going to promote World Wide Ventures as a holding company. I wanted George to feel important, so I decided to make him the Chairman of the Board of World Wide Ventures. I would become the chief executive officer and the president. The Vice President of World Wide would be Don Sheppard. Don was a good team player. I wanted Don in this deal with us. He was good with numbers, and he knew how to write a good business plan. I would use him as a buffer between George and me.

George had his Real Estate Offices set up with a lot of desks. They were the old, small metal desks. He must have had at least twenty of these desks lined up in two rows going to the rear of the building. I was looking at these surroundings, and I couldn't imagine myself ever working there. I needed a private office.

George wanted to build me an office downstairs in the basement, or the dungeon as I called it. There was no fucking way I was going for that. I had the idea to build an office all the way in the back of the building. It would have a walkway from the front door entrance straight back to what would soon be the door to my new office. George asked me if he could share an office with me. I reluctantly agreed to let him.

We had a really nice new office built inside that shit hole. We had two executive sized desks butted up next to each other. If I were in the office at the same time as George, we would be facing each other. I sat facing the door, and George sat with his back to the door. I ordered a level two NASDAQ machine. Only Brokerage Firms were allowed to have them, but I managed to get one installed in the office so I could watch the market. I could see what brokerage firms were making a market in the stocks I would be trading. I made up a name of a brokerage firm just to get the machine installed. When they were installing it, they actually believed it was for a brokerage firm.

With new phones, a NASDAQ machine, and a new deal, World Wide Ventures Corp., I was now ready to do business. I needed a brokerage firm to make a market in World Wide for me and to act as our investment banker.

Ben Tarimina was the President of Norbay Securities. George, Don, and I went to meet with Ben at the headquarters of Norbay Securities, located in Bayside, Queens, New York. I informed Ben that I was going to build World Wide into a corporate holding company and that I planned to do mergers and acquisitions. Ben was really excited to be working with me. I assured him that he would always get World Wide stock at a discount under the bid price. He assured me that he would do whatever I needed him to do.

The stage was set. I had everything I needed. I called Mickey at Troster Singer. They were a big trading firm, and I could always count on Mickey to buy a big position for me if I needed him to. With him and some of my other friends trading this stock, it would be easy to get it moving. Now I had to acquire a company for World Wide with little or no money and make a public announcement of the acquisition.

Marc Bateman, one of my lawyers and the mortgage lender who lent me the money that I gave to Mike Gardner, told me about a company in the Pocono Mountains of Pennsylvania. It was a building and loan company. They owned hundreds of buildable acres and had been developing this property and building homes on it for years. The owners were from New Jersey, and they wanted to sell and cash out. I met with them in their offices in Montclair, New Jersey. I knew within the first twenty minutes of the meeting this would be the deal that would kick off the World Wide Ventures stock promotion.

I wanted to see the property and all the homes that the company had built. This company was real. It had assets, sales, and a bottom line income. It was exactly what I was looking for. I made a point of telling them that my company was a publicly traded company. It is what people referred to as a Penny Stock. I explained to them that it was easier for a penny stock like mine to go from a penny to a dollar than another stock to go from a dollar to a hundred dollars.

A penny to a dollar is the same as a dollar to a hundred dollars. It's the same profit margin, but no one looks at a stock if it is trading in the pennies. However, let a stock move from fifteen dollars to twenty dollars, and everyone is running to buy it.

To impress them that I was sure of my company's success, I told them to watch the price of my stock over the next week and they would see it going from a penny to a quarter. Think about how big of a jump that is. It's twenty-five hundred percent. Let's put it this way: If the stock was ten dollars, it would be two hundred and fifty dollars. I wanted a Letter of Intent from them between their company and World Wide Ventures. I needed a Letter of Intent so I could make a public announcement that World Wide Ventures would be acquiring Indian Mountain Lakes Building and Loan Company. I was going to move the stock up, but I needed news about the company so the stock would not appear to be manipulated or moving up on its own.

We hammered out a deal. The purchase price would be five million dollars, cash. The company's assets were close to twelve million dollars, eight million of which were first mortgages on homes that they built and sold. They asked me to put up a fifty thousand dollar good faith deposit in order to review their books and records. I requested that should I agree with the deposit, the money would be held in my attorney's escrow account, and should this deal not be consummated, the fifty thousand dollars would be refunded back to World Wide Ventures Corp. Fifty grand was deposited in Jay Surgent's Escrow Account. Marc Bateman was mad at me that I wasn't using him to close this deal.

I agreed to pay the five million dollars on or before 180 days from the signing of the contract. With those terms agreed to, I arranged for a small group of brokers and investors to spend a weekend in the Poconos at Indian Mountain Lakes. My whole thought process behind telling the Principals of Indian Mountain Lakes to watch the price of World Wide Ventures Stock was to convert the deal from an all cash deal to a deal for stock and cash. Preferably, I would want them to take more stock than cash.

Three days after my first meeting with the Indian Mountain Lakes group, I signed a Letter of Intent. I put out a press release to all the major outlets including the AP wire and Reuters. I had the announcement printed on the front page of the Pink Sheets so all the brokers in the country would see it. Working closely with Ben at Norbay and Mickey at Troster Singer, we started to move the price of World Wide Ventures up. In fact, there was so much buying the first two days we had to hold the price back. I didn't want it to go up too fast and cause bells and whistles to go off at the NASD or the SEC. The announcement was a huge success. In less than one week, World Wide Ventures' stock was trading at seventy-five cents to one dollar. My favorite line is "a penny to a dollar." It's a rush when you know you're the guy that makes it happen. You know you're the best at it and very few people can pull it off.

George Livieratos was counting his millions already. Between George and I, we owned fifty-five million shares of World Wide Ventures. On paper, in just one week, we had become mega-millionaires worth fifty-five million dollars. This was a stock promoter's dream, and no one in the country knew how to play the game better than me.

I left for the Poconos on a Friday night with Robin. I was excited I was going away with Robin, which always seemed to be good back then. I was sitting on a fortune I created with the stock. I also knew that on Monday morning when the Stock Market opened, World Wide Ventures would be higher than what it closed at on Friday. George and Don drove up together. Ben Tarimina arrived with his wife, and Ben's son and his wife came as well. I had other brokers from different firms there too. I had brokers calling me wanting to come, but there were only so many rooms and I wanted the best of the best there. This would be what promoters call a "Dog and Pony show." The setting could not have been better if I wanted it to be. There were these small white cabins that we all stayed in, and the business office was a stone's throw away from them. A little bit down one of the roads was a tiny little bar/restaurant that was also owned by Indian Mountain Lakes.

It was the dead of winter. I was wearing a fur coat and George was wearing a brown suede coat with a white lamb wool collar. We walked into the woods for whatever the reason was. I think God only knows, but there we were in the woods in the freezing cold. I think we just wanted to walk the property we were about to buy for stock and not for cash. We discovered two things: the first being we were lost, the second being that it was hunting season.

George and I made perfect targets with the coats we had on. We could hear the shots from the rifles, so we quickly decided to take our coats off before we got killed. The next big decision was which way we should go. I wanted to go left and George wanted to go right. We were freezing our asses off in the cold, and we were lost for a good two hours. I don't mind saying it; we were a little scared at this point that we weren't going to make it out of the woods alive. George sat down on a fallen tree.

"I'm not going to go any fucking further," George said.

"If we stay here much longer, it will get dark," I said. "I'm not gonna be in these fucking woods in the dark."

I started walking, and George followed me.

"Maybe we should scream for help," I suggested. "Maybe someone will hear us."

We started screaming at the top of our lungs for help, and someone yelled back at us.

"What's wrong? You guys okay?" someone shouted.

"We're here. We're here," we yelled back.

"Okay, stop yelling. I see you," the guy said, approaching us through the trees. "What's wrong?"

We were really excited. We were jumping up and down, thanking God that we were saved.

"You fellas are only twenty feet from the road," the guy said.

There we were, ready to freeze to death and not take another step, and we were twenty feet from the road. I didn't care if we looked stupid. I was really happy to be out of those woods. Everyone got a big laugh when we told them what happened.

All the brokers and the investors went on a guided tour of the property. Everyone was convinced this would be a great deal and that the assets would give World Wide Ventures a strong foundation. The weekend was a great success for our new company, and it ended with an ice storm. My God, we were all almost killed trying to get home from the Poconos. Cars were slamming into each other everywhere. I decided Robin and I would go back, stay one more night, and go home in the morning when the road conditions were better.

I had been dating Robin a little over a year and she never knew I wore a hairpiece. I would always tell her I didn't like my hair touched. I never let her touch it. I was lying in bed with Robin. I got up and went into the bathroom and I took off my hairpiece. When I came out of the bathroom, Robin almost went into shock when she looked at me.

"Oh my God," Robin said, putting her hands to her mouth, "don't ever let anyone see you like that."

"Seriously, is it that bad?" I asked.

"I never would have gone out with you if I would have seen you without your hair piece."

I believed her.

Morning came, my hair was back on, Robin was still in shock, and the roads were safe to drive. I couldn't wait to get back to talk to the brokers and get them all excited about World Wide Ventures.

Morty Burger was talking to me about an inventor named Amos Walls. Amos lived in Indiana, and he had invented an escape device. It could be used to escape fires in high-rise buildings. It was called the "SAFE-T-SCAPE." Morty thought we might be able to get the worldwide rights to distribute the Safe-T-Scape. I was very interested, and I wanted to see how this device worked. I took a plane to Indiana to meet with Amos Walls. Amos was a really cool guy. He reminded me of Q from the James Bond movies. Amos took me on a tour of his workshop. I was in awe of the cool things this guy had made.

He showed me the Safe-T-Scape. He explained how it worked. Amos pointed to the harness attached to the unit. It looked like a parachute harness. He explained that the unit was a metal box with gears inside it that looked kind of like a pulley. It had airplane cable wound around the pulley that came through one end of the box and attached to the harness. The other end of the box had a cable coming out of it that allowed you to attach it to anything that would hold your weight. If you saw the movie *Mr. and Mrs. Smith*, Angelina Jolie used something almost just like it jumping off a balcony in the movie.

Amos told me he designed the Safe-T-Scape so that if you had to jump off a balcony, it would drop you quickly, and then the pulley system he designed would kick into low gears and slow your descent. By the time you got to the ground, your knees would just about bend when your feet touched the ground. After seeing the product and hearing Amos Walls presentation, the only thing I could think about was promotion, promotion, and more promotion. Amos had an inventory of ten, thirty, and ninety story Safe-T-Scape units. I agreed to buy all of them from him. I wanted World Wide Ventures to be the distributors of Safe-T-Scape. I sealed a deal with Amos Walls before I left Indiana to return home.

On the plane coming home, I was thinking about the press releases. Now I had something to really promote. Safe-T-Scape had sizzle, and it was exciting. I would try to get fire departments to endorse the product and maybe do some demonstrations. Morty Burger told me his friend, Marshall Zolp, had the original distribution deal with Amos Walls and fucked it all up.

Marshall, being the asshole that he was, tried to go around Amos and cut Amos out of the deal. Marshall took a Safe-T-Scape unit and had it reproduced by another company. He then hired a video production crew and a stunt man and had a video made of the stunt man descending to the ground of the MGM Grand Hotel in Las Vegas. I must admit, it was a very cool sales presentation.

The MGM had caught fire in the early eighties, and Marshall had used actual film footage of the fire. He had the video editing people edit the tape so it looked like the guy was coming down right through the flames. It was a very powerful visual effect. Marshall also had retired Fire Chiefs singing praises to his "Safe-A-Scape." Marshall was a pretty smart guy, but as smart as he was, he was also just as dumb.

Marshall took in some investors on his new invention that he ripped off from Amos Walls before Amos could even sue over patent infringements. Marshall was already in big trouble. Marshall took in a partner who was in the heavy equipment business. This partner would let his son and girlfriend go to the top of a crane and then jump off using the Safe-A-Scape device Marshall had made, and then, instead of sending it back to the manufacturer to be rewound, they rewound it themselves. They kinked the cable when they were rewinding it and when the cable hit the pulley where the kink was, the cable snapped and the two kids fell to the ground to their death. The Safe-T-Scape was not meant to be rewound; they were designed as a throw away product, never to be reused. Morty gave me a copy of the tape Marshall made, and I re-edited it and used it for World Wide Ventures.

"Larry, what the fuck? I can't believe the stock is a dollar," Jay Surgent said over the phone. "You're fucking crazy. Be careful, man."

"This is just the beginning," I said. "I'll be there to see you soon. I've got something for you. I hate your seating in your office. I hear Lenny and his boys are keeping you busy with their book making charges."

"Yes, it seems I'm the lawyer they all come to now."

"Maybe it's you that should be careful."

We both laughed.

George was jealous. He knew that I had a limousine and a Rolls Royce, and although I had sold my limo shortly after Royer Securities went out of business, it seemed George was obsessed with getting one. The stock price of World Wide Ventures was now over a dollar. We were selling our shares into the buying that we created through our press releases and through other brokers that we recruited to retail World Wide Ventures.

I was making deals left and right with brokers. If a guy bought fifty thousand shares, I would give him ten thousand free trading shares in what we call "street name." That's when the stock is signed off on the back and whoever has the certificate owns it. We were raking in the cash. I called my friend, Sandy Wallach, and asked him if he had a nice Stretch Lincoln Limousine. I wanted to surprise George with the car, and I had it delivered to our office.

I will never forget that day. George was so excited. He sat in the damn car all friggin' day playing with the TV and the VCR. He sent someone out to buy bottles of a Greek Whiskey, Metaxa Gold, and other booze to stock the bar that was in the car. He hired one of his flunky people to act as a chauffeur. George was dying to take the limo somewhere, so he asked me if I wanted to go to Atlantic City.

"What are we waiting for?" I said.

This car was one of the turning points with my relationship with

George. He was really happy I did this for him. George and I had about ten thousand in cash on us and we figured that if we lost it, we would at least have had a good time and a comfortable ride home in our new limo.

It was so cold out that night. In fact, I think it was the coldest night of the year. We were on the Garden State Parkway and had just passed the Little Egg Harbor tollbooth when the fucking car just shut off. We rolled off to the side of the road and waited for help. It was really freezing, and the car was getting colder by the minute. I couldn't believe there were no State Troopers passing by us. Whenever a car did come by, we would take turns trying to flag it down.

"We're going to fucking freeze to death in here," George said.

"Stop crying," I told him. "Someone will stop soon."

About two hours later, a Trooper pulled up behind us and called for a tow truck. When the tow truck arrived, all three of us climbed in the front seat to get warm. The tow truck driver was cool. He drove us the rest of the way to Atlantic City and then dropped the car off at a Lincoln dealership. George and I gave him five hundred dollars each. We asked him if he wanted to be our guest for the night at the casino, but he had work to do and was very grateful for such a large tip. We kept his number in case we would ever need him again.

Although we were tired when we arrived at Harrah's by the Sea, George and I went straight to the black jack tables and gambled into the early hours of the morning. George had an unconventional way of playing blackjack. I cringed as I watched him hit on 17 and split picture cards. He had no idea what the hell he was doing, but he was having fun. We stayed at the blackjack tables until we lost all our money. I still think, even with the crazy way George played cards, the car was a jinx to us, and it was probably the reason we lost that night.

My meetings with the Wise Guys were now held at Steve Polverino's video store. Steve and I made up a name for Lenny, "The Golfer," because of his passion for playing golf. Steve was just a couple of years older than I was. He went to high school in North Caldwell at West Essex Regional High School, which was not far from where I lived. Although we didn't know each other, we knew a lot of the same people from that school.

Our meetings were of no real value. It was all the same bullshit, and the Indian, Steve's Father, was always complaining about someone or something. The Indian never liked George, and I found myself defending George many times for things he didn't do or say. Lenny was pretty much middle of the road. If the Indian didn't like George one day, neither did Lenny.

I explained the Indian Mountain Lakes and Safe-T-Scape deals to them. Lenny never really understood the deals, but he pretended too, and the Indian was only concerned with how much money he was going to earn. Steve caught on, and he would ask me intelligent questions, maybe because he was younger and closer to my age. I'm not really sure.

We would never talk on the telephone, and if there was something serious we needed to talk about, we would walk around the corner to Bloomfield Avenue and sit in a restaurant and talk there. The Indian hated phones. I can't remember a time that I ever spoke to him on the phone.

Lenny and I had become good friends from the Chapter 11 days, and we liked going out together. If we met people he knew, he would introduce me as his partner, and I would do the same. Lenny liked me because he knew I wasn't a punk. He had watched me in Chapter 11 when fights broke out, and he knew I could handle myself pretty well.

One night, we were in the Parsippany Hilton drinking with some of our friends. The Hilton was another Wise Guy hang out, and most of the people knew who we were. Lenny and I were at the bar drinking, and Lenny started talking to some chick who came up to the bar for a drink. Her girlfriends soon joined her, and we were all having a good time. Then some guy comes up to Lenny and starts giving him a hard time about the girl he was talking to. Lenny tried ignoring the guy, but that didn't last long.

"Get the fuck away from me before we have a big problem," Lenny warned.

The guy was pissed and walked away, saying something to the girl as he walked past her. As far as I was concerned, it was all over before it started.

I was standing next to my barstool talking to one of the girls, and the guy who started trouble with Lenny came up to me.

"You're blocking my seat," he said.

"I don't think so," I said. "Your seat is down the bar further."

"Oh, another Italian jerk. You want to step outside?"

I was never one to step outside with anyone. I always figured if a guy wants to fight me, why go all the way outside?

"You wanna go outside? Let's go," I said.

With that, I hit him and hit him again as he was falling to the floor. I kicked him a few times too. Lenny and a few of the boys grabbed me and got me off the guy.

"Larry, get the fuck out of here. The cops are coming," Lenny said.

I left the club and watched from the parking lot as the police cars and an ambulance pulled in. I found out later from talking to Lenny that the guy must have hit his head on the brass foot railing when he hit the floor. He must have cracked his head open pretty good. The people that were there all said the guy hit me first. The cops must have thought the guy was going to die, because they were questioning everyone separately, and they were trying to find out my name. I don't think they ever found out who I was, and the guy turned out to be okay.

"You're fucking crazy," Lenny told me. "You're worse than me."

*   *   *

I had the most beautiful leather couch. I paid twenty-five thousand dollars for it, and I had it delivered to Jay Surgent's office. I wanted to talk to Jay about the guy I hit at the bar in case they found out who I was. Jay assured me he would take care of it if they did and it would go nowhere. Jay loved the couch. I told him it was from my heart.

"Don't ever get rid of it," I said. "Make sure you keep it."

The weather sucked outside, and I was sitting in my new office at World Wide Headquarters when I received a phone call from a guy in Wayne, New Jersey. He was a mortgage broker, and he knew Marc Bateman. He asked me if our company would be interested in doing a joint venture with Jilly Rizzo, Frank Sinatra's road manager and bodyguard. He told me it involved some land in the Poconos and that these guys needed money and might be looking to go public. I told him we were interested, but I wanted to meet with the principals. If this was Jilly Rizzo's deal, then I wanted to meet with him personally to make sure it was for real and not just someone using his name.

The meeting was set, and before going to the meeting, I went to see Joe the Indian. I told Joe that I was meeting with Jilly Rizzo about a deal in the Poconos. I knew Wayne Newton had tried to put something together in the Poconos. It was called Tamiment Resorts, but he went broke with it. Joe didn't like Jilly Rizzo, not even a little bit. He warned me about Jilly and said he was a real asshole and wasn't liked in our circle of friends.

Jilly was around a "Skipper" in the Gambino Family named Davie "Little Davie" Icivette. Davie was the Boss in the Boston area and parts of Miami, Florida. Like Joe the Indian, Davie was an old timer—a dying breed. Guys like the Indian and Little Davie were tough as nails and as ruthless as they come. Joe didn't want me to mention that I was with anyone. If anyone mentioned "Wise Guys," I was supposed to act like I didn't know what they were talking about.

We met at 6:00 p.m. at a closed catering hall off of Route 10 in Randolph Township. I arrived with George Livieratos and Don Sheppard in our limousine. We had our driver pull right up to the front doors and make sure that everyone noticed our arrival.

Jilly Rizzo was wearing a nice, well-tailored suit. He was a tall, balding man about 5'11" and about 200 pounds. He also wore dark tinted glasses that covered a glass eye. Jilly had a couple of people with him at the meeting: Tony DelVecchio, who was introduced as Jilly's partner, and Frank Miller, an adviser to Jilly and Tony.

Tony did most of the talking. He told us he was from Newark, New Jersey, and that he lived in the Poconos not too far from where they planned to build a hotel and sports complex. I was very interested in the idea of doing a joint venture with these guys. Tony was sure gambling was coming to the Poconos, and if he was right, then we would have a gold mine with the hotel and sports complex that they wanted to build.

They showed us some drawings and plans they had for the project. It was going to be built on Echo Lake, which backed right up to Caesars' Pocono Palace property. Jilly and Tony had purchased the land with some other investors, and they were having problems with these people. The property was going into foreclosure, and they needed money right away to save it.

Tony DelVecchio and I were from the same neighborhoods in New Jersey, and we knew a lot of the same people. One of the things Tony and I agreed on from the beginning was that we would keep the Wise Guys out of this deal. I was never going to let Jilly and Tony know I was with anyone, although I knew I wasn't kidding Tony anymore than he was kidding me.

Tony worked for Jilly at his famous nightclub in New York, Jilly's. Jilly's was known for the celebrities that would frequent the place, especially Frank Sinatra, Jilly's long time friend and associate. The celebrities weren't the only ones known to be seen at Jilly's. The Wise Guys were there too, and they would come out in full force. Jilly was Frank Sinatra's bodyguard.

The first meeting was a success, and I went back to structure the deal to purchase fifty percent of Jilly's Enterprises for stock in World Wide Ventures, Corp.

CHAPTER 18: THE GREEK SPENDS BIG

I spent the next few weeks putting the Jilly's deal together. George Livieratos was worried about doing the Jilly's deal. He didn't want to spend the kind of money it would take to make the deal happen. I told George he was being short sighted, and that the price of the stock was where it was not because of George Livieratos but because of Larry Formato. George and I were selling our shares faster than I ever imagined, and the money was flowing like a raging river. He had no concept of how big this could be, but I did. I knew that if I used key words like gambling, Frank Sinatra, and hotel sports complex, the stock of World Wide Ventures would triple.

Frank Sinatra was still playing at Caesar's Palace in Las Vegas. My idea was to hire a female model from Gallery Magazine to kick off the Jilly's announcement at press conferences in Denver and Las Vegas. I wanted to use a hot model to jump from a high-rise hotel using the Safe-T-Scape and invite the press there to film her descent safely to the ground. Then we would hold a press conference with Jilly Rizzo and announce that World Wide Ventures, along with Jilly's Enterprises, had entered into a joint venture to build a Hotel and Sports Complex. I had my doubts about using the Safe-T-Scape, and to be honest, I really wasn't sure the damn thing worked.

I called Amos Walls, the inventor, and I grilled him about it. I wanted him there with us at the two events we had planned, and I wanted to make sure it was going to work. This was going to be some stock promotion. I couldn't remember in my years as a stockbroker anything like what we were about to do.

I had Ben Tarimina, the owner of Norbay Securities, and his best brokers, as well as other big hitters that I knew in the brokerage business scheduled to fly to Denver and then to Las Vegas—all paid for by World Wide Ventures. George Livieratos thought I lost my mind. I also had all the top producers from firms in Denver join us at the press conference. The producers who gave me orders for blocks of stock were invited to go onto Las Vegas with us. I arranged for another twenty-five brokers from California to join us in Las Vegas. In the end, the press conference, performing the demonstrations with the Safe-T-Scape, and booking hotel accommodations and airline tickets, it was going to cost George and I about three hundred thousand dollars.

World Wide Ventures was trading at about $1.25 per share, and leading

Larry and George
Promoting Jilly's Resort

up to the Denver trip, there was already talk on the street that something big was going to happen with World Wide Ventures. I was trying to keep the price of the stock down until the press conference. I didn't want anyone front running the stock. (Front running means buying ahead of all my people and then selling back into my buying.)

This was like a heavyweight fight that everyone was waiting for. You could feel the anticipation and the excitement. We booked our rooms at the Stapleton Hotel in Denver. If the Hotel knew that we were going to have a girl jump off their balcony, they never would have allowed us to do it. Their insurance would not cover them for such a stunt. We knew it, and we had a hell of a hard time pulling it off without the hotel catching on to what we were doing. It is hard to imagine all the feelings that one has when they are about to do something no one has ever done before. I knew that if the Safe-T-Scape worked, at the end of that day, World Wide Ventures would be trading over $2.00 per share and that would make George and me worth over one hundred million dollars, but if it didn't work, George and I, and World Wide Ventures, would be broke.

The weather in Denver that morning was cold, and we originally planned to have Vicki jump from the balcony in Hot Pants. Tony DelVecchio, without knowing it, saved the day by suggesting that we have Vicki jump in a Snow Suit, because it was so cold out. I agreed to the idea. I figured what the hell. We're in Denver ski country, so it will work.

The news trucks started to arrive. Amos Walls, along with his son, Mark, were on the 11th floor with Vicki and Don Sheppard. I was down in the parking lot in the rear of the hotel with Jilly and Tony. The TV cameras were rolling and the photographers were everywhere. Vicki moved out onto the balcony, and I could see she was wearing the harness to the Safe-T-Scape. My heart was racing. I could not help to think if something went wrong, that it would be the end of World Wide Ventures. I had gambled millions of dollars on the fact that Amos Walls knew what he was doing.

All Vicki had to do was hold onto the straps above her head and jump. Vicki lifted one leg over the railing of the balcony and then the other. On the ledge of the balcony with her back to everyone looking up at her, it happened. Vicki jumped off the balcony in what looked like a backward swan dive—not holding onto the straps. She flipped upside down. I could hear the cable of the Safe-T-Scape. It sounded like a fishing reel that was peeling off-line when a big fish hits it. Vicki fell very quickly, bouncing off at least two or three of the balconies below.

Don Sheppard, Frank Miller, George Livieratos,
Jilly Rizzo & Tony Delvecchio

It's over, I thought, watching her bounce off two or three of the balconies upside down. We're finished, and it's all caught on film.

Jilly moved under the falling model, later claiming that he thought he was going to have to catch her. All of a sudden, the braking device kicked into gear. Right before Vicki hit the ground, it slowed her descent and she was able to right herself and land on her feet. The crowd went nuts, clapping their hands and cheering.

Tony DelVecchio and I grabbed Vicki by each arm, and this kid was a champ. I knew she was scared half to death and she could barely stand.

"The cameras are on you," I whispered to her. "Smile."

And that's exactly what she did.

If Tony had not suggested putting her in a snowsuit, she would have been all cut and bruised from hitting the walls and balconies. The press asked me if I felt that the demonstration was a success.

"We proved that the Safe-T-Scape works," I said. "It is only to be used as a last resort. If a fire is about to burn you, and you are choking from the smoke, you can be sure that the Safe-T-Scape will get you to the ground quickly and safe your life. World Wide Ventures proved this fact today."

We invited the press to a conference room at the hotel that we rented and had catered. It was in the conference room that I made the announcement that World Wide Ventures had entered into a joint venture with Jilly's Enterprises to build a Hotel and Sports Complex. I then walked over and unveiled a portrait of what the Hotel and Sports Complex was going to look like. I also welcomed Jilly Rizzo to the podium and he fielded some questions from the press. I felt like I was holding the winning ticket to the long shot at the race track as the press kept asking more and more questions, some about if Frank Sinatra was going to be involved and when we expected gambling to come into the Poconos. I knew that we would be all over the news that evening and the following morning.

That afternoon, some of us watched on the news what could have easily been the downfall of our company as Vicki bounced off the balconies of the Stapleton Hotel. But the news coverage was great, especially when they said Frank Sinatra's long time pal, Jilly Rizzo, is building a Hotel and Sports Complex in the Pocono Mountains in Pennsylvania with his new partners, World Wide Ventures, a publicly traded company.

I was right about the price of World Wide Ventures Stock. It opened at $2.50 the following morning.

"Larry, I will never doubt you ever again," George Livieratos said.

Prior to leaving Denver that day, I met with Will Smith, a Stock Promoter from Denver. He was truly excited about World Wide Ventures and what the company could do in the future. Will told me he wanted to get all his people involved in the World Wide deal, and that he believed in it. I told him I thought that would be great. I also told him that, for every 100,000 shares he could prove his people purchased, I would deliver to him, at any place he wanted, another 20,000 shares to be put in any name he requested. Will told me he already started buying the stock. We shook hands on our new deal, and I invited him to Las Vegas with us.

Mark Thompson was a young broker who loved the money and the excitement of the brokerage business. I could see the greed in his eyes when we talked. He would look at my watch that I was wearing and would make comments that it was really nice. I told him he could have the watch I was wearing, or we could go down to a jewelry store and I would buy him a new one. A ten thousand dollar watch would be a cheap price to pay for a kid that could buy a half a million shares of stock from me and put over a million dollars in my pocket. I told Mark to get one or two of his best brokers and to meet us in Las Vegas. I would pay for everything. When we were in Vegas, I would buy him a new Rolex watch, and I would show him how to make more money than he ever dreamed of making.

I was a great salesman, and I just sold Mark Thompson on World Wide Ventures. I believe that, between Mark and the two brokers he took to Vegas, they bought for their customer's accounts over one million shares of World Wide Ventures. Will Smith and Mark Thompson were happy to be on my team. They made a lot of money for themselves, and between them, they put over three million dollars in my pocket buying World Wide Stock from my accounts.

Everyone was in a good mood that Friday morning on the flight to Las Vegas. Jilly Rizzo and Tony DelVecchio had me in stitches. I was laughing so hard at Jilly telling the story of how he thought he was going to have to catch Vicki falling from the 11th floor of the Hotel.

"I thought I was gonna get fucking killed," Jilly said. "I didn't know what I was going to do if I did catch her."

Jilly could be a pretty funny guy when he wanted to be, and Tony was always good for telling funny stories. Jilly, Tony, George and I sat in first class, but I kept walking to the back of the plane to talk with our guests and make sure everyone was happy. With the success we had in Denver, I was sure that Las Vegas would be even better. This time we would not get a hotel with balconies. We were going to use the Sahara Hotel, and we actually got permission from the hotel to do it.

George and I took a limo to Caesars. We had beautiful suites reserved for us. I will never forget walking into Caesars that day. As I entered that beautiful Hotel, I could feel all the money from the casino, as if it all belonged to me. I actually believed that when we were done with our demonstration of the Safe-T-Scape and we announced our joint venture with Jilly's enterprise in Las Vegas, I could own a casino. I was on a roll, and I was not going to lose. This was my time to win.

We booked a suite just to have meetings in, and I had room service bring in extra large shrimp, caviar, hot and cold hors d'oeuvres, antipasti, pastries, champagne, liquor, and soft drinks. It was nothing short of a banquet, and there was nothing short of the room service bill that day either—over seven thousand dollars. Even I thought I might have gone a little overboard just so people could have some snacks when we were in meetings.

The messages were piling up for me with the hotel operator. Brokers from all over the country were calling me, wanting to come to Vegas. The word was out on the street. Every broker who was anybody was on their way to Vegas for a piece of the World Wide Ventures deal. I had picked the cream of the crop and flown them to Vegas. Everyone else that wanted to come was doing so on their money, but if they bought enough stock and could prove the buy orders, I would reimburse them for all their expenses.

George and I split up. I was letting him handle the public relations, and I was handling all the brokers. This was in no means a pleasure trip for my team. It was all business, and we had a job to do. I was making sure it was going to get done right. I was holding private meetings with brokers and taking their commitments on how much World Wide Stock they were going to buy. From the time George and I arrived at the hotel, we started working. I finally went to my suite around 3:00 a.m. and just crashed from a long day, a pretty fucking exciting one at that.

Larry, Tony and Vicki after a successful
Safe-T-Scape demonstration in Las Vegas

DANGEROUS WAYS

SUN Metro

Street Talk / Gaming / Local / State

Touch-and-go for a moment

In photos at top right and far right, it was supposed to take a couple of minutes to descend on the safety harness, but it was more like 10 seconds. Demonstrators of the lifesaving device, bottom, were only slightly embarrassed by the test Thursday at the Sahara Hotel. Vicki Whitten, cover girl on the May issue of Gallery magazine, is the model.

SUNfoto by JIM LAURIE

I had the rest of the weekend to meet and greet brokers from all over the country, while George was busy meeting people and showing them a good time. George and I were a good team. I let him do what he did best, and that was party, while I handled the business. I would send George to all the parties and functions. I wanted him to be a big shot. I let people buy into thinking George was a big "Greek Tycoon".

The weekend went by fast, and some brokers didn't stay for the Safe-T-Scape demonstration on Monday morning. They wanted to get back to call their clients and start buying World Wide Ventures stock. I felt that this time Vicki was going to do great. She had hot pants on, and she looked good. Vicki was going to jump from the 16th floor and just like the first jump in Denver; I was risking the whole company on a safe jump.

The setting was much the same. Jilly, Tony, and I were outside in the parking lot along with the TV cameras and the photographers. I couldn't count all the brokers that were there, and a big crowd had gathered. Don Sheppard came to get me. He told me we had a problem. Vicki was afraid to jump this time, and she didn't want to do it. My stepbrother, Rick, had been sleeping with Vicki since we got to Denver, and I told him to go up there and push her off the fucking ledge if she doesn't jump herself.

Everyone was getting antsy. No one knew what was taking so long. We were thirty minutes past the scheduled time for the jump. I went into the hotel and up to the room where Vicki was at.

"You're going to be fine," I assured her. "There are no balconies this time. All you have to do is remember to hold onto the straps."

I tried to comfort her and give her courage, although I got to tell you, I wouldn't jump out that window for a hundred million dollars. But getting your picture in the newspapers and on TV is worth more than money to some people, and Vicki was one of them.

"You're going to be on talk shows and in newspapers all over the world," I told her.

She thought about what I said, and I guess that did the trick. She took a deep breath.

"I'm ready," Vicki said. "I'll do it."

"I'll be at the bottom waiting for you, just like in Denver," I said.

When I got back downstairs, Vicki was already out on the ledge. As I looked up, she just stepped off. This time, unlike in Denver, Vicki seemed to just float to the bottom, and in fact, she waved to the crowd as she passed the last few floors. I was right about what I told Vicki. Her picture was everywhere.

World Wide Ventures pulled it off. Every news station covered the story, and with the announcement of the joint venture with Jilly's Enterprises, we were really rocking.

That night, we had a dinner party, and I said my goodbyes to everyone. I thanked them all for coming, and I told them I looked forward to making a lot of money with them. The last few days were so busy for me I almost forgot all about Mark Thompson and the watch I promised him. I called Mark at his room and asked him to meet me in the lobby. I took him to a jewelry store and bought him a Rolex Submariner.

I was on my way home to New Jersey. Jilly was going home to Palm Springs where he owned a home not too far from Frank Sinatra. I couldn't get back fast enough. I wanted to be in my office, answering my phones, telling my story about how great the jumps were in Denver and Vegas—telling brokers, "You should have been there."

I met with the Indian at his son's video store, and I filled him in on everything that was going on. The Indian was not happy about how expensive everything was, and he did not grasp why I needed to spend all the money I did to bring everyone together for the demonstrations and the press release.

"Joe, think about this," I said. "Not too long ago, I gave you five million shares of World Wide Ventures stock, and when you got it, it was worthless. Now it's almost three dollars per share. So what if I spent maybe half a million or more? Look at what you have because of what I did—almost fifteen million dollars."

"You guys are making a lot of money, and I have to split mine with a lot of people," Joe said.

"We all have a lot of people we have to share with."

I arranged to have two million shares of Joe's stock bought from him at $2.50 a share. Five million dollars I put in his pocket, and he still had three million shares left. I figured that would keep him happy for a while.

I hated going there to see Joe. It wasn't the same as when I used to go see my old friend, Red. Man, did I miss him. I wished Red were there to see what I did with World Wide Ventures.

The Jilly's deal was going to cost somewhere around fifty-five million dollars to build, and I had started looking for investment bankers that would raise the money for me in a public offering for Jilly's Enterprises.

George and I would go to the Holiday Inn in East Orange, New Jersey for dinner and drinks, and it became our hang out. George was getting good at playing his role as a Greek Tycoon. I actually think he started believing it. George was really starting to grow on me, and I was getting to like him. Now that Red wasn't around anymore, there was no reason for me to stay on top of George. I told George that I had set out to set him up for the Wise Guys so they could take whatever he had because he beat Gyp De Carlo on a gambling debt. George admitted to me that he did beat Gyp and that he made the story up about paying him off.

"From now on, no more fucking gambling," I warned.

George was always taking the limousine everywhere he went because his car was a real piece of crap. He was driving a 1980 Cadillac Seville, and I couldn't stand for anyone to see him in it. I called my old friend, Sandy Wallach, and asked him what high profile cars he had available. Sandy told me he had a nice Rolls Royce Convertible. I told Sandy to get the car ready, and I was coming to get it with my partner, George Livieratos, and to title it to World Wide Ventures. I asked George to go for a ride with me to Apple Chevrolet in Rutherford, New Jersey. Apple Chevrolet was a dealership Sandy Wallach bought for his Son, Jimmy Wallach. George had no idea why we were going there. I was always trading cars, and I told George I was going to look at a Mercedes and I wanted his opinion.

Jimmy had the Corniche all cleaned and shining when we arrived. I walked right past it, and George stopped to look at it.

"You look like you should be driving that car," I said.

"I would cut off my prick to have a car like that," George said.

"You better get your knife out, because it's yours."

George couldn't believe his ears.

"Really?" he kept asking me.

The keys were in the car already.

"Go ahead, drive it home," I said. "It's all yours."

As crazy as things are, I did wind up looking at a Mercedes. It was a really old two door red convertible, and it looked brand new.

"Jimmy, call your dad and tell him I want this one too," I said.

I was really happy as I drove my new old Mercedes home that Friday afternoon. I was glad I was able to get George a Rolls Royce, and he loved that car. George could have bought ten Rolls Royces with all the money we were making, but he was too busy fucking everything with a heartbeat to be thinking about buying cars.

I needed a break, so I picked up Robin and my son, Sonny, in the little red convertible and took a ride to the New Jersey Shore. It was a good weekend. We had some fun on the boardwalk, and we stopped at my uncle's house for a short visit. Driving home with the top down was fun until the sun started going down. Robin and Sonny started to get cold. Robin and Sonny were so mad at me for driving with the damn top down. You would think I was trying to kill them or something. We stayed at the Holiday Inn that night and went home in the morning.

I arrived at the office Monday morning to find George sitting at his desk. He looked like death warmed over. I could tell he didn't have much sleep, if he slept at all, and he was smoking one cigarette after another.

"What's wrong with you?" I asked.

"I need to talk to you about something very serious that could break our partnership and our friendship," he said.

I knew he didn't screw my girlfriend because I was with her all weekend, so nothing else could possibly be that bad.

"Okay, George, tell me what it is that is so bad," I said.

"I left for Atlantic City shortly after getting back on Friday with the new car," George said.

"Yeah? So what's the big deal?"

"Larry, I fucked up. I took fifty thousand dollars of our money and I lost it."

I just looked at him.

"Great. Come on, we're going back to Atlantic City," I said. "I've been dying to play Blackjack. And who gives a fuck? It's only money."

We took our limo and one hundred thousand dollars and went to Harrah's on the Bay. We had a blast. We were there for three days and we left with our hundred thousand, plus the fifty thousand George had lost over the weekend and another twenty thousand on top of that. In the Limo on the way home, George thanked me for being the best partner he had ever had. We both agreed that if he spends one dollar, I spend one dollar. We shared equally in everything. From that day forward, we never questioned each other again about any spending or what we were buying. It turned out that if I bought a big screen TV, I would buy two, one for me and one for George, and George would do similar things.

Jilly was coming to New York on business for Frank Sinatra, and while he was in town, Tony set up a radio interview in the Poconos for Jilly, George and I. The interview was on a Saturday, and Robin and I took the Mercedes Convertible to the mountains for a nice drive. I was a little late getting there, and so were George and Jilly. We were in a rush to get into the building for the interview and piled into this tiny elevator, and we all got stuck in that damn thing. I thought for sure we were stuck in there for the rest of the weekend. After a few minutes of ringing the bell, we were saved, and we did manage to pull off the interview.

I asked Jilly to introduce me to some people on the West Coast. I felt we needed to penetrate that market, especially since we were going to look for fifty-five million dollars in funding. We made arrangements to meet in Los Angeles in two weeks. George and I were going to stay at the L'Ermitage Hotel in Beverly Hills. This was without a doubt, in my opinion, the finest hotel in Beverly Hills. It had great suites with a spiral staircase to the master bedroom. I didn't realize it when we first arrived in Beverly Hills, but George and I would end up living there for almost a year. To this day, I still tell people when they ask me how I liked living there, that I flew back home to New Jersey on weekends just to keep my sanity.

The phone system in the newly designed L'Ermitage Hotel was horrible. It was so frustrating for me to make calls to my brokers and to receive calls. I was complaining so much to the management that they had the phone company come in and install all new phones just for me. In my world, everything happened on East Coast time, and here I was on the West Coast. I would get up at 5:00 a.m., order room service, and start hitting the phones for the opening of the stock market.

I wasn't interested in the LA nightlife. I was interested in keeping my deal going, and that meant bringing more and more buying into the stock of World Wide Ventures. I thought it would be a cool thing to have a portable VCR/TV that I could bring with me to brokerage firms and show them our promotional tape of the Safe-T-Scape. In 1983, an item like that would cost a couple of thousand dollars. Now you can buy them in the stores for under two hundred bucks.

One smoggy morning, I took a cab to downtown LA and went to the offices of Sutro & Co, a member of the New York Stock Exchange. The manager of Sutro was a man by the name of Harrison Lee, and he was familiar with World Wide Ventures. It seems some of his clients had made inquiries of World Wide with him, and he also knew Jilly. When I showed him the Safe-T-Scape tape, I knew I had him. Here he was, the manager of a big board firm in downtown LA, and he was practically begging me to get him a position of World Wide Ventures Stock. He was hooked.

Harrison Lee started putting his clients into World Wide, and by the time I got back to my hotel that day, he had called me three times and wanted to take me to dinner. I was still very much into playing chess, and I had the electronic chess game in my suite with me. I would spend my nights playing chess against the computer game and thinking of ways to continue the buying of World Wide Ventures stock.

George was out on the town every night, and he was entertaining all of fucking LA. I could see that I created a monster. He was up all night drinking and smoking, hitting all the clubs, and making quite a name for himself in Beverly Hills, but the smart people knew who they needed to get close to. The whisper around town was about the guy who was hard to meet, George's partner, Larry Formato. And with all the money George was spreading around and the partying he was doing, people were more interested in the mystery man who stayed in the suite and very rarely came out. Everyone wanted to get close to me, from movie stars to singers.

Just about anyone who was anyone in the entertainment business in LA knew Jilly Rizzo. They could call him, but people were going around him to try to meet with me. Harrison Lee called me and asked me if I would have dinner with him, Steve Lawrence, and Eydie Gorme. They were also friends with Jilly, and I found it strange that they had Harrison Lee call me and set the dinner date without Jilly. We had a nice dinner at the L'Ermitage, and they were very nice people. They also became shareholders in World Wide Ventures. People would leave their numbers at the front desk for me to call them. If they were not in the brokerage business or I felt they were not going to buy stock, I would not talk to them, whereas George was talking to everyone. He thought he was a fucking celebrity.

Tony DelVecchio stopped in LA on his way to Palm Springs. We had planned a party in Palm Springs, where Jilly lived, to kick off the Jilly's Enterprises joint venture with World Wide Ventures. I can remember walking down the stairs from my bedroom into the living room of my suite and seeing the sofa bed pulled out, and there was Tony popping his head out from under the sheets. He was a fun guy. We talked about the plans for the Hotel and Resort and discussed the best way to raise the fifty-five million we would need to build it.

Tony stayed in my suite on the first floor, and he flew to Palm Springs with George and I. There was a new restaurant in Palm Springs that opened, and Jilly's nephew was in the orchestra. It was the "big band" sound, and I thought it was very cool. The band dressed in black tuxedos, and it was like stepping back in time to 1940. It was my favorite place in Palm Springs for dinner and music. We planned to have the party for Jilly at this restaurant.

We all stayed at the Spa Hotel, and it was great. I was getting daily massages and working the stock from my suite at the spa. Of course, George and I picked up the tab for everyone's rooms and guest services. George and I stumbled upon a jeweler in Palm Springs and bought so much gaudy jewelry. The jeweler had made a ring for Liberace, but he didn't like it. When George saw it, he flipped out. He had to have it. It looked like a woman's ring. It was sapphires and diamonds built like a cone with a diamond on top of the crown. George wanted that ring. The price was forty thousand dollars. George wore that ugly ring on his pinky, and I couldn't stand to look at it. There was a medallion that I thought was a scorpion. It was gold on black onyx, and since I'm a Scorpio, I bought it, along with a thick gold rope chain to put it on. I also bought a fifteen thousand dollar diamond and blue lapis gold ring. It was big and dripping gold. I bought it for Robin. George and I spent close to one hundred thousand dollars that day in the jewelry store, which turned out to be our favorite place to visit when we were in Palm Springs.

The party was set, and as became our custom, the press was invited along with some of Jilly's friends like Tommy Lasorta, Leo Durocher, and Burt Reynolds. George, by now, had acquired a following of his own, and he invited some of these leeches to tag along with us. We would use them as gophers. One of these people was a kid who went by the name "Nick Valenti." Nick had a great story. He claimed his father was a wealthy entrepreneur living in Beverly Hills, and he was rebelling against his father. He wanted to work for George while we were on the West Coast. I accepted Nick, but I never warmed up to him. There was something about him I just didn't like.

The party went off without a hitch except for one thing: George and I had been living off of our American Express Card. We purchased everything with it. If we wanted something and the merchant didn't take American Express, we would make them get it. We even made our lawyers and accountants take it, but the restaurant where we had the party didn't take American Express. They wouldn't take an out-of-state check either. Jilly convinced the owner to take our check and that it wouldn't bounce. The bill was almost twenty thousand dollars, so the owner had plenty to be worried about.

"Please, Larry, whatever you do, don't let Jilly get embarrassed," DelVecchio told me. "Don't let that check bounce."

I was in charge of making the money, and George was in charge of paying the bills. Our whole entourage left Palm Springs and headed to wherever their homes were.

I will never forget the look on Robin's face when I presented her with the gift of that ring. She looked as though it were a joke I was playing on her.

"It looks like you got it out of the twenty-five cents machine," Robin said. "That has to be the ugliest ring I've ever seen."

I have to admit, looking back on it now, she was right. But back then, I took the ring back. I was so mad at her for being ungrateful that I returned it and bought something for myself.

I called George and reminded him to make sure that the check to the restaurant got covered. George, who always waited until the last second to do anything, didn't make the bank in time, and of course, the check bounced. I could hear Jilly yelling at Tony from Palm Springs to the Poconos. Tony was quick to call me.

"What the fuck happened?" Tony asked me over the phone.

"It was a mistake," I told him. "We're already correcting it."

Jilly wasn't too happy with that response, but what was I to do? Say George is a fuck up and that he didn't care enough to take care of it right away? Jilly and Tony were already getting used to George fucking with them, and they weren't getting along too well with him. I almost think George let that check bounce on purpose.

Tony had invited me up to his house in the Poconos not too far from where we were going to build our Hotel and Sports Complex. I drove there with Robin and my son, Sonny. I liked driving to the Poconos and we planned on making a day of it. Tony's boys were close to Sonny's age, so he would enjoy himself, and later we were going to go to Bushkill Falls. I was almost at Tony's house when my car phone rang.

"It's an emergency," George said. "I need you here right away."

"George, I'm on my way to the Poconos. I'm almost at Tony's house." I said.

"I'm in trouble with some Wise Guys from Newark."

"Who are they?"

"Andy Gerald, Tony Devingo, and John Riggiliro."

"Where are they?"

"At our office."

I put my hand to my face, pinching the bridge of my nose.

"Put one of them on the phone," I said.

After a brief pause, I heard someone pick the phone back up.

"Yeah go ahead," he said. "What do you got to tell me? Is this fucking guy with you?"

"My name is Larry Formato," I said. "I'm not available to be there until tomorrow, but I know some very nice people, friends of ours, if you know what

I mean. I want to meet with you to resolve this problem with the Greek."

We set a time for 11:00 a.m. the next morning. I told George to relax and that nothing was going to happen to him. I called Lenny and told him I had a sit down with Andy Gerard over George and asked him to meet me at the office at eleven to hear the bullshit. George said that they were pressing him for twenty-five thousand dollars over some real-estate deal that went bad. He was just a small part of the deal, but they were trying to get all the money from him.

George was acting tough, like he wasn't scared in front of me and Lenny, but when Andy showed up with his partner, George was visibly shaken. I let them start the conversation and listened to them talk about George and how he tried to beat them. I was watching Lenny very closely to see what his reaction was going to be. When they asked for the twenty-five grand, Lenny wanted to make a settlement and a payoff arrangement.

"Hold it," I said. "We're not fucking paying anything off, and we're not accepting responsibility for this money."

I turned to George.

"Do you owe these people twenty-five grand?" I asked.

"No fucking way," George said.

"Andy, because there were other people involved in the deal, it's not fair for George to pay the money," I said. "Unless anyone else is going to pay anything, George isn't going to pay anything either."

If I didn't stop Lenny from talking, we would have looked weak, and George would have paid the money. It wasn't that Lenny was unsure of himself. He just didn't know how to handle himself in sit-downs. He learned from this one. George was off the hook again, and I saved his ass one more time.

Our stock was doing great, and we were selling a lot of shares. We increased our market makers to over twenty-five firms. Surprisingly, we were getting calls about the Safe-T-Scape from all over the country, and people actually wanted to buy it.

I had just sent my Rolls Royce into the shop to have it painted. I was talking to Sandy Wallach and he told me I should get rid of the little Mercedes I had and buy this new 500 SEC that he just got in. He also told me about a Mercedes Limousine he had. It was a 500 SEL, and it was beautiful. The price for the Limo was $125,000 and the 500 SEC was $62,000. I told Sandy to come get the little red car, pick up the piece of shit Lincoln Limo we had, and bring me both new cars. This Mercedes Limo was the shit, and I do believe

George and I were one of the first people to have a new 500 Mercedes Stretch Limousine. I was feeling pretty good during that time, so I also bought Don Sheppard a new Cadillac Eldorado. When Tony saw Don's car, he wanted one too, but George said no fucking way.

"Don't worry," I told Tony. "Go pick out the color you want. You got the car."

After all, Tony was our partner, and we were making money off our stock because of the Jilly connection to Frank Sinatra.

My friend Ronny Testa, the DJ from Chapter 11, was now the DJ at a club in Bloomfield, NJ called Jocks Place. Billy Stravacas, a nice kid who started with me as a bouncer and moved up to a bartender, was working there too. I started going there when I was not on the West Coast. It was a club a lot like Chapter 11, but not as big or as exciting. I always traveled there with at least two or more people, and a cheap night at Jocks Place was a couple of grand. All the waitresses and barmaids wanted to go out with me because of the money I would spend there and the big tips I would leave. I was comfortable there. It was like my own place. Jocks Place also had an oldies night, and when I was there, I got to sing with all the oldies groups. I made it my business to be there when my good friend, Freddy Paris from the Five Satins, was playing. Freddy wrote and sang one of my all time favorite songs, "In the Still of the Night."

One night at Jocks Place, Ronny's wife, Helen, had a few too many drinks. We were close friends, so I told Ronny I would drive her home and get her there safely. I had gone to the club in my Limo that night, and I had my driver bring the car around to the front doors so we could get right in and leave. Helen could hardly even walk to the car. Wise Guys have a rule: You don't fuck with another man's wife or girlfriend. That makes you wrong, and it also makes you dead if there's a beef. I had everything to do to keep her off me in my limo that night, and I was really glad to finally get her to her house. I never said anything to Ronny, and Helen never said anything to me about the way she had acted. It would have been easy to take advantage of her, but I wasn't that kind of guy. I believed strongly at the time that you abide by the rules set by the Wise Guys, but not my fucking partner, George.

We had a friend named Danny De Benadetto, a really nice older guy. Danny was harmless, but he had a brother who was a Wise Guy named "Louie Coke." Danny was married to a younger woman whose name was Dottie, and she was infatuated with George. Danny was hard of hearing, and because of that, his speech was also impaired. Dottie and George would sometimes laugh at Danny. I warned George to stay away from her and that he couldn't get involved with her, because it would be bad for all of us. Danny loved Sinatra and wanted to get to know Jilly, so George got Danny to put up fifty grand to buy stock personally from George's account. George promised to introduce him to Jilly. I was so fucking mad at George for that. I really liked Danny, and Dottie was flirting with George every chance she could. I made plans to go back to LA for a couple of reasons, but the most important one was to get George away from Dottie so I could try to talk some sense into him. The other reason was we were now going almost everywhere Sinatra was, because that's where Jilly was too.

George had his entourage meet him in LA. He had these two fat, ugly broads staying with him at the hotel, and they were disgusting. I have no idea what the hell George was thinking, having these girls there. I think he flew them in from New Orleans, and it seemed as though they were there to stay. And then there was Nick Valenti, waiting to kiss George's ass. It was all a bit too fucking crazy for me.

Jilly made a big mistake and introduced George to Laverne Gunther. Laverne was a big woman and wasn't very good looking, but she had connections, and George took advantage of them. Now, George didn't need Jilly anymore to get favors or to be introduced to anyone. By being with Laverne, who traveled in Hollywood's high society, George was now able to meet with famous celebrities as well as important state and government officials. Laverne would take George to every event that was important, and George just ate it up, getting his picture taken with the "Who's Who in America." George was really starting to believe he was a somebody—a big shot. It was all going to his head.

"I'm going to invite Danny and Dottie to Vegas to see Sinatra," George told me.

I looked around the people in his suite: the two fat broads he was fucking, Nick, and some other guy that I didn't know.

"Why don't you all go for a walk," I said. "I need to talk to George alone."

I couldn't wait for them to leave the room. I was so fucking mad. When they shut the door behind them, George lit a cigarette nervously.

"Do you think I work my ass off every night and sit in this fucking hotel room while you're out spending thousands and thousands of dollars that I made, for you to fuck it all up because you can't keep your fucking dick in your pants?" I started.

George acted like he didn't know what I was talking about.

"If I find out you're fucking Dottie, we are through," I said. "I will kill you before Louie Coke gets his hands on you. You're not going to get me killed because you have to fuck every woman you meet. Don't test me, George. I'll fuck you up, and I'll let the Indian know why I'm calling it quits."

"Fuck the Indian," George said. "Do you think I'm scared of that fucking asshole? I am George the Greek. Nobody fucks with me."

I got up and slapped him across the face.

"Now what, tough guy?" I said.

"Okay, okay, Larry. If it means that much to you, I won't fuck the bitch," George said, rubbing his face.

I turned and headed for the door.

"Remember, don't test me," I said, and then walked out.

George and I hadn't talked to each other at all after the argument until the next day when we had a meeting by the pool. We met because we were meeting one of the Reynolds', from RJ Reynolds Tobacco, to talk about possibly doing a joint venture together on the Hotel and Sports Complex. I thought the meeting went really well, but later when we had the chance to talk with one of the Reynolds representatives, he informed us that Mr. Reynolds was not interested in doing business with us because he thought that George and I were too flashy. We wore too much gold and gaudy jewelry.

That was it for me. I learned a new lesson—no more flash. I gave all my flashy jewelry to my brother and started wearing very conservative watches and rings, no more gold chains dripping from my neck or big gold rings with diamonds. I didn't get the Reynolds deal, but I did learn something money can't buy: how to look. I guess Old money can see new money coming a mile away, and if you want a piece of that old money, you need to act and look conservative.

Mateo's Restaurant was the place to be if you were a somebody. With the money George was spending there every night, I guess you could say he was a somebody. Me? I was a lot less noticeable, but Barry Huntsman wanted to know me. He was a friend of Jilly's, and was here in this country watching the interest of his crime family in London.

I met him in Mateo's one night with Jilly, and we started talking about stocks. He was interested in buying a position in World Wide Ventures. He wanted to trade in and out of the stock. I liked this guy. He was up front, and he didn't pull any punches.

"I can't stop you from buying World Wide Ventures stock, but I really don't need anyone unloading a bunch of shares on my market," I said.

We spent about two hours talking about World Wide Ventures.

"Why are you tied up with George?" Barry asked me. "People around town are all talking about how much money he throws around. You should be a little more careful."

Barry wanted to make money with me, but he was scared of the way George spent it. Mateo's was well known because there was always someone of some name value there, from Sinatra to Clint Eastwood. As usual, George would pick up the tab.

I didn't feel much like hanging out there anymore, and I was going to have the limo take me back to my hotel. Barry offered me a ride because he was leaving too. He had a very cool, custom-made, white Rolls Royce.

"What else would an English gentleman drive?" Barry joked.

"I own a Silver Shadow 11," I said. "What else would an Italian stock promoter drive?"

By the time I arrived back at my hotel, I had agreed to get Barry one hundred thousand shares of World Wide Ventures between the bid and the ask. Barry got a good deal.

Rick Johnson, Light Heavyweight Champion Michael Spinks and Nick Valenti in Larry's Mercedes Limousine

CHAPTER 19: MISSING IN ACTION

George came to my room and apologized to me for the way he was acting. He agreed with me that I was right. George suggested that I fly Robin out to spend some time with me, and then maybe I would relax a little and have a sort of mini vacation. I thought that was a great idea, and I really looked forward to seeing Robin.

I made plans for Robin to fly into LAX airport in LA, but George, Don Sheppard, and Tony DelVecchio were leaving for Palm Springs. I was going to wait for Robin and drive to Palm Springs with her, but instead, at the last minute I decided to fly to Palm Springs with the rest of the guys. We were going to meet Jilly and Frank Miller there. I had talked to Nick Valenti and arranged for him to meet Robin at the airport and drive her to Palm Springs. We made all the arrangements for rooms for everyone, and I was really excited about seeing Robin. I estimated that by the time Nick picked up Robin and got on the road, they should arrive in Palm Springs around 6:00 p.m.

Everyone went to dinner while I waited at the hotel for Robin to get there. It was starting to get late, and there was still no word from Nick or Robin. They were three hours late. I was getting really worried because I couldn't imagine where they were or why I had not heard from them. I started calling the airport to see if her plane landed on time, and it did, but they would not tell me if Robin was on the flight.

If something happened to her, what would I say to her mother? I thought.

I really didn't know this guy Nick, and for all I knew, he could have killed her on the way there. I was told that the road to Palm Springs was dangerous to drive on. At times, strong winds could kick up, and cars have been found in ditches off the side of the road. I was on the phone with the California Highway Patrol, asking them to check the highways. As time went on, I was losing my mind. Robin would have called me if something was wrong or she was delayed.

Tony, George, and the guys came back. It was sometime after midnight when I told them Robin and Nick had not arrived, and then everyone got nervous. Don Sheppard was on the phone with the Palm Springs Police, and I was calling all the hospitals from LA to Palm Springs. I just can't explain the feeling of sickness that came over me with every minute that passed by with no word from Robin.

It was about 6:30 in the morning when Robin pulled up to the hotel with Nick. It was like I couldn't believe my eyes. I was certain that something bad had happened to them, but there they were, right in front of me.

"What are you doing up so early?" Nick asked me, stepping out of the car.

"Where the hell have you been?" I asked, blood boiling.

"We were sightseeing all night."

I lost my mind. I attacked him. I was going to kill him, right there in front of everyone. Don and George had to restrain me.

"I'm okay," I said. "Let me go."

They let go of me as Robin got out of the car. I then turned to her.

"Where were you?" I asked.

"We were out sightseeing," Robin said.

Don and George grabbed me as I lunged at her. Everyone there had all to do to stop me from killing her. I was never so mad. Don got Robin away from me and took her to his room to find out what really happened. Nick was told to go to another hotel and to stay as far away from me as possible until this was resolved.

The hotel called the police. They wanted to arrest me because I was out of control. They wanted to see Robin and talk to her, so she came to the lobby and started telling the police she didn't know anything was wrong. Nick kept telling her she didn't need to call me and that I would know she was safe with him. When she told them he took her to the beach and they walked on the boardwalk, I lost it and attacked her again. All I wanted to do was get my hands on her. The police were trying to hold me back, and Don and George were getting in the middle of it. One of the cops drew his gun, but things calmed down again for the time being. They allowed me to go to my suite, as long as I didn't go near Robin. Robin was going to go and get the next plane out of Palm Springs back to New Jersey.

I owned a gold Piaget watch that I bought from a friend of Barry Huntsman. It was the watch to own at that time. I put the watch on when I got back in my suite. Don came to my room to try to explain what happened with Robin and Nick.

"It's fucked up that they didn't call, but she swears nothing happened between them," Don said. "She can't stop crying. If you can be calm, you should go talk to her."

"I just want her to leave," I said. "But I'll go hear what she has to say."

I went to Don's room to talk to Robin. I was like a detective questioning her and re-questioning her. I didn't believe her story.

"I just want to go home," Robin said, tears still streaming down her face.

"Then get the fuck out," I said. "We're through."

"Good!" she yelled with the full force of her Irish temper.

We went out into the hallway, still fighting back and forth. She said something to me, and I grabbed her arm. She swung around and grabbed me, trying to push away from me. When she grabbed my wrist, my Piaget watch broke into a million pieces all over the floor. I think we were both shocked, because it seemed to have stopped the fighting for the moment.

Robin was set on getting to the airport and going home. Half of me wanted her to go, and the other half wanted her to stay, but she was all for leaving. At that time, she didn't want any part of me. She said I was crazy. Maybe she was right, because I was crazy that night with worry. When I found out there was nothing to worry about, then I was mad. I look back at it now, and I think how crazy it really was. I tried to kill Nick, then Robin; I almost got shot, and I made a fool of myself, all in one night.

Robin went back to New Jersey, and I stayed in Palm Springs until I went on to Las Vegas. Frank Sinatra was playing at Caesars, and of course, we had the best seats in the house. Laverne Gunther handled all of Sinatra's tickets and traveling. Laverne had the hots for George, and George was never one to pass up pussy, no matter how old, fat or ugly the women were. In fact, I can't remember ever seeing George with a good-looking woman. George had Laverne head over heels for him, and she would take him everywhere with her and introduce him to all the celebrities and Who's Who in the entertainment and political worlds. We went to all the Sinatra shows, and when Sinatra played at the Meadowlands in Jersey, George and I split one hundred tickets up that Laverne got for us.

It was some juggling act I was doing during these times. I was out at clubs in New York at night and bribing stockbrokers during the day to buy World Wide Ventures Stock. I fought with George over everything and answered to Joe the Indian, because Joe and the other guys in the crew hated George. They weren't happy with the way George would show off and flaunt everything he had in everyone's face. The Wise Guys were giving me a pretty hard time back then because they had a taste of the kind of money that penny stocks could generate. World Wide Ventures was spending about fifty thousand dollars a week. George and I were traveling back and forth from Jersey to LA weekly. George hated Jilly and Tony but loved to tell everyone he was Jilly's partner with Frank Sinatra. It seemed wherever I would go, I would run into some Wise Guy trying to get in on my deal.

Jilly knew a stock promoter from LA named Richard Carey. Rich was pretty connected with the Beverly Hills click and knew a lot of people. While I was in Vegas, Rich flew into town to meet me and see if he could fit in to help place some stock. Rich was married to Terry Moore, a famous actress, and that is how he made all his connections. I liked him, and decided to use him for my West Coast operation. We made a deal while we were in Vegas, and Rich flew back to LA with me and George. There wasn't a hot nightclub that Rich didn't know, and he knew the doorman at every club. We just walked right in without waiting everywhere. Rich introduced me and George to Clint Eastwood. We had a meeting with Clint at his ranch in Carmel, CA. George chartered a jet to fly from LA to Carmel. I sent Rich and George to go to Clint's place while I took care of business in LA. I worked the phones, calling my brokers and brokerage firms. Rich and George pitched Clint on doing a development deal on property Clint owned in Carmel, but it never happened.

The days and nights were running together for me. There was always so much going on. Movie stars, recording artists, and Wise Guys were around me almost every second of the day. Brokers were calling me constantly, wanting more news on World Wide Ventures. I didn't have time for myself anymore, and everyone was tugging at me. My biggest problem that I could foresee was the Wise Guys. They wanted to know what was happening to all the money. Joe the Indian was having Lenny call me every day for an update. It was getting unbearable, and George didn't help. Every time he came home from the West Coast, he had more stories to tell of who he was with or what be bought.

While we were staying at the L'Ermitage during Oscar week, Brooke Shields was staying in the suite next to mine. I asked her if she would like to join me and Jilly for dinner in the restaurant on the top of the hotel. I told her James Caan and some other people were going to be joining us. When George found out that I had this dinner arranged, he had his flunky, Nick Valenti, rent every limousine in the hotel so he could pick up Jilly and James Caan, and drive everyone to and from all the parties after the Oscars. He was like a kid. He ordered dozens and dozens of roses for Brooke, and the only one that took any notice was Brooke's mother. Brooke's mother and George seemed to really hit it off, I think.

The restaurant in the hotel was on the top floor, and the elevator opened up right in the restaurant. If you were sitting at the right table, you would see everyone coming off the elevator and into the restaurant. That night we had

---

a big table right in front of the elevator. We were having a nice dinner. At the table was Jilly, Tony DelVecchio, Brooke Shields, James Caan, and some other women who were guests of Jilly's and Tony's. George and Brooke's mom were nowhere to be found. They were off having a good time by themselves.

I can remember ordering champagne, and just as I was toasting to good friends, the elevator doors opened, and George and Brooke Shields' mom fell to the floor, they were leaning against the doors screwing. So there they were, on the floor, right in front of everyone. It was really embarrassing for everyone, especially Brooke. We tried to act as if we didn't see what we all knew we saw. That night was an unforgettable night, and the tab for all the flowers, limos, dinner, booze, and extra help came to forty thousand dollars.

When Joe the Indian heard about that tab, it was almost curtains for George. What started as a simple dinner turned out to be an extravagant affair that cost a lot of money. I never blamed Jilly and Tony for wanting more money from the World Wide Deal. They had a firsthand experience watching George spend money like water. George and I were living in Beverly Hills at the most expensive hotel. Barry Huntsman suggested to me that we move from the L'Ermitage Hotel to the Beverly Hills Comstock Hotel. It was one-third the price, and as far as I was concerned, it was just as nice. I think I had just checked in when I had to fly back to PA for a meeting. The funding of the money for the Hotel and Sports Complex was not going to be as easy as we all originally thought.

We had a meeting with Middle Smith Field Township in PA where Echo Lake is. We were having problems with them too. It seemed as though nothing we did with this project was going right. The only thing going right was the sale of the stock, and we were selling more stock than we could get our hands on. I was driving the price of the stock up with all the buying, and to make it better, I had applied for an NASDAQ listing for World Wide Ventures Corp. Finally, after a lot of going back and forth with the SEC, World Wide got listed on the over-the-counter NASDAQ exchange with the symbol WWVC. Now we were right up there with other big companies. We were no longer a pink sheet or a penny stock, and it was going to be hard for anyone to discredit us.

I was in our office in Orange, NJ, and I was fighting with a trader about shorting World Wide. Shorting is when you sell without actually owning the stock. As an example, sell at $3.00 and hope to drive the stock down to $1.00. Then, buy it for $1.00, covering the sale of $3.00 and making a profit of $2.00. The trader said he worked for Eric Wynn. Eric was a stock promoter out of New York who wanted to be a Wise Guy and had an affiliation with the Bonanno Family. The trader was afraid of Eric, but he was more afraid of me.

"If you continue to short my stock, I'm going to have someone come over there and throw you out a window," I told the trader. "Start buying and stop selling. If Eric has a problem with that, have him call me. If you do the right thing, I'll see to it that you make a lot of money with me."

It took about ten minutes for Eric Wynn to call me. My secretary told me Eric was on the phone. Eric didn't even know who he was calling. He was just calling some guy named Larry.

"This call is going to be fun," I told George.

I picked up the phone.

"Who the fuck do you think you are?" Eric said.

"I'm Larry Formato," I said.

"Hey, asshole, I'm not mentioning names, and I don't think you should be either."

"Hey, Eric, I'm not mentioning names you jerk-off. I'm telling you who I am."

There was a long pause.

"Larry, I meant no disrespect," Eric said. "I thought you were just some guy hassling my trader over that stock. I apologize."

"Eric, go fuck yourself," I said. "Next time you call someone acting like a tough guy, you better know who you're talking to. You dumped thirty thousand shares of WWVC, and now I want you to go in and buy sixty thousand shares. I want to know what brokerage firm you use to buy the stock."

I swear, when Eric got off the phone, he asked himself, "What the fuck did I just do?"

I was happy to be back in NJ for a little while. I was getting to see my family and spend some time with Robin. I was still not over Robin being out all night with Nick, and she was still mad at me. I needed alone time with Robin to make up. George, Tony, Jilly and Frank Miller decided to go to Europe. There was no way I was going to make that trip. I wanted a vacation, but not to Europe with all those guys. I told everyone to have a great time, and I took Robin to my favorite place in Ft. Lauderdale, Pier 66.

I always stayed in the Mercedes suite. I would charter a private fishing boat, and Robin and I would go out deep-sea fishing. I loved being there with her and away from everyone and everything. The American Express Card was averaging about three hundred thousand a month with George and all those guys on a buying spree in Europe. He must have pushed it over six hundred thousand dollars.

I received an emergency phone call from George. He was frantic. He was stuck in Europe with Jilly and the boys, and they cut off our credit card.

Well, I wasn't happy either. My bill at my hotel must have been at least ten thousand dollars, but I had that on me in cash. They wanted to throw George in jail if he didn't make good for the money he owed in Europe, and they were serious.

I called American Express, and as luck would have it, their collection offices were in Ft Lauderdale. I was right there. I never had to go to their offices. I simply got them on the phone and told them my partner was stuck in Europe and was about to be put in jail. I was staying at Pier 66, and that if they didn't turn the card back on, I was never going to pay it. If they let us continue, I would get them out a check when I got back to my office for six hundred thousand. The card was back on, George was saved, and everyone had a great time.

I got a call early in the morning from George. He was in a hotel room with five girls—yes, really, five girls. He wanted to know if I wanted to talk to them.

"Are you crazy? I'm with Robin,' I said.

"Larry, you won't fucking believe what happened," he said. "I was eating this one girl's pussy, and she got so excited that she grabbed my hair. My hairpiece came off; she lost her balance, and fell backwards, almost right out the window."

"Great, George. I'm glad she didn't fall."

I hung up the phone.

Three hours later, Tony called me, laughing his ass off.

"Larry, the hotel got girls for all the guys, but no one wanted them," Tony said. "George took them all."

"I know," I said. "George already called me."

"You had to be here to see this to believe it. This fucking guy wore those five broads out. They looked like they were in a war, but George never got tired."

"Don't spend too much money."

"Yeah, okay."

He was still laughing when he hung up.

It was the trip of trips. I didn't think George was ever going to come home. Jilly and the boys all came home with new clothes, shoes, and jewelry. Who paid for it? George, on our American Express card. If Joe the Indian knew one tenth of this, he would have had George killed. I was now rested from my trip to Florida, and I was on my way back to the West Coast to all the insanity and craziness.

CHAPTER 20: LITTLE DAVIE AND THE ONE-EYED COCKSUCKER

World Wide Ventures was the "Over The Counter" stock to be involved with. I was doing the promotion of the century; between the West Coast and the East Coast, every OTC (over the counter) brokerage firm was either buying from the hype or from the bribes I was giving to their brokers. George was spending big money, upwards to $100-$200,000 a week. We were living off of our American Express Cards, and back then, American Express would allow you to spend as much as you could prove your net assets were.

Norbay Securities was the main market maker for World Wide Ventures. All of our stock was deposited into Norbay's trading account. Literally every time the stock moved up, George and I got richer, and Norbay reported our stock holdings and its net worth to American Express. Basically, we had an unlimited American Express Credit Card. Due to the increasing value of the World-Wide Stock, George and I became multi-millionaires. When we were on the West Coast, it was nothing for George to blow through a million dollars a month on parties, girls, and gambling. Jilly was getting upset because he was watching first-hand the money George was spending. All of Jilly's friends had heard by now about George the Greek Tycoon, the multi-millionaire who was living at the L'Ermitage Hotel in Beverly Hills; they were flocking to him as if he were the Pied Piper.

No one really knew who I was, I very rarely left my hotel suite. There were rumors that George's partner was the brains and the real money behind everything. Lots of people tried meeting with me, but I stayed in the shadows never wanting to meet with anyone. I only cared about working the stock. I was the mystery guy, and a lot of people had heard I was a connected guy from Jersey. I was happy to let George do his thing, it was good promotion for the stock, and although his social life may have been a bit overboard, he was doing exactly what I needed him to do. There were a few times I had warned him to tone down his spending, because people were getting jealous, especially Jilly.

Jilly couldn't take all the gossip, and he called me and asked what the fuck George was doing with all his friends, and he wanted to know where his end of the money was that George was spending. I knew it wouldn't take long for Jilly to call for a "Sit Down". On more than one occasion, Lenny had mentioned to me to make sure we kicked money upstairs to Joe. These guys were no fuckin joke, and if they didn't see their end, or if they felt you were holding out, the very least you could expect was to get a beating. I knew for sure that if Joe had any idea how much was being thrown away by George, George would be killed. If Jilly let it be known at a sit down what was happening in Beverly Hills with all the money that was being spent, it would be big problems, and I was the one who Joe was going to hold accountable. They would kill George and make me pay them all the money.

I told George, "We need to get Joe some money, and soon, or we're gonna get fucked."

George's response was, "Fuck Him."

"Stop with the fucking bullshit George, you're going to get us both killed," I told him.

I would wake up every morning expecting to get a call from Lenny that Joe wants to see me. Sure enough, that call came while I was in Vegas meeting with some brokers. When the Boss calls for you, you drop everything and you go. That's exactly what I did.

I was on the next flight back to Jersey. As soon as my plane landed, I went straight to my vault for my emergency funds and I counted out $250,000 dollars. I knew this would appease Joe and at least keep him off of George's back for a while.

Joe was sitting in the back of the club, and I had just sat down when Lenny walked in. I gave the shopping bag with the cash in it to Joe.

He asked me, "how much?"

I told him, "Two Fifty Large."

Lenny said, "Minga."

I knew by Lenny's reaction that they would be happy with that amount. Joe's favorite name for Jilly was One-Eyed Cocksucker because Jilly had a glass eye. Joe told me, "We're going to Miami tomorrow to meet that One-Eyed Cocksucker and the Little Guy" (Little Davie Iccavitte).

Davie was a Capo in the Gambino Family, a ruthless old-timer who was known for whacking out guys. He controlled most of Boston and Miami with fear. Joe told me that Jilly was making a beef about George.

He asked me straight out, "Do we really need this Greek Mother Fucker?" It was then that I knew they were gonna whack George.

Lenny and I met Joe in Miami where we had dinner with Jilly and Little Davie. Jilly was complaining that George was embarrassing him out in Beverly Hills. I sat and listened as Jilly talked about George, and how much money he was spending.

I was really getting sick of hearing all this bullshit, and I said to Jilly, "What difference does it matter to you how much fucking money George spends, he's not spending your money."

Jilly said, "You fuckin guys are making millions off of this stock because of me and Frank" (Frank Sinatra).

I said, "Most of the money being spent is for promotion, how the fuck do you think this stock got so high?"

Davie asked Joe. "Is there any room here for us to have a taste? I mean, come-on, this fucking guy's all over the fuckin place! Jilly told me this fucking Greek spent a few hundred thousand just on broads."

Jilly jumped in and said, "I want that mother fucker out of California and I don't want him using Sinatra's name anymore."

Joe's answer was, "The Greek goes where Larry tells him to go. If he gets out of line, Larry will straighten him out. As far as a taste is concerned, we haven't seen a fuckin dime yet, we're waiting to see where this all goes. This Kid knows what he's doin'," pointing his finger at me.

"You guys got a lot of stock, and because of him, it's worth a lot of money, so what the fuck are we talkin about here?"

Joe hated Jilly, and I knew he was waiting to tell him to go fuck himself. Jilly was not happy after hearing what Joe had to say.

Davie had a suggestion to keep the peace between everyone, he had a stock he got from a guy that owed him some money. He wanted me to get rid of the stock for him, and he would take care of Jilly and Frank from what I sold the stock for. We went back and forth, and I finally agreed to do it, letting him know there would be expenses attached to the sale of it.

I told Jilly, "When this is done, I don't want to hear any more shit about George and his spending." Jilly felt as though he had won the sit down because he was going to get some money from the sale of Davies stock, and although I knew Davie would never give up any money, it's just not the Wise Guy way. Jilly walked away a winner in his mind.

It was a relief to be done with all the bullshit from him.

Now I just had to deal with Joe and his plans for the Greek.

CHAPTER 21: THE TROUBLE WITH BLINDER ROBINSON

It was a cold, almost freezing morning. My Rolls Royce was slipping and sliding on an icey Route 280 highway in New Jersey. I was on my way to the headquarters of World Wide Ventures, where George and I made a fortune selling World Wide Stock to stockbrokers. I was thinking just how lucky George was to have escaped the wrath of Joe, and I knew it was going to be just a matter of time before George got clipped. I tried to clear my mind from these thoughts as I reached for my car phone.

"World Wide Ventures, can I help you," said Rose, our secretary.

I said, "Hey, it's me. Where's George?"

Rose said, "Larry, I was just trying to reach you on your car phone. George is in your office, screaming on the phone with the SEC. You need to get here fast, he's calling them names and telling them he's owns the most successful penny stock company in the country – oh, wait, he just hung up, hold on."

I yelled at George right up until the time I pulled into the parking lot of our offices. I hated when George acted like a jerk, and I was always left to clean up his mess. I walked into the office and went straight back to my private office, and George tried to talk to me, but I just put my hand up and said to him, "don't say a fucking word."

I sat down at my desk and turned on my Level III Machine, which allows you to enter bid/ask quotes as the trades are being executed right in front of you. These machines are typically found only on the trading floors of brokerage firms and market makers. I was able to have one installed at our office; I paid a guy three thousand dollars to put it in for me.

WWVC was the trading symbol for World Wide Ventures Corp., and I could see Norbay Securities was the main market maker, and right behind them was Troster Singer and Wilson Sloan followed by a slew of Big Board Firms like Michell Schwarber, Oppenheimer, and Merrill Lynch. I could see the trades clicking by, and Norbay was getting hit with a lot of stock.

Ben, the owner of Norbay and head trader, was standing firm on his high bid - he was buying WWVC five and ten thousand shares at a time. I called Ben as quickly as I could to find out where all this stock was coming from, and why someone was dumping trying to hurt my market. Ben told me Blinder Robinson was doing all the selling. They hit him for fifty thousand shares. I told Ben to drop his bid and move out of the way.

I then called Mickey at Troster Singer, and told him to drop his bid, and I did the same thing with Wilson Sloan. That only left the big board firms.

I had so much power with a phone call to the market makers, I could move a stock up or down.

Don Weis was the head trader at Blinder Robinson. I called him and said, "What the fuck are you doing with WWVC?"

He said, "who is this?"

I said, "I'm Larry Formato, and your gonna buy back every single share you dumped into the market today, or I'm gonna break your fucking head!"

"Larry, I didn't know it was your deal, Meyer" (Meyer Robinson, owner of Blinder Robinson) "told me to short one hundred thousand shares. I don't want any problems."

I fucking hated Meyer Robinson, going back to my First Jersey Days.

"Look", I said to Don, "I know you were just following orders, so this is what I'm going to do. I've got ten thousand free-trading shares for you to put in any account you want it to go to. You go back into the market and buy back all those shares you dumped. Tell Meyer the stock started to run the other way, and you had to cover your short or the trading account was going to lose two- to three-hundred thousand dollars. I'm going to lift the market so you look like a hero to Meyer, and I'll get you that ten thousand shares, but don't you hit my bids with it. You sell it into the buying."

Then I said, "My word is good, and if Meyer gives you a problem, call me. I've got other firms that will take you if I tell them to."

I also said, "Make sure you go to Norbay and buy back the all the shares you dumped, and make sure to lose twenty-five thousand in your trading account, that's me letting Meyer off easy. I'll be watching the trading, Don. Do the right thing, don't fuck me on this."

The rest of the day seemed to go by pretty good, and World Wide ended up a quarter of a point higher on the trading day. This type of thing with Blinder Robinson always happened, and it was my job to stay on top of our trading to make sure no one ever fucked with us. George and I went back to being partners with business as usual.

CHAPTER 22: SIT DOWN AT PALS CABIN

It was 11:00 pm. I had just turned on The Honeymooners when my phone rang. I recognized the voice immediately.

Red said, "Meet me in one hour at the place."

I knew the place he was talking about; it was Pal's Cabin in West Orange, New Jersey that was our meeting spot. We never met there late at night, and this was really troubling to me. I grabbed my car keys and was out the door, thinking the whole time while I was driving, what the fuck did I do now?

Red was already inside sitting at our usual booth. The steam from his coffee was still rising from his cup as he picked it up for a sip.

He said, "We're gonna wait for Lenny, and then we are gonna take a ride."

I wasn't sure if I should ask where or if I should just shut the fuck up. Red pulled out a pack of Kent 100s and offered me one; I motioned *no* and grabbed a Parliament from my shirt pocket.

It seemed as though the waitress and Lenny came to the table at the same time. Red waved her off and Lenny bent over and kissed Red on the check, and as he was sitting he kissed me on the check and sat down.

"What's up, Fellas?" Lenny said.

Red answered, "Did you take care of that thing with that guy?"

Lenny said, "Yeah, we picked him up coming out of his office in New York, and we have him at the house in Livingston. The Blade and couple of the boys are sitting with him."

I was trying to figure out who they were talking about and what it had to do with me. Red never brought me into this side of his world; he always wanted me to keep legit and stay clean, but yet here I was trying to figure out who Lenny and the boys picked up.

Red said, "Come on, we don't have time for you guys to have coffee - you drive," and he tossed me his keys.

We were not far from Livingston, and the conversation in the car had nothing to do with the guy they were holding. Lenny gave me directions to the house, and as I pulled in the driveway, it appeared to be completely dark.

Now, I was really wondering what was I doing here with Red and Lenny. The hair on the back of my neck was standing up. I have heard of guys getting whacked in these exact circumstances, and I couldn't help think I was gonna be next. Lenny told me to pull around the back, and I could see lights coming from the basement.

Red said, "Lets get this over with."

Lenny lifted up the metal cellar doors and he walked down the steps, followed by Red and I.

Lenny knocked on the door, "it's me," he said to the guy on the other side. The door opened and we all walked into this dingy, barely-lit basement.

The Blade came up to Red and kissed him on the cheek, and then he greeted me the same way. The Blade told Lenny, "This guy's been a real pain in the ass. He keeps saying, 'I'm with people'."

Lenny laughed, and said, "*We* are people."

Sitting on a chair in the corner, I got a good look at Eric Fink. It was just the day before that I had a huge argument with him on the phone. He was fucking with one of the stocks I was promoting, so I called him and told him he was going to have to buy back all the shares he was dumping into the market, and that, because he was shorting my stock, he would have to buy an additional One Hundred Thousand shares.

Eric said, "Fuck You! Who do you think you are." He came on like a real telephone tough guy.

I said to him, "Me, I'm Larry Formato, and you're going to find out just who I am!"

Eric had gained some attention because he was making big money. He caught the eye of some wise guys from Brooklyn, and he was claimed by the Bonanno Family. This meant they owned him and gave him the confidence he needed to bully his way around the street with the traders. Eric thought he had enough juice to fuck with me and my market. He told me on the phone, "Fuck you, and whoever you're with."

Red walked over to Eric, and then he motioned with his finger for me to come closer. Red said to Eric, "You see this guy?" pointing at me. "Don't you ever fucking disrespect him again." With that, Red punched him in the face splitting open his eye.

Eric screamed, and then started yelling, "You can't touch me; I'm with Porky from Brooklyn!"

"Oh, we can't, huh, tough guy?" Red said as he hit him again; I think Red must have had something in his hand like a slap-jack or a roll of quarters, because Eric started spitting out blood and some teeth.

"Listen to me you piece of shit!" said Red, "You tell Porky what you told Larry on the phone. 'Fuck you and who ever you're with.' Isn't that what you said, tough guy?" Red continued, "Now, I'm gonna send you back to Porky so you can tell him Larry's with Red."

Red told the Blade, "Beat the shit out of this punk and dump him by Porky's in Brooklyn."

Red mother-fucked that guy all the way back to Pal's Cabin, and just when I was about to leave, Red said, "Listen to me, you own the street, not one of these fuckin' jerkoff wannabes."

Then he grabbed my hand and pulled me close to him and said, "No one fucks with us, I don't care who they are or who they're with."

They broke Eric's arm and his jaw that night, although I really think it was Red who broke his jaw when he hit him.

The Over-the-Counter Wall Street Guys, the movers and shakers, the real moneymakers, are a very small, almost secretive, selective group of guys, and word travels fast in that circle. Red wanted to send a message to them, and he did it with Eric Fink.

Whether you were new or old to Wall Street, if you didn't know who Larry Formato was, you sure knew who he was after the Eric Fink incident.

Larry Formato was the guy you don't fuck with.

CHAPTER 23: A TURN FOR THE WORSE

I hated being on the West Coast. People were leaving cocaine for tips in restaurants. It was totally nuts back then. Sonny Bono had opened a restaurant in Palm Springs, and he was telling me he was thinking of running for Mayor. I was thinking he was smoking too much whacky weed.

Tony and I just had our first falling out over the phone because of George. He wanted to meet me in LA with Jilly and George.

We set a meeting at the Beverly Hills Comstock, where I was living. George flew in from Europe. I was so pissed at George that I was ready to throw in the towel.

"I think Jilly and Tony are going to try to shake us down for more money," George said.

"Can you blame them, the way you throw money around?" I asked. "You better listen to me, George. We need to give Joe and Lenny some money or they are going to fucking kill you and maybe even me, me maybe more than you, because I'm supposed to know better."

"Fuck them. They're parasites, and Jilly and Tony are the biggest ones."

George was always brave when no one was around.

"This time, you're gonna be on your own," I said. "I'm not going to cover for you anymore."

We had the sit down at the hotel poolside. George was sitting with his back to the pool, I was across from Tony, and Jilly was facing George.

"People are talking about George fucking everyone in LA," Jilly started. "He's spending way too much fucking money."

How many times have I heard this before? I thought.

"Yeah, George and Larry are living like kings, while me and Jilly pick up the scraps," Tony said.

"Do you think that I'm going to just give you my money?" George asked.

"I want money, or we're going to take this up with the Indian," Tony said.

George was talking and making no sense. I knew I had to say something, or I would look like I was soft.

"Shut the fuck up, George," I said.

I turned and looked at Tony.

"Listen to me carefully," I said. "If George and I want to go out and eat steak, that's our business, because we're spending our money. We don't have to give you anything, and if we choose to give you something and you can only buy hamburgers, well, be glad you got that. Now, if you want to make a problem out of this, let's go see my friend."

"Okay, you're going to be shocked," Tony said. "We're not going to lose another fucking penny."

The meeting was over. I felt bad because I knew in my heart George was wrong. We made a lot of money using Jilly's name and his connection with Frank Sinatra.

Later, George told me he was planning on grabbing Tony and pulling him into the pool to the bottom and holding him there. I almost doubled over laughing. I told George he would have gotten himself killed. I knew I needed to patch things up with Jilly and Tony, but now it was out of my hands, since they said they were going to reach out to Joe.

I caught a plane the next day back to the East Coast. I met with Joe and Lenny at Steve's video store.

"Fuck that one-eyed cocksucker," the Indian said. He hated Jilly. "Let's see who shows up for him."

I gave Joe a hundred grand at that meeting. I told him that stock sales were slow and our expenses were going up because of accounting bills, and our annual report was due. I hired my brother-in-law, Louie, to take the pictures for the annual report. It was very cool. We went to a library in Paterson, NJ. The library had a huge globe taller than me. George and I stood in front of the "world" and that was the cover picture of our annual report.

Little Davie, or Davie Iccavitti, was a Captain in the Gambino Crime Family from Boston. He was the guy Jilly and Tony reached out to. Davie and Joe went way back to the old bootlegger days together. The tension on both sides was high. There was a lot of money at stake.

The sit down was set, and we were to meet in Florida. I thought this was somewhat unusual because, what the hell, the only thing I did in Florida was vacation, but it turned out that Joe had a son in Florida and Little Davie owned a seafood restaurant in Miami. So, the two Captains, one from the Gambino Crime Family in Boston and the other from the Genovese Crime Family in Newark, were meeting in Florida.

Joe was still mad because of all the big spending we did with World

Wide Ventures. He could never grasp that promotion is everything in selling something, and that promotion is what cost the most money, but it was the over-spending that George was doing that put it over the edge. Jilly and Tony had a much better idea of the over-spending than Joe ever did, and that was my concern. I knew the shit was going to hit the fan from my end, because I allowed it to continue without kicking back more to Joe and our crew.

Tony was like a guy getting ready for a slugfest. He loved the drama, while I on the other hand hated it. I hated it all. I just wanted to promote my stock and make money.

"The Greek is gonna lose. Don't even show up," Tony said.

"Don't underestimate my crew," I warned him.

I knew that if push came to shove, we had the backing of the most ruthless crime family in the country, but what were we going to do? Start a war over some bullshit stock deal involving Jilly Rizzo and George the Greek? What a joke. I'll tell you what wasn't a joke. It was these little bullshit deals that guys get whacked over, and I knew it. I also knew the blame would fall on me if things went bad, and I didn't like being in that seat.

Tony knew all too well that I was the one in that seat, and I don't blame him for trying to use it to his advantage. George was not allowed at the meeting, and I think it was a good thing he was not there. I could just see him opening his mouth and all of us from our side of the table would look like fools. Plus, I think Joe would have killed him right there.

Here we all were, having dinner together: Jilly Rizzo, Tony DelVecchio, "Little Davie" Iccavitti—Captain of the Gambino Crime Family, Lenny Maccalusso, the Indian, and me.

The Greek was getting slammed pretty well by Jilly and Tony.

"Ask Larry. He can't deny it," Tony said every time he brought up the wild spending.

I was too smart to fall into that kind of a trap. I just sat there and didn't say a word. I let Joe handle the meeting.

"Wise Guys don't get nervous," Red used to tell me. "Just keep your head in the soup."

I knew what it meant: Keep your head down, listen, and don't talk unless you were asked to speak. That was great advice, and I always remembered it.

My God, they complained about everything from hotel suites to jewelry. They complained about how we would always fly first class and about George fucking everything that walked in LA. They said he was embarrassing. Although I would never say it aloud at the table, I agreed with them about most of their complaints.

"What are we going to do about George?" the Indian asked me.

"Let's keep him out of LA unless we really need him," I suggested. "I'll handle everything on the West Coast."

In my mind, I had already accomplished everything out there that I needed George for anyway.

"Can you throw Jilly and Tony some expense money?" Davie asked.

I waited for Joe to answer. I just knew Joe was going to say, "No fucking way," but he didn't. Instead, he turned to me.

"Can we take care of their expenses?" the Indian asked me.

Wise Guys always have to put someone in the hot seat, and here I was again.

"Look, we already pay for Jilly's hotel suites when he's in New York staying at the Doral," I said. "When he's not flying for Frank, we pay for him to fly. We always pay for Tony wherever he goes. We even bought him a car. If it's a World Wide Ventures expense, I have no problem paying for it as long as the company has the money, but right now, there is no extra money. We have big expenses: accountants, lawyers, printing, mailings, et cetera. It's costing a lot of money to make this all happen, and I don't know that we'll be successful getting the money to build this project."

I learned that you always have to throw a bone so people will think they got something.

"I will be more than happy to share the pie if we do something together," I added, "but as for now, the best I can do is pay for any World Wide expenses that Jilly and Tony have."

"I think that's fair," the Indian said.

Lenny never said two words about the beef. He only had casual conversation with everyone. Dinner was over. We all kissed each other goodbye with smiles, but I knew this wasn't going to be the last sit down for us. I have no idea what was accomplished at the meeting except that it was one more dinner I paid for.

Tony called me at my office in Orange. He told me he needed a favor. He needed my help.

"My brother is in trouble for twenty-five grand to the bookies, and I have to come up with the money," Tony said.

I was in a difficult situation. I wanted to help Tony, but I would have to explain what I wanted twenty-five thousand dollars for. There was no way I was going to tell anyone I wanted to give Tony that kind of money after just having a sit down with him.

"I'll help you if I can," I told him.

I called my friend, Marc Bateman, and told him I was short on cash and needed to borrow twenty-five grand. Mark knew I was good for the money. He wanted to write me a check, but I told him I needed cash. The following day, I arranged to meet Tony. I gave him the money, thinking the whole time how fucked I would be if anyone from my crew found out. However, Tony was desperate. My relationship with Tony was never the same after that first sit down in Florida, but we always had a common respect for each other.

We had a meeting in Little Falls, NJ with Jilly, Tony, and two of their friends, Al Procrevia and Mike Fusco. Al was a builder, and Mike was a bullshitter. Al was going to help, along with Mike, on the beginning stages of the project in the Poconos. This was going to cost World Wide Ventures more money, but I felt if people would see things happening there, like roads being put in, it could bring more interest to the stock. Mike Fusco really liked us. He wanted to hang with us and do whatever he could for World Wide Ventures. I never trusted Mike. I always thought he was a cop, but overall, he was a fun guy most of the time to be around.

I had a big pool party and cookout at my home in Roxbury, NJ. Some of my guests stayed the night. In the morning, we were sitting in my kitchen drinking coffee and just bullshitting about World Wide and gambling coming to the Poconos, when someone who was looking at my closed circuit security system said that there was a car stopped at the end of my driveway, and they were throwing all my garbage in their trunk. I knew it was the FBI looking to see what they could find, and it wasn't one minute later that I received a call from Tony. He said the shit hit the fan in the Poconos, and we made the front page. Tony said that the paper for the most part had called our project a scam and that Larry Formato, the President of World Wide Ventures, had problems with the SEC—just what I didn't need.

I was still dealing with the assholes who were stealing my garbage. I didn't feel comfortable leaving my guests at my house, but I wanted the newspaper. I had Robin take my Mercedes 500 SEC and drive to the Poconos to get a newspaper. I told her to go as fast as she could, and on her way back, they put up roadblocks for her because they could not catch her.

The newspaper article was worse than what Tony described. It was the whole front page and a big article in the middle of the paper. They had tied me to organize crime, and with the mention of Frank Sinatra, it wasn't too hard to believe. I viewed this as the real beginning to the end of World Wide Ventures. I had a lot of damage control to do before Monday morning.

I was calling brokers all night and letting them know that this article was just an attempt by some local and federal authorities to stop the success of WWVC. It was no secret that George and I were high profile, and the way we ran our company was high profile too. World Wide Ventures had the attention of the New Jersey Bureau of Securities, the SEC, the FBI, and the Wise Guys.

"Except for the Wise Guys, fuck 'em all," I told George. "Let them try to do something to us."

Larry and George Livieratos
Annual Report, 1983

CHAPTER 24: THE INSIDER AND A BAD HONEYMOON

After the bad press we received, the stock of WWVC took a little beating, but I had an army of brokers that were loyal to me and would do enough buying to keep up with the selling. George got a call from a guy that called himself Jim Rossof. Rossof convinced George that he should come to New Jersey and help George restore World Wide's credibility with the public. Rossof was recommended by Walter Crudenton, who was the Branch Manager of James Alexander, a Brokerage Firm out in CA.

Rossof was supposed to be connected to the newspapers, and he was going to get WWVC more visible to the stock buying community. Rossof was a skinny little guy who smoked a pipe, and like most of the stragglers George would find, he was dead broke. In fact, he slept in the basement of the office, and I have no idea where he took a shower, maybe at the YMCA. George would brag to me about how good Rossof was and about all the good things he was going to do for us. I thought the guy was a misfit and was trouble.

Steve Wynn, who was going to be opening the Golden Nugget Casino very soon, was holding a benefit at the Waldorf Astoria in New York for Retinitis Pignatosis, an eye disease that renders its victims blind. In fact, Steve Wynn had the disease. This was a big event. Frank Sinatra, Sammy Davis Jr., Dean Martin, and Liza Minnelli were starring in the show, all of them on the stage together once again. Frank was trying to pull Dean out of his depression. Dean never got over the loss of his son, Dino, who died in an Air Force plane crash. I was with Dean in the elevator going up to a suite we had, and he was so drunk he could barely stand. I really felt bad for him. He was a really nice guy.

I took Robin with me, and she looked great. I thought to myself as we were sitting in the Waldorf surrounded by all these celebrities and politicians, I have finally made it to the top. I was sitting with the best of the best in the entertainment business and the political world. George was with Laverne, who always made sure George got his picture taken with important people. I am pretty sure this was the last time that all these superstars appeared on stage. It was really something to see.

Sinatra was closing out his contract with Caesars Palace and going to work for Steve Wynn at the Golden Nugget, so of course, we all flew out to Vegas to watch Sinatra's farewell to Caesars. I was in the lounge at Caesars near a private blackjack table shortly after Sinatra's show. I was considering playing some blackjack. Mickey Rouden, Sinatra's Lawyer, and Sinatra came down to the lounge and went to the table. I joined them for a short while, but the cards were really bad. I quickly got out of the game, but I did stay and watch. Sinatra asked to have the limits raised, and they were really taking a beating. Mickey Rouen lost over one million dollars and Sinatra must have lost at least two hundred thousand.

The next night there was a beef, and Sinatra wasn't going to do his show unless he got his money back. That night they played again, and he won his money back. Mickey Rouen even won back some of the money he lost the night before, too.

Sinatra closed Caesars, and I went to Palm Springs with George. I was looking at real estate there. I decided to buy the home of Robert Wagner and Natalie Woods. It was really cool. The only problem George and I had was deciding who would get the main part of the house. While we were busy thinking of ways to spend our fortunes, Jim Rossof was busy back in our offices in New Jersey making copies of all our documents and sending them to the FBI and the SEC. Mike Fusco was doing a lot of work for World Wide at the time. He managed to work his way into the company. He mentioned to me that he thought something was up with this guy Rossof, and I told him to keep his eyes on him.

Robin was living with me now at my house in Roxbury, and I was considering moving the World Wide Headquarters to my home and converting a 2,000 square-foot section of my home into offices. I returned from Palm Springs thinking that I was glad to be home. I had got in late from the airport, and drove straight home.

It felt as though I had just fallen asleep when my phone rang. It was Mike Fusco. He was going by the office after leaving a nightclub and noticed Jim Rossof making copies of corporate documents. George was on his way, and Mike was holding Rossof. I got up, dressed pretty quickly, and drove as fast as I possibly could to the office. When I got there, I could see that George was upset and Mike had Rossof scared, but Rossof knew when I got there he was probably going to die. He knew he would not see the sun come up when I found out what he was up to.

Rossof had been making copies of all our checking account statements and all our brokerage accounts. Mike had already smacked the shit out of him, and Rossof told him he was working for the Government to bring down WWVC. I grabbed Rossof and threw him over one of the desks, and when he got up, he ran and jumped right through the big plate glass window in the

Jim Rossof

front of the office. I couldn't believe my eyes.

"Did you fucking see that?" I said, completely shocked. "Mike, go outside and see if that asshole is bleeding to death on the street."

I turned to George.

"This is your fucking fault for bringing this asshole around here," I said.

In minutes, the Orange police were at our door. They said they received a call that we were trying to kill someone and they wanted to have a look around. George, with his big fucking mouth, told the cops that we were invaded by the Government with a secret agent. Talk about embarrassing. Two of the cops looked at each other and laughed.

"Is his name James Bond?" the cop asked.

After about an hour of hanging around, I went home. James fucking Bond. Are you fucking kidding me? While I was driving, I decided that night that I wasn't going to work out of that office ever again.

I was busy making plans to move my offices to my home, when George called and told me the FBI came to our office to talk to him about me, and ask him if he wanted to tell them anything about me. I knew this was all from the newspaper articles and Jim Rossof.

"Fuck them all," I said. "We're going to fight back."

I went to see Marc Bateman. He recommended a law firm to me in West Orange, NJ. World Wide Ventures filed a lawsuit in federal court against the United States of America under the Civil Federal Racketeering Law (RICO). WWVC held a big press conference in Newark, NJ to announce the lawsuit. We had a long table set up with Jay Surgent, George, Don Sheppard, and myself. We fielded questions from the press, and made it clear that the Government acted illegally in their pursuit of World Wide Ventures, Corp. I was thinking that we would spend around one hundred thousand dollars on the suit, but I was quickly proven wrong. The Government's lawyers came at us with more paperwork that made our law firm work around the clock. The suit became too expensive to keep up, and we finally caved in to the high cost of following through with it. World Wide had its day. We received a lot of press, and we weren't afraid to use the Government's own laws against the FBI.

I opened my offices at the house, and Mike Fusco was working directly for me now. I was hardly seeing George or Don Sheppard.

*　*　*

I asked Robin to marry me, and in May of 1984, Robin and I were married. It was a great wedding, and the list of people and the wedding films were much sought after by the FBI. My aunts and cousins from my father's side of the family, people I did not talk to since my Mom remarried, were all calling to get an invitation to the wedding, because they heard through the grapevine that Frank Sinatra was going to be there.

My wedding was a Who's Who in organized crime and the entertainment business. My dear friend, and one of the original "Teenagers," Jimmy Merchant, called me and told me he would be honored if the Teenagers could perform at my wedding.

"In thirty years, the Teenagers never performed at a wedding, but I wanted to do this wedding as a special gift to Larry and his new bride, Robin," Jimmy said, making an announcement at the wedding.

Jimmy Merchant really touched my heart by saying that.

I had one big table just for all my lawyers, and the Wise Guys had tables in the back near the bar. My wedding was kind of a truce between Jilly, Tony, and their crew. They all came, which showed me that they at least had respect for me. Marc Bateman could not resist the chance to have a meeting, since everyone was in one room, so he held a bullshit meeting about finances and borrowing money from Federal Flushing Savings and Loan, a Bank in Flushing, New York. Gabe Palusso, a friend of mine, had arranged a five hundred thousand dollar loan for World Wide Ventures Corp. Carl Cardaccia was the bank's president, and he had his hand out for every deal he could. I was mad at Mark for pulling that crap on my wedding night, but I was going to wait to let him know until I got back from my honeymoon.

Robin and I were to fly to Jamaica the following morning, but I missed the flight because I couldn't get up. We took a later flight out. I didn't let many people know where I was going or how to reach me. I wanted to be left alone to enjoy my honeymoon. Robin and I were in Jamaica for a day and a half when the phone in my villa rang. It was George. There was a big problem with Tony, and the Indian ordered me back immediately. He had George tell me to leave right away.

What the fuck? I thought.

Larry and Jimmy Merchant

The Teenagers

Larry and Robin

I asked George if he knew what it was all about and if he could fix the problem, but George was no help. I had to tell Robin. I asked her if she wanted to stay and I would be right back, but Robin did not want to stay there alone, and she cried all the way home. There was nothing I could do. The Boss sent for me. I had to go.

When I got back, I went straight to Bloomfield, NJ to meet the Indian. I was really pissed that he called me back from my honeymoon. I had to rethink what he actually thought of me.

"I got a call from Little Davie," the Indian said. "Jilly and Tony are upset that World Wide is using the property as collateral for a loan."

"Who gives a shit? We own it. We paid for it. It belongs to us," I said. "This is just a move to try to get some money out of the deal."

"Well, I'll be happy as long as I get my piece." the Indian said.

That was it. They just wanted to make sure they got their end. That's why I had to come home from my honeymoon. I wanted to rip Marc Bateman's head off. I was really getting tired of these fucking guys.

I owned a Cabin Cruiser that I kept on Lake Hopatcong in New Jersey. I asked Robin if she wanted to just go there and stay on the boat, or if she wanted to go back to Jamaica, but she was destroyed and hurt, so we did nothing. I felt bad for her and started hating the Indian and the rest of the Wise Guys for all this petty bullshit. It could have waited.

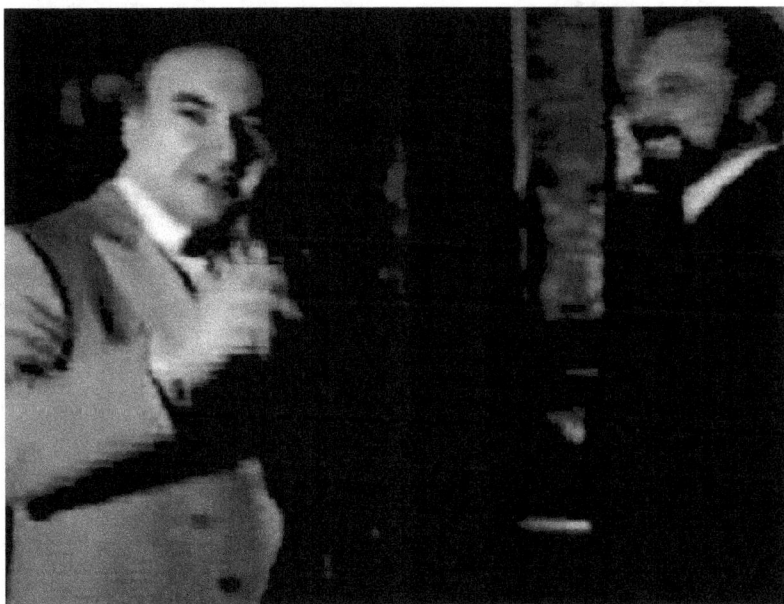

George Liveratos and John Tobin

CHAPTER 25: WORLD WIDE VENTURES, PART TWO

I was working from my office in my home in Roxbury, NJ. I was comfortable there. I had security cameras and big iron gates blocking anyone from just driving up my driveway. I was safe and secure in my own environment. I only had to deal with George on the phone, and I was playing it pretty cool with the Indian since the incident with my honeymoon. I was not talking to Jilly or Tony, and I was just doing my own thing without anyone else around me.

I had thrown myself into a deal I made while I was in Beverly Hills with Josef Shaftel, the Academy Award winning Director of the hit TV series *The Untouchables*. I purchased fifty percent of TPL Productions and was negotiating a deal to get a loan against a six million dollar contract we had with the Playboy network. We just finished a film for Playboy called *Erotic Images* with Britt Ekland, Peter Sellers' wife. Josef did some films with Peter Sellers and also brought to the table Stirling Silliphant, a great screenplay writer. They were almost like soft porn movies, and Josef knew how to make a low budget movie look good. I felt I would have no problem getting money for TPL Productions. I was happy, and doing something I liked, and as always in my life, when things are going good, something happens. Tony called me and asked me if I could meet him and Jilly in New York the following day. He wanted me to meet some people that he felt we could make a lot of money with together. He told me they had a scheme to make millions of dollars, and they needed a guy like me.

"Why are you calling me if these guys are so good?" I asked.

"They need my connections to the brokers and banks," Tony said.

I agreed to meet Tony and his people, but before I could go there, I would have to go see the Indian and let him know what was happening in case there was a beef later, I would be covered. The meeting was at the Waldorf Astoria in Manhattan. I met Tony downstairs in the lobby, and he quickly started telling me we were going to make millions with these guys.

"You shouldn't take that sit down in Florida personal," Tony said. "Jilly thinks you're a great guy. He just hates George."

"Yeah, right," I said.

"Come on, Larry. You know it was all about the fucking Greek. If you work with me on this and leave the Greek out of it, we can all make a lot of money."

I followed Tony into the elevators.

"These guys are big," Tony said.

How many times have I heard that before? I thought.

Once in the hotel suite, Tony introduced me to Lionel Riefler. He was about fifty years old, 5'11", and 160 pounds. He was wearing a three-piece suit and had a thin black mustache. He was slightly balding, and sported a dyed black combover to hide his receding hairline. He was soft-spoken and a bit classier than most of the people I had been meeting with lately through Tony and Jilly. The other player, a guy by the name of Michael Rapp, who was also about fifty years old, but appeared to be older at first glance. Rapp had on a white dress shirt and boxer shorts, and I couldn't tell if he was getting dressed or undressed. His hair was grey, and he was about six feet tall and a bit over weight. It appeared to me from first glance that Rapp was the main guy.

I was making small talk with Lionel and Tony. Rapp was on the phone talking about transferring five million dollars. I wasn't sure if he was doing this at that moment to impress me or if he really needed to arrange for the transfer.

"So this is the guy I've heard so much about," Rapp said to Jilly, hanging up the phone before turning to me. "Your reputation precedes you, Larry."

"The last time someone told me that, they were taking me away in handcuffs," I said. I waited a few seconds before adding, "Just kidding."

Rapp said he had a deal where he could purchase CD's (Certificate of Deposits) from the Union Pension Funds. All he does is move the money from one bank to another. He has no control over the money, just where it goes. A Savings and Loan bank can make loans based on a ratio of its deposits verses its loans, and most Savings and Loan banks, or S&L's, were starving for deposits. Rapp knew from Tony I had just made a five hundred thousand dollar loan, and I had the bank president in my pocket. He asked me if I would call the bank president and ask him if he could use deposits ranging from five million to fifty million dollars. We all knew what the answer was going to be. It was going to be yes, but there is always a catch. Rapp wanted ten percent in unsecured loans for every five million he had transferred to the S&L.

An unsecured loan is one that is not collateralized by anything except a person's signature. My job was to make the bribe and secure the loans. For doing that, we would divide the loan, less the cost of actually buying the CD's, between three groups: Tony and Jilly, Rapp and Reifler, my group, whomever that may be. The cost for buying them was about fifty grand, and the smallest unsecured loan we would take would be five hundred grand, so each group would net at least four hundred and fifty grand. I had the plan and understood what they wanted to do.

"I will think about it and let you know in the morning," I said.

Everyone was hungry, and we went to eat.

"You know, I think what you did with World Wide, getting it on NASDAQ, was pure genius," Lionel said to me in the limo. "I don't know how you did it, but it has got to be the biggest coup ever pulled on the NASD and SEC."

"I was involved with stocks once, but it has been so long since my involvement that I'd be lost now," Rapp said.

These guys were really buttering me up, but I was smart enough to see through their game. I really just needed time to tell the Indian what was happening and get his okay on it. The idea of moving money from one bank to another bank was really cool, and I felt I could get Carl Cardascia, the President of Federal Flushing Savings and Loan, to accept the offer.

Lunch was interesting. I could see that Lionel Reifler was a not really partners with Michael Rapp, as they would have wanted me to believe. Reifler was the money guy. He was putting up the money to buy the CD's. Rapp was a deal guy.

Reifler invited me to his offices in Ft Lauderdale, Florida. He told me he wanted to do some stock deals and wanted my advice.

"I visit there quite often," I said.

"I would like to have you there as my guest," Reifler said.

"I'll let you know, but first I want to see if this bank deal can actually be done."

When I left them, I went straight to Bloomfield, NJ to meet the Indian and tell him what was going on.

"Do you think these guys are real?," the Indian asked me.

"The only way to know is if they do what they say they're gonna do," I said.

I had been around for a while now, and I knew most of the movers and shakers in the business, but I had never heard of either of these two guys, Reifler or Rapp. I called later that night at their hotel suite.

"I'm in," I told them. "I'll be going to the bank in the morning, and if it's a go, I'll come straight to the city to meet you."

The following morning, I called Carl Cardascia.

"Hey, Carl, do you have a few minutes?" I asked him. "It's really important."

"We can meet right after lunch," he said.

That was perfect timing for me.

I walked into Carl's office at 2:00 p.m. After we said our hellos, I asked him for a piece of paper and a pen. When he gave them to me, I put my finger to my lips to signal him not to say anything. I wrote in letters big enough for him to read from his side of the desk: I WILL GIVE YOU FIVE MILLION DOLLARS IN DEPOSITS; YOU GIVE BACK 10% IN UNSECURED LOANS FOR EVERY FIVE MILLION. SHAKE YOUR HEAD YES OR NO.

The reason I did not hand the paper to Carl was that I did not want him to have it with my handwriting on it. Carl shook his head yes a bunch of times. I kept the paper with me and asked Carl if he would walk me out to my car. Once outside, I told him I would be back with someone for him to meet who would explain everything to him. Carl was excited to get these deposits; he really needed them for his bank. What made this deal so good was that Carl had the power to lend up to five hundred thousand dollars without having to get approval from the bank's Board of Directors. He could just okay the loans, and no one in the bank would know anything or ask any questions.

I called Michael Rapp and told him it was a done deal. We needed to meet and go to the bank. Tony, Rapp, and Reifler went with me to the bank. Jilly couldn't go. He was doing something with Sinatra. When we arrived at the bank, Carl came out to greet us in the waiting room. It was decided that I would introduce Reifler and Rapp to Carl and Tony, and I would sit in the waiting room while Reifler and Rapp told Carl how they wanted to do the deal.

While we were waiting, Tony confided in me that Michael Rapp is not his real name. Tony then goes on to tell me that his real name is Michael Hellerman, and he was an old friend of Jilly's.

"Rapp was in the Witness Protection Program for ratting on Johnny Dio," Tony said.

Dio was a made guy in the Gambino Family.

"Rapp had ratted on some other Wise Guys back in the seventies," Tony continued.

At first, I thought Tony was just fucking with me.

"Yeah, right, and Lionel Reifler is a government spy I suppose," I said.

"No kidding," Tony said. "The guy even wrote a book about it."

I couldn't believe my ears. I could not understand how Tony or Jilly could be around a fucking Rat.

"Does Davie know about this?" I asked.

"Rapp was a good friend of Davie's too," Tony said.

I about fell off my fucking chair. Here was a Captain in the Gambino Crime Family with a known fucking rat who is in the Witness Protection Program. I wanted to know who this guy Reifler was. Tony told me he was just a guy Rapp was doing business with. I just didn't know what to say after that. Tony saw the look of concern on my face, and he tried to tell me that the guy had no choice but to rat on those people. They had beaten him, robbed him, and even raped his wife.

"They deserved to be ratted on," Tony said.

Oh my God, how am I going to explain this one to Joe the Indian? I thought.

Everything I knew about the Wise Guy world told me this guy Rapp should be whacked. Hell, I could get whacked just for doing business with him. However, sometimes money is a very powerful tool, and it can be used to buy protection. Tony also told me Rapp had a problem with "Brother Moscotto," another Wise Guy, and Davie had to step in. I couldn't even breathe listening to this, fucking Davie stepping in for a rat. It was unheard of.

The meeting with Carl was over. Reifler and Rapp came out to the waiting room with Carl, who had loan applications for everyone to fill out. It appeared that the first round of money to go into the bank was going to be fifteen million dollars. I didn't do a loan. I let Tony and his two new partners do the first loans. I couldn't wait to get back to my car and get the fuck out of there. I felt as if I was just set up for a big fall. Tony and Jilly had me bribe a bank president for a fucking Rat. I knew this was going to come back to fuck me. I had to get to the Indian so he could reach out to Little Davie.

When I told the Indian what I had just found out, he was really pissed.

"These guys are a bunch of jerk-offs," the Indian said. "I'm going to reach out to Davie for another meeting."

The next few days went really fast. Tony was calling me to make sure Carl wouldn't fuck them once the money hit his bank. I was more worried about Rapp fucking all of us, and I told that to Tony. I was hoping the Indian would meet with Davie before the deal went down, and as luck would have it, Rapp was having trouble moving the money. It was taking longer than expected. The Indian reached out for me and wanted to see me right away.

I went to Bloomfield to his son's video store, where we always met. I got there before the Indian, and Steve, the Indian's son, couldn't believe these guys were keeping this fucking rat bastard around them.

"I met with that guy," the Indian said, walking into the video store. "Davie told me he has nothing to do with that fucking guy, Rapp. I know he's lying. He's making a lot of money from Rapp, or he wouldn't be alive."

The Indian turned to me.

"Be careful of Rapp and Jilly," he told me. "I let Davie know that there better not be any trouble from that motherfucker or that one-eyed cocksucker."

"Our end of the deal should be around four hundred grand," I said.

"Yeah, let's see if this cocksucker does what he says he's gonna do."

The money was being transferred, and the loans were being processed. I knew these loans were never going to be paid back from these fucking guys. It would just be a matter of time before I got a call from Carl asking for payment.

Rapp wanted all of us to come to Miami. We stayed at the Sheraton Bell Harbor. While we were there, George called me and told me Nick Valenti's father died in California and he told me Nick was all upset. I told George I wasn't going to fly to LA to go to the funeral and to just send flowers from the people at World Wide and from Jilly and Tony. I let Tony know that Nick's father died, and he said he might go out for the funeral. George sent the flowers to the address he got from Nick, and to no surprise of mine, the florist called and said the address George gave him was to an abandoned building. I told George something was wrong.

Nick finally had a wake for his father. Tony went and paid his respects and called me not long after.

"You're never gonna believe this one," Tony said.

"Okay, tell me," I said.

"Well, I went to the viewing with Nick, because I felt bad that he didn't have any family. When we walked in and Nick went up to the casket, he threw up all over the fucking place. That's when I knew Nick pulled a scam, because no one would throw up looking at their own father."

"Are you fucking kidding me?" I asked.

"I cornered Nick and pressed him for the truth. He was pulling an insurance scam, and he's been working on it for the past two years. He purchased an insurance policy two years ago using a fake birth certificate. Then he got a friend who worked at the coroner's office and stole a John Doe body. He's been paying on an insurance policy for two years on a man that didn't exist."

Tony told Nick he wanted an end of the insurance money, and I told Tony I wanted an end of his end.

Lionel Reifler had asked me again to visit him in his office in Ft. Lauderdale. Lionel was pretty much on the ball and seemed to be the sharpest out of all of these guys. He was also the guy who seemed to have most of the money. Lionel wanted to do stock deals, and he wanted me to move to Florida and work with him. I was considering his offer.

Dominick Fiorese, who was the owner and President of Southeast Securities, was also mixed up with the Wise Guys. He was coming to Florida to meet Lionel, and Lionel asked me if I would sit in on the meeting. Dominick was now working with F.D. Roberts, a brokerage firm in East Rutherford, New Jersey. Members of the Gambino Family operated it under Joe Butch, a Captain known for his ruthlessness. Dominick's biggest problem was he was always jumping from one ship to another. First, he was with Eric Wynn and the Bonanno Family. He got his ass handed to him, so he then took shelter with F.D. Roberts, earning them huge sums of money, so they protected him.

I knew all about Dominick, and I also knew all the people he was involved with. As usual, Dominick was having problems with the Wise Guys. When I met him with Lionel, he told us he owed a lot of money to the Wise Guys and needed to get them paid. Lionel wanted Dominick to retail a stock for him and offered him a lot of money. It would be enough money for Dominick to pay back the people he owed money to and still have some left over for himself. He took the deal. Because I was there in the room and no Wise Guy had actually claimed Dominick, I did. This meant Dominick belonged to my crew now, and no one can touch him without a meeting. It also meant Dominick was not going to fuck me, either.

I don't think I was back home a day after leaving Florida when Michael Rapp wanted to meet in LA. I wasn't seeing enough of my wife, so I stepped out of character and took Robin with me. We stayed at the L'Ermitage hotel, and I couldn't help but to think that when Mike Rapp gets this bill he is gonna shit himself. I knew only too well how expensive it is to stay there. Rapp got us rooms. I wasn't used to staying in just a room at that hotel. I didn't like it, so I upgraded to a suite. We completed our business there, and by the time we left, I had my belly full of all Mike Rapp's bullshit. I had Dominick in my pocket. I also had him retailing World Wide Ventures Stock.

Going back to LA reminded me of when we would travel from LA to Palm Springs and on to Las Vegas with Sinatra. I was thinking of a time when Sinatra had Jilly fire his long time friend and opening act, Pat Henry, and hired Frank Gorshin. The poor guy was so upset. He never saw it coming. He was Frank's friend, or at least he thought he was, but Sinatra told Jilly to get rid of him.

We were at Mateo's, and Jilly drank a whole bottle of booze. Jilly really felt bad about having to fire Pat Henry. Jilly had just been to the doctor's with Pat Henry a few days earlier, and the doctor told Pat that he needed to calm down and not allow any stress in his life. I'm pretty sure Sinatra just didn't want to see the guy working so hard, but a lot of people saw it differently. After Jilly delivered the bad news to Pat Henry, Pat died from a heart attack that night. Sinatra didn't even have the guts to tell him why he was letting him go. He made Jilly do it. I never could stand to be around Sinatra very much after that. I thought he was a real asshole, but on stage, the guy was pure genius. No matter how much I disliked him, every time I saw him perform, it was like magic. I never witnessed anyone command an audience like he could. Everyone loved watching and listening to him, and so did I, but he was still an asshole, and my days of running around the country with him were over. I was way over it.

I was becoming bigger and bigger, not only financially, but with the Wise Guys as well. I was making everyone a lot of money, and I was gaining more respect in the Wise Guy world—except from my own crew. I never got along with the Indian since Red had the stroke. They were just using me, and I knew it, but unlike Dominick, I couldn't jump from one crew to another. I was with my crew forever, and I hated it.

"I wish I could get away from the Indian, but I'm a stand up guy," I remember telling Robin. There was no getting away from the Indian. He was my Boss, and it didn't look like he was going to retire any time soon.

CHAPTER 26: THE WORLD STOPS SPINNING

I had pretty much decided that I was going to work with Reifler in Florida. This would allow me to move away from George the Greek, as well as get some separation from the Indian. Although, there would never be any getting away completely from him. I mean, you just don't resign. I still had to report to him.

Reifler had wanted me to make a deal with George to buy the rest of his free-trading stock, as well as all his shares in World Wide. I made the deal with George and bought him out. With George out of the picture, I was going to run the shit out of World Wide, pushing the price higher and higher before bailing out.

Reifler was making a power play for World Wide. I'm pretty sure he was in a dick-measuring contest with Mike Rapp and Tony. Getting World Wide Ventures, in his sick brain, would make him the big Dick in town. Dominick told me about a guy, Lincoln Dastrup, in New York who owned a Member Firm. He had just lost a ton of money with a guy by the name of Larry Powers. I knew Larry from an old firm on the street, Brooks Hamburger.

Larry was a big hitter, but he buried Lincoln in some bullshit stock. Lincoln was desperate for fifty thousand dollars. Lionel and I flew Lincoln to Ft. Lauderdale to meet with us, and we were going to make a deal to become partners in Lincoln's firm. I gave Lincoln 100,000 shares of World Wide Ventures to put into his brokerage firm for capital. World Wide was trading at $3.00 a share at the time. I had Lincoln make a market for World Wide, and we started buying the hell out of World Wide with Dominick's sales people and all my contacts. We pushed the price of World Wide to over $9.00 in one week, and World Wide became the most actively traded over-the-counter stock for a week straight with its daily volume and price listed in USA Today Financials. I was the fucking king. No one but me could pull that off, and everyone in the business and in the Government knew it. Things were going great. Lincoln was out of trouble with the stock he was buried in, and Reifler and I were on our way to making a shitload of money together with our new partner, Lincoln Dastrup.

Reifler made a deal to purchase 500,000 shares of some piece of crap stock for a penny per share. His idea was to get Lincoln's firm to make a market in it, and we would retail it out around $2.00 per share. You don't have to be a genius to pull that off. You just need a boiler room with lots of retail buying. I wasn't happy about this. I didn't know the company, and I couldn't get a fix on how many shares really existed in the public's hands. I didn't want to get bagged on some worthless stock.

Lionel opened an account at Lincoln's Firm, and I went back to New York to actually sit in the trading room so I could keep my eye on things. Reifler and Mike Rapp had a big falling out over money. It seemed that Reifler never got back the money he put up to purchase the CD's to put into Federal Flushing, and he never got any of the loan money either. I was on Reifler's side because I never got any of the money either.

It was coming down to another sit down. Jilly and Tony were convinced that Michael Rapp was going to make them millionaires, and I was convinced, along with Reifler, that Rapp was going to put us all in jail. Tony wanted to break the partnership with World Wide, and he wanted his half of the Echo Lake Property back. Jilly and Tony were also looking for more money.

On a cold Wednesday morning, I met Joe the Indian and Jimmy Higgins in Bloomfield, New Jersey. Jimmy Higgins was a Boss, another older guy who had been friends with Joe for fifty years. He was going to be acting as the middleman between the Indian and Little Davie. This was not just some little beef: this was as serious as it gets. If Jimmy Higgins goes with the Jilly side, it could cost me millions of dollars, or maybe even my life.

I was surprised that I met Jimmy Higgins with The Indian. It usually didn't happen that way, especially since Higgins was supposed to be a neutral party. Higgins asked me some questions about what was going on with the loans that Rapp had made with Jilly.

"Do you still want to do the Jilly's deal?" Tony asked me.

"I think the deal is dead," I said. "The financing is too difficult to obtain, and it doesn't look as though gambling is coming to the Poconos."

Higgins had heard enough.

"Let's go see these jerk-offs," he said.

I liked Higgins. Anyone could easily see this guy was tough as nails. He had salt and pepper hair and was a thin-framed guy with big hands. He looked like he should have a glass of scotch in one hand as he puffed on a Camel with the other.

The sit down was at the Park Sheraton in New York. On the way there, Higgins and the Indian talked about Jilly, saying if he's not careful he is gonna wind up getting whacked for bringing that fucking rat Mike Rapp around. They both agreed that Rapp could not be allowed to be in the same room with them, and that I was to let everyone know that when we arrived.

Jilly Rizzo, Davie Iccavitti, Tony DelVecchio, Mike Rapp, and some other guys I didn't know were all in the hotel suite when I walked in.

"Where are your friends?" Little Davie asked me.

"They won't come up until Mike Rapp leaves," I said.

"Aww, that's a bunch of bullshit," Tony said.

Little Davie knew better, and he also knew he would have some explaining to do for letting this fucking rat be around him if this went bad.

"Jilly, tell Rapp to go into another room until the meeting is over," Little Davie ordered.

I went back down to the lobby to get the guys, and when we walked into the room, it was as if I wasn't there just five minutes earlier. It was all hugs and kisses going around the room.

"Jilly wants his half of the Echo Lake property back," Little Davie said, starting the conversation. "Larry and George made millions while Jilly and his people made nothing."

The Indian glanced at me when Davie said George and me made millions. I could hear his thoughts. I knew he was thinking where the fuck his end was.

"I need another million dollars," Little Davie demanded. "I feel it should have been Jilly and Tony's part of what Larry and George made off the World Wide stock."

I just listened. I wasn't about to say anything yet.

"Jilly and Tony can go fuck themselves," the Indian shot back.

"Who the fuck are you?" Tony asked the Indian, jumping into the conversation.

Did he really just say that to the Indian? That is enough right there to get whacked. Tony wasn't a Captain. He wasn't even a made guy, and as far as I knew, he wasn't even a proposed guy with any family.

I've seen the Indian when he got mad, and Tony was way out of line. I knew this was about to get ugly. Jimmy Higgins acted quickly, right before things got out of hand.

"I just want to talk with Davie and Joe," Higgins said, hinting for Tony to leave.

Tony didn't want to leave. He was heated, but Jilly got him to walk away.

When the three Captains from the different Families were finished, they told us it was decided that the land would go back to Jilly and that there would be no money paid. Jilly and Tony could keep our end of the loan money from Federal Flushing, and we would not be responsible to repay any of the loans.

Fucking Joe came through. I couldn't believe my ears. I thought this was a great deal, because I didn't think we were going to see the loan money anyway. Better yet, if they didn't pay these loans and a problem came down, it was going to fall on them. I was off the fucking hot seat.

"I want all the World Wide stock back that I gave to Jilly and Tony," I added. "Since it was a transaction in a public company, I need the stock back to reverse it. Normally I wouldn't care, but the SEC will be all over us if we gave back the land and didn't get back our stock."

That was bullshit, of course, but they believed me. I got all the World Wide stock back. That was it—a done deal. Our partnership with Jilly and Tony was over, or at least I thought it was.

Lionel Reifler was pacing the floors, waiting to hear from me. I told him I would call him as soon as I was free to talk. I filled him in on what went down, and he was excited that I was away from the bullshit with Rapp and Jilly. He couldn't wait for a shareholders meeting and for me to introduce Lionel Reifler as the new Chief Executive Officer and Chairman of the Board of Directors of World Wide Ventures. I gathered up all my shares of World Wide that I had in my sister Patty's name and turned them all over to Reifler. I felt there was no way he was going to screw me. He knew he would get himself killed if he did.

The stage was set for the takeover, and I was set to work with Lincoln at our new firm on Wall Street. Reifler wanted to sell 300,000 shares from his account of a stock he bought for a penny at $1.50 per share and then have some other firms come into the stock and buy it back from us at $2.00. This game sure wasn't new to me. I have been doing it since I started with stocks. Lionel and I would get $450,000, and the firm would get $150,000. That would be a really good score.

Lionel told me he had a buyer arranged for the stock. The way the brokerage business works is that a firm has a trading account it buys and sells out of. At the end of the month, the firm has to have enough money in all its accounts to be in compliance. If it over buys, or owes money, it is termed as "out of net capital." It was almost month's end for the firm, and we had just bought $450,000 of stock from Lionel Reifler with no money. When you buy or sell a stock, they have what is called a settlement date. Usually, it takes a stock trade five business days to settle, but on special request, you can ask and receive what is referred to as a next day settlement. If you are selling, you can receive your money the next day. We did the Reifler trade as a next day settlement, and the clearing firm was getting worried that there would not be enough money to pay for the trade. I knew that, unless Riefler had someone come in to buy this worthless stock, Lincoln was going to be stuck with it, and it would put him out of business. World Wide was at $5.00 now, and the firm still had enough capital deposited with its clearing firm from the shares of World Wide to do the Reifler trade without setting off any bells or whistles.

I was starting to get feelings of déjà vu. This was reminding me of Data Force.

"Where's my buyer for the stock?" I asked Reifler over the phone.

"I'm still waiting for the buying to come in," he said.

The clearing firm did some checking. They found out that there was no legitimate market for this stock and tried to put a stop on paying Reifler. Reifler was smooth and forced their hand by calling the SEC, and he got paid. Lincoln had to come up with the money, but the only way he had to do it was from the stocks in his trading account. The clearing firm sold out his trading account. The worthless stock was still worthless, and they sold the 100,000 shares of World Wide, forcing the stock to fall under a dollar.

With the stock coming down like that, every one jumped on the bandwagon and bailed out. World Wide Ventures was where it started—at a penny. Lionel's attempt to take over World Wide was unsuccessful, but the damage was done. Nothing was going to bring World Wide back over a dollar ever again.

Lincoln Dastrup was out of business, and I had to explain to Joe the Indian what had happened. I knew Reifler was going to be killed over this; I just didn't know when. I also knew there would be an SEC investigation, and I knew that it would be soon. George the Greek was going to have a heart attack and scream that he was fucked, but as far as I was concerned, we had a good ride. The world of World Wide Ventures stopped spinning.

CHAPTER 27: THE TROUBLE WITH EVE

I moved from my home in Roxbury, New Jersey to Andover, New Jersey. I also opened a new company, International Trade Management (ITM). My offices were just five minutes up the street from my house, and I was happy I wasn't working out of my house anymore.

Morty Burger was still my SEC attorney, but he was more interested in music than he was in law. As long as Morty and I had known each other, we always talked music. Morty was the attorney for Grandmaster Flash and the Furious Five. I was pretty friendly with Grand Master Flash. In fact, I had lent him some money, and he was late paying me.

I met Barbara Baker and Vinny Castalanno through Morty. They were music executives and producers. I especially liked Barbara. She had a real flair for life, and she was a very classy lady. Vinny was a drunk, and I could never understand what Barbara was doing with him.

In 1979, Vinny and Barbara had a hit record with Ray, Goodman & Brown called "Special Lady." Barbara had a huge home in Englewood, New Jersey, and I always enjoyed visiting her house. I became very friendly with some of the people in the music business that Barbara knew, and I was moving ever so close to getting back into music full time. I was doing a one-man oldies show at the marina where I kept my boat. It was my passion, and I missed playing and singing. The show was a hit, and the audience was getting bigger every week. It never seemed to fail that the closer I got to music, the harder I was being pulled away from it.

Norbay Securities was struggling to stay in business. They did an IPO for a company in East Rutherford, New Jersey called Computer Technologies Inc. Norbay was the underwriter for the IPO.

Just like with Levin Computer, an IPO is the first round of public financing where a company puts its shares up for sale to the public. The President of the company was Chuck Rothstein, and his lawyer was Marc Bateman. Chuck had gone through all the money that Norbay had raised for him, and with Norbay going out of business, Chuck was now looking to raise more capital. Norbay was about to fall, and there was nothing I could do to save them.

I went to meet with Chuck as a favor to Mark, and I discussed becoming a consultant with him and helping him raise another two hundred and fifty thousand dollars.

"I need ten grand up front to get started," I told Chuck. "We'll talk about a more significant fee later."

Computer Technology Inc., or CTI as we called it, made computers called the Eve. It was equivalent to the Apple. In fact, it was exactly like the Apple computer. Chuck sent an Apple computer to Japan, had them make an exact duplicate of it, and just change the name to Eve. It didn't take Apple long to file patient infringement complaints against CTI. The Feds moved in fast against CTI and confiscated their entire inventory, and with that action, CTI was almost out of business.

I liked what I had seen, and I also liked that CTI had a deal with the Government of Pakistan to build computers for them and ship these computers anywhere in the world on PIA, Pakistan International Airlines. I knew this was a company I could take and remold. I was just looking for the right opening, and Chuck handed it to me on a silver platter by lying to me about some money he took from some guys out of New York. He made a deal with them to promote the stock of CTI, and they advanced him twenty-five grand against free trading shares that Chuck never gave them. It was just pure coincidence that I was there the day they came for their stock.

Chuck didn't want me to meet these guys because he had told me he had no other deals with anyone. I was in Chuck's office when they came in

"Can you give me a few minutes to talk with these guys?" Chuck asked me.

I didn't know them. I just figured they were there for some computer business, so I waited outside the office. I was only sitting there for about five minutes when I heard shouting and cursing.

"Hey! What the fuck is going on?" I yelled, opening the door and walking in.

"Get out of here, pal, before you get hurt," one of the guys said. "This is none of your business."

"Who the fuck do you think you're talking to? This is my business, and Chuck is my partner. Isn't that right, Chuck?"

Chuck shook his head, motioning yes.

"If this is your business, then you owe me fifty thousand shares of stock in CTI and twenty-five thousand dollars," the guy said.

"Are you two tough guys or business men?" I asked them.

"Both," said one of them.

"Good, I'm really glad you're tough guys, because if you were business men, I wouldn't talk to you the way I'm going to now. Chuck doesn't owe you anything, and you are not getting any stock. You fucking assholes can run to whoever you need to, but you're not getting a fucking penny. Don't ever come to my place of business again and act disrespectful, or they will find you in the trunk of a car."

The tough guys were pussies. They left apologizing to me for Chuck owing them money. One of the guys asked me very politely for my name.

"I'm Larry Formato," I said. "Now get the fuck out."

After they had gone, Chuck was really thankful.

"I'm your new partner," I told Chuck. "Have an office set up for me. I'll be coming here every day from now on."

As usual, I reported to the Indian and let him know that we just took over the computer company.

Chuck was doing business with a guy from Pakistan named Anwar Fancy. Anwar didn't like Chuck. The Pakistan Government owed CTI about one hundred thousand dollars for computers, and they were not in a hurry to pay CTI. Anwar had an office in New York, and he was the middleman between CTI and Pakistan. I went to see Anwar to find out why Pakistan wasn't paying. I expected that I was going to have to threaten him for the money. I found Anwar to be a really nice guy, and he explained to me that the Government of Pakistan was honorable and would gladly pay, but CTI never did what they promised to do. Anwar told me that Pakistan is interested in putting their people to work. They would build factories and supply the labor at a cheaper rate than Japan, but they do not have the technology to build things. CTI was going to send technicians to Pakistan to teach their people how to build computers. I told Anwar to arrange a meeting and that I wanted to go to Pakistan. There was no way I was going to let anyone, not even a government, owe me one hundred thousand dollars.

Driving from Andover to CTI in East Rutherford everyday was a pain in the ass, but I would stop at night to see Barbara Baker and Vinny and talk music. It turned out that Vinny's uncle owned the studio where I recorded my first record, Vantone Studios in West Orange, New Jersey.

I learned from Barbara that Morty was talking shit about me, so I was looking to have it out with him. Vinny had a young black kid doing some music for him. His name was Guy Vaughn, and I really liked this kid. He was from the neighborhood where I grew up in East Orange, New Jersey, and all he wanted to do was be in the music business. I told Guy I would help him if he didn't get anywhere with Vinny. I didn't want to step on Vinny's toes, but I knew he would never go anywhere with Vinny. Vinny was washed up in the music business, and he was a drunk. He did have some kind of a chance with Barbara because she had all the contacts.

"Can you raise some money for me and Vinny?" Barbara asked me. "Can we be partners?"

"I would like that," I said, "but there's something that I want first."

Morty was the attorney for Grand Master Flash and the Furious Five. Flash owed me some money, and I wanted to take over their management contract. Barbara thought she could get Morty to agree to let me have management because he really didn't do anything for them anyway. Morty heard through the grapevine that I was making a move on the group and called me to ask about it.

"I want to manage the group," I said. "I feel, through my connections, I could do better for them than you could."

We got into a pissing match, and he really got me mad.

"Keep the fucking group," I said. "You tell your fucking DJ Flash that if he doesn't pay me the money he owes me, he's gonna be spinning records with his elbows because I'm going to chop off his hands."

A few days later, Morty caved in, and I became the Manager of Grand Master Flash and the Furious Five.

I was in my office at CTI when I got a phone call from a friend of mine named Tommy Quinn. He was looking for work, so I told him to stop in my office and see me. I really liked this kid. He was loyal and would do anything I asked him to do. I hired Tommy, and he soon became my right hand man. Where I went, Tommy went. In fact, he was the driver most of the time. When I started bringing Tommy to Bloomfield to where I would meet the Indian, I would make Tommy sit in the car and wait for me until everyone was comfortable with meeting him. Now, like the Indian, Red, and all the other Wise Guys that traveled in twos, I had my sidekick. Much the same way Red taught me, I was teaching Tommy.

I decided that I wasn't going to put any more money into CTI and that Chuck Rothstein was useless. I made Chuck sign over everything to do with the Pakistan deal, and I even took the secretaries that worked there and made them come to my office in Andover. I was in the music business, and with Flash, I was making serious money. I had a meeting with the Indian and told him I was going to stop doing stock deals and concentrate on music.

I was deeply rooted in the music business at this point. Everyone wanted to get close to me. The biggest people in the music business had become my partners, like Freddy Heinz, the former President of Polydor, and Kuhn Suenfeld, the Chairman of the Board of PolyGram. Red was right. I had money, but with him, I would have power. The Indian let me know how powerful we could be in music, and we were connected to the business. So just when I felt I could get away from the Indian with my news that I was quitting stocks, the Indian let me know we are still attached to each other.

Steve, the Indian's son, was even getting into it. He came to my office and built a studio for me. Things were going great. I wanted to buy a major record label, and at that time, it was not an impossible thing to do. I had my sights on the record division of RCA. I was going to do a leveraged buy out. That's where you use the assets of the company you are buying and some of your cash. I figured it was going to cost me fifty-five million dollars to do the deal. I knew I could put it together. I needed to do just one more stock deal. I would then retire from doing stock promotions.

My last stock deal was going to be 21 Entertainment, the record company that Freddy Heinz and I owned. I was going to take it public. I told the Indian this one deal will make us all rich beyond our dreams. This was a statement I have never made over the years with the Wise Guys, and I knew I was the only guy who could pull it off. After everything I had accomplished, maybe I was a stock whiz kid. I had money and power with the Indian. I always made the people around me money. Maybe this was what I was born to do.

I was going to do a "blind pool," an IPO that has no business plan and discloses that the company will use the money it raises to seek a business to purchase. The blind pool would be a unit deal. I would offer one share of common stock and five warrants convertible into common stock.

Wise Guys never forget. With the biggest deal of my life about to unfold, I was feeling really good. I had the idea that I could bring Pakistan in on my deal too, as well as get the hundred grand they owed me. I called Anwar and told him I was ready to go to Pakistan. He made the arrangements, and before I had the chance to change my mind, we were off to Pakistan. I left Tommy Quinn in charge of everything. I had a lot of faith in Tommy, and I trusted him completely.

Anwar and I flew first class on PIA, Pakistan International Airline. It was a real eye opening experience for me. We had an armed guard standing right at the door of the plane, something I had never seen before. The flight was really long—twenty-six hours. I was happy that we made a quick stop in Turkey. One hour later, we were on to Karachi for a few days, and from there to Islamabad.

I was treated as if I was the President of the United States. Anwar was a powerful man in Pakistan, and he knew all the right people. I was meeting with Air Marshal Wickham, who definitely seemed like the guy in charge. I was amazed at his office. He had a long table that was at least 60 feet long with people sitting in chairs on both sides. They all had a phone in front of them. At this time, Pakistan had achieved nuclear power, but they could not get a phone system that would roll over, or even a switchboard for that matter. These people were answering phone calls and having messengers run the messages to Air Marshal Wickham. They were at least twenty years behind the times.

They loved me in Pakistan because I didn't try to bullshit them. I told them the computer deal was dead, that Chuck had fucked them, that I was stuck with picking up the pieces, and that I needed the money they owed for all the computers. Air Marshal Wickham wanted me to move my family there. They offered me the exclusive rights to bring products to Pakistan and have them shipped all over the world for free using their airlines. It was a tempting offer, but I was juggling too many things and wasn't sure if I wanted to plunge into all this.

Although I loved the country, as it was really beautiful, I didn't think I could live there. I wanted to get back to the States and to my music business and family. I made deals with all the right people in Pakistan, and I was sure that they would join me in any venture I wanted to pursue. They wanted to buy a big position in the blind pool I was doing and that was, pardon the pun, music to my ears. The one hundred thousand dollars was released to me just as they promised at the Bank of America in New York. I had a personal open invitation from Air Marshal Wickham to return to Pakistan anytime I wanted to go.

CHAPTER 28: THE JUGGLING ACT

The music business was all I could think about. Grand Master Flash just finished a new album on Electra Records that I was really excited about, and 21 Entertainment was about to drop an album on Alvin Lee, the famed lead guitarist for the group Ten Years After. I thought this was a fucking great album. The name of it was "Detroit Diesel," and it had features from Eric Clapton and George Harrison on it. Freddy and I also did a deal with Gregg Allman and a new album with Golden Earring. I was putting together a deal with Zachary Starr, Ringo's son, and John Entwistle, the bass player from the Who. Vinny and Barbara soon learned that they couldn't keep up with me. Vinny held Barbara back. I wasn't letting anything hold me back. At least, I didn't think anything could hold me back.

I was at a boat show with my wife Robin and we looked at a new 28-foot Century Cruiser. It was really nice, and I thought it would be great for us to have a new boat since our first child together was just born, Christian John Formato. I was thinking it would be good to spend weekends on the boat and it would be a good family thing, but Robin never saw it that way. In fact, she thought I was nuts.

"Who brings a baby on a boat?," Robin said.

My lawyer, Jay Surgent, reminded me that we had a meeting with the Morris County Prosecutors office about a gun charge I caught in 1982 when a gun was found in my desk during the raid of Chapter 11. I met him at the office, and I think that was the day my life changed forever. We were there thinking that we were going to be talking about some gun charge, when two police detectives walked into the room and informed me that I was under arrest for child molestation of my oldest daughter, Angel, from my first wife.

Holy shit; charge me with murder. Charge me with extortion. Charge me with anything, except that. I was going to take a big fall but not without a fight. I knew everyone, including the Wise Guys, would look me at differently. Tommy Quinn delivered the cash bail, and I was home. I was literally sick to my stomach.

The next day, it was on the radio and in the newspaper, but it was there for one day and it was gone. Now I had something else to take up my time, and I wasn't losing any ground with this. I hired the best private detectives, and with Jay Surgent, we mounted a legal defense that was second to none. I was sure I would win at trial and there would be no plea for these charges. I was determined to prove my innocence.

If that wasn't bad enough, Morty Burger called me and wanted to see me. He was really concerned for me, so I went to his home in New York.

"If you need anything, I'll help with the case in Morris County," Morty said. "I have more bad news for you, though. The United States Attorney for the District of New Jersey contacted me. They want to indict you, Larry. Come in with me and cut a deal."

"Let's go see what they're after," I said.

I met with Robert Warren, the Chief of the Fraud Division in the District of New Jersey, and an FBI agent who had put together a "failure to report income" case against me. Warren wanted me to plead out to three charges, but I was against that. I was weighing out my options. They wanted me to take a hit for failure to pay income tax and some money laundering trumped up charge stemming from Royer. It was from when I did that deal with the old man, selling all that stock to Royer's trading account. I needed time to think about this. I also needed to tell the Indian what was happening before he found out on his own.

Morty thought the worst I would be facing with these federal charges would be one year on a federal farm, but he really thought I would get probation. This was because, although I had been arrested many times, I was never found guilty of anything. I had no criminal record. I wanted to wait to decide what I wanted to do.

"Buy me time with the feds," I told Morty.

Right out of the fucking blue, the Indian gets a message that Little Davie wants another sit down. I couldn't figure out what this was all about.

"This has to be nothing but bullshit," I told the Indian. "Are we really going to Miami?"

Yet there we were, the Indian, Lenny, and me, sitting in Miami at another restaurant. We were listening to Little Davie complain about Federal Flushing Savings and Loan and that these guys were taking down Pass Book Loans and not paying. Reifler had a stock deal to get all the loans paid. He wanted to do it through Joe Butch's firm, F.D. Roberts. Little Davie was talking about the new RICO Laws, saying that they were really powerful, and he made a threat right to me.

"If anything goes wrong, someone is going to pay for this," Little Davie said. "I'm not going to ask for permission."

I was really pissed. I had enough shit on my head.

"What the fuck does that mean?" I asked.

"It doesn't mean anything," the Indian said. "Let me remind you, Davie, that you brought Rapp and Reifler around. These guys are trouble."

Davie had a hard on for me. He made it clear that if he caught a charge, he was holding me responsible. Red taught me to just keep my head in the soup, but this time I had enough.

"Davie, with all due respect, by rights you were supposed to whack Rapp a long time ago," I said. "You let Jilly bring this fucking rat motherfucker around us. Don't fucking threaten me, when you're protecting a fucking rat."

Everyone looked at me.

"Larry, you can't talk like that," the Indian said.

"Well, everyone sitting at this table knows I'm right," I said.

"Larry, I meant no disrespect to you," Little Davie said, much to my surprise.

Yeah, right, I thought. I'm sure this motherfucker would have me whacked if he thought he could get away with it. This was his way of testing the waters.

I left the meeting with Lenny, and he knew I was upset. He tried to calm me down.

"Don't worry," Lenny said. "I was about to say something to Davie just when you did."

"Yeah, well you didn't," I said. "I didn't hear you get threatened at the table."

I hated these fucking guys. They were all alike, always out for themselves. If Red was at that table, that never would have happened. Joe was shocked. I was way out of line, but you know what? Davie was more out of line, and by rights, he should have got whacked for keeping that rat cocksucker around. So, another bullshit sit down came to an end, except this time I wasn't taking any more bullshit from anyone.

I had to keep myself focused. I had too many irons in the fire. I felt like I was in the frying pan. I actually, for the first time, started to feel like things were closing in on me. Reifler brought Dominick Feroreese back into the picture to help coordinate the stock deal. I told the Indian no one was going to make any money with this deal, and everyone was gonna get in trouble. He instructed me to just oversee our interest so we get what we are supposed to get. I was so busy with my court case in Morris County that I hardly had time for anything else.

The investigators were doing a great job for me. I went to see a forensic psychiatrist to show I wasn't a pedophile and help me with the case against the State. With the information that my lawyers supplied to the State, including that I passed a lie detector test, and the fact that my ex-wife was in a mental institution, we could not believe they weren't dropping the charges. The State offered me a deal to plea out to a lesser charge, some 4th degree bullshit that would carry probation, but I told them no fucking way. I wasn't pleading out to anything like this.

I had Jay, my state case attorney, calling me, and I had Morty, my federal case attorney, calling me. I had Wise Guys calling me about this fucked up deal that Reifler was putting together, and I had my music business that I had just started. Things were starting to get a little crazy. My home life was coming apart. There was so much stress put on my marriage, and my new assistant GiGi, who was a little hottie and a big flirt, didn't help. I was convinced that I was going to beat the State case. I knew I would have to take some plea deal with the feds, but I needed to wait on that until I finished my state case. I wouldn't be able to take the stand with the State if I was a convicted felon. I would lose all my credibility with the jury, and there was no way I was not going to take the stand in my defense.

Rapp had everyone fucked on the Federal Flushing deal. He took phony passbooks from the Cayman Islands and pledged them for loans. He used Tony's name, his wife's name, Tony's nephew, Pete, and Jilly's name. George's name was used, and so was Reifler's. Jilly claimed he knew nothing about the loans, and I'm not too sure he wasn't telling the truth. Rapp fucked over everyone. The only way to save it was to pay it. I was never too concerned about the Flushing Bank Deal, because the only loan I did was with World Wide, and we gave financials and real security. I told the Indian that something about this bank deal stank, and it had Little Davie really spooked.

I wonder if Rapp did some loans in his name too.

CHAPTER 29: THE CHILLING EFFECT

Morty Burger, my friend and my attorney, called me at my office.

"I need a big favor," Morty said.

"If I can do it for you, I will," I said.

"Do you remember Marshall Zolp?"

"Are you kidding? Of course I do. I still want to kill him for fucking me at Royer."

Marshall, who is a George Hamilton look alike, came to see me at Royer Securities and walked out with some of my letterheads from Royer Securities. He then went to Las Vegas and wrote letters of intent to do underwritings (IPOs) for companies on the West Coast, using my letterhead and collecting twenty-five thousand dollar advances. I had no idea what he had done until I started getting phone calls from all these companies wanting to know when I was going to take them public.

"I really hope this favor has nothing to do with Marshall," I told Morty.

I knew Marshall and Morty were friends. Morty told me that Marshall was stuck in Florida. Reifler fucked him on a deal, and he is broke and couldn't get out of there.

"You're breaking my heart with this sad story," I said. "The only reason I'm still on the phone is because I hate Reifler more than Zolp."

"Can you get Zolp here to New Jersey?" Morty asked. "He has a stock deal. Marshall needs to get some stock placed in a company he has. If you help Marshall, you'll get fifty percent of the deal."

"I think I have enough going on right now without adding another deal into the mix."

"Come on, Larry. Don't be a fool. You can make a lot of money with this deal."

"What is this deal, anyway?"

"I'd rather have Marshall explain it to you, but I feel you can make yourself at least a million dollars really quick."

I thought about it for a moment.

"Fine, I'll do you the favor," I said. "Is this a real deal?"

"As real as it gets," Morty assured me.

I called Marshall at a hotel in Ft. Lauderdale, and I got him a plane ticket to New Jersey. I had Tommy Quinn pick him up at the airport and bring him to my office. Marshall was motherfucking Lionel Reifler from the time he walked in until I told him to shut the fuck up. I asked him about the deal that Morty called me on and Marshall started to pitch me on it. I looked at him like he had three heads on his shoulders.

The name of the company Marshall needed help with was called Laser Arms. According to Marshall, it was a shell that, at one time, was in the arms business. A shell is a public company that has no assets, only shareholders. Marshall had a brand new product that had never been introduced to the public. It was a special can, a "Chill Can," and it was designed to chill in your hand when you popped it open. I asked Marshall if he had one I could see and he told me he was having some shipped to him.

Marshall needed to sell some stock to raise some money. He needed not only a way to sell the stock, but he also needed nominees, people whose names he could use to sell this stock through. I called a trader I knew that owed me a favor. His name was Bobby Bosse. I had Bobby buy fifty thousand shares of Laser Arms at $3.00 per share, which was a start for Marshall to get some operating money to do some advertising, including a TV commercial. I put about ten market makers in the stock and gave them all cheap stock, I had the stock trading at three dollars, and I was giving it to my market markers at two dollars. Morty said I could make a million dollars with this deal, so I was all over it.

One of the people I used as a nominee was a kid my stepbrother brought around, Paul Genovese. I called him Big Pauly. Although I always suspected something wasn't right with him, I let him continue to come around and prove himself to me, like putting this stock in his name. If he did the right thing, he would be closer to getting into my crew.

Marshall was a fugitive and was wanted in Las Vegas for stealing a car. It seems he walked out of a casino and was mistaken for George Hamilton.

"I'll get your car right away, Mr. Hamilton," the parking lot attendant said.

So, Marshall drove off in George Hamilton's Rolls Royce.

Marshall was acting as the transfer agent for Laser Arms. The transfer agent is the company that keeps track of all the shareholders and is responsible for cancelling the shares of the selling party and issuing the shares to the buying party. Morty lied. There was nothing real about this deal. What all that means, in a nutshell, is Marshall could issue all the shares he wanted to in Laser Arms, and no one would be the wiser.

As is with most stock promoters, Marshall was into some Wise Guys in Bay Shore, Long Island, in New York. One of the fellas was Les. He owned a big car dealership out there called Bay Shore Subaru. Les was around "Carly the Blind," and Marshall owed them some serious money. I reached out to Les and asked him for a meeting to straighten out his problem with Marshall. Unlike most other Wise Guys, Les was one of the few that I actually got along with, and we were becoming friends. I made sure Marshall paid Les, and Les wanted to get involved with me in the music deal I was doing.

The checks from the sale of the stock were getting bigger and bigger, so we needed someone who could get them cashed for us. I had every trader I knew working this stock, and everyone was making money. I contacted Danny De Benadetto, the guy whose wife George was fucking and whose brother was "Louie Coke." I had that big fight with George about it. Danny had a nephew who had great banking connections at a bank in New Jersey. Danny took me to see his nephew, and we went to see the president of the bank.

"We have large checks coming from brokerage firms in New York," I explained. "We need to cash these checks. We would be happy to give you ten percent of each check if you would cash them for us."

The checks ranged from one hundred thousand up to two hundred and fifty thousand dollars. The bank president wanted in.

"I'll need a day in advance to order the money," the bank president said. "I'll do it."

This was working like magic. I was having the brokers selling the shares that Marshall was literally making in one of my back rooms at my office. Marshall and I would take my limousine to the bank, walk inside, and literally walk out with hundreds of thousands of dollars in big green trash bags over our shoulders. We were running out of places to keep the money.

In Long Island, New York, there is a place called the Zurich Depository. What made this place so good is that we could enter it twenty-four hours a day, seven days a week. You could rent small deposit boxes or huge safes big enough to put a car into. The Zurich Depository didn't require you to show proof of who you were in order to rent a safe. There was no identification required. If you wanted to say you were Batman, you could, and they didn't care. It was underground and bomb proof. To get in, you used code names and numbers that only you would know, and if you forgot your code name or numbers, you were pretty much fucked. Marshall and I rented walk-in safes next to each other at a cost of ten thousand dollars per year, payable in advance.

Marshall took out full-page nationwide ads in The Wall Street Journal advertising the Chill Can and making mention that Laser Arms was talking to the big bottling companies like Coca Cola and Pepsi. The whole country wanted to buy stock in this new company that had a can that would chill in your hand when opened. The whole fucking industry bought into it, along with the public.

I introduced Marshall to my friends in the music business, Barbara Baker, Vinny Castalanno and Freddy Heinz. Marshall wanted in on the stock deal with Freddy Heinz and 21 Entertainment. I wasn't really sure what Marshall could contribute to the deal since everything he ever did was bullshit. I was putting a lot of pressure on Marshall to show me the cans that he said worked. People were beginning to believe it wasn't true. Vinny and Barbara loved Marshall, and Marshall, along with his good friend Morty Burger, convinced them that he could be their savior and help finance them in the music business. All this was done behind my back.

I planned a big party at the 21 Club in New York to announce the public offering of 21 Entertainment. Freddy and I had just released Alvin Lee's new album, "Detroit Diesel," and the single was starting to get good radio play. The party was timed perfectly. What else could I ask for? I had a company called 21 Entertainment and I was announcing its public offering at the 21 Club. I was going to open the stock at twenty-one cents and bring it to twenty-one dollars. We were in line to make hundreds of millions of dollars, which would buy us the RCA Record division.

The party was a huge success. Stock traders and brokers were there, along with some big names in music: Alvin Lee, Tommy James from Tommy James and the Shondells, Roger Daltrey and John Entwistle from the Who, George Harrison, and Grand Master Flash. I talked with record executives from major labels including Bob Krasnow, the President of Elektra Records, who I signed a six million dollar, five-album deal with for Grand Master Flash under the management company that I owned and operated, Bentley Management Co. The Wise Guys from my whole crew and from other families were there too.

The booze was flowing, music was playing, and all was going well, until I passed by a broker who was a friend of mine—Paul "Little Pauly" Schoengold. He grabbed my arm and asked me to help him out with some guy who was giving him a hard time. I looked at the guy, and I didn't know him. I figured he came in with one of the Wise Guys, or maybe he was a friend of a friend. It really didn't matter. He was giving my friend a hard time.

"Come over to the bar with me," I told the guy, approaching him. "I want to talk to you."

"What's up?" he asked, not knowing who I was.

I started to walk towards the bar. I wanted him to follow me. There weren't a lot of people by the bar in the back, and I thought it would be a good place for me to tell this guy to leave my friend alone.

"Who the fuck are you?" he started, like most half-ass Wise Guys.

"Paul is a friend of mine," I said. "Can you please leave him alone so we can all go back to enjoying ourselves?"

"Fuck you."

I hit him in the face, grabbed him, and bent him back over the bar and started choking him. Then, I dragged him down the length of the bar, knocking glasses all over the floor. Lenny Macalusso was there in a second, and he grabbed the guy.

"Get the fuck out of here before you get killed," Lenny told the guy, shoving him towards the door.

The management of the 21 Club wasn't happy with me. They said they never had anything like that happen in their establishment. I told them to fuck off, and if they didn't like it, try to get paid for the party.

The stock deal that Reifler was putting together with Dominick wasn't going well. Little Davie was getting upset, and Tony DelVecchio was blowing a gasket. Joe the Indian told me they wanted another sit down, and because all the families were promised so much money, they were getting itchy. I told Joe that if Reifler was heading the deal, everyone was going to get fucked.

"The Federal Flushing deal will be brought up at the sit down," Tony told me over the phone. "If you think I'm going to rely on Little Davie, you're wrong. Davie is Jilly's guy, not mine."

"I really don't care," I said. "The Indian is handling things from my end."

"I can't give a name on the phone, but my guy's initials are JG."

I knew who Tony was talking about; or at least who he wanted me to think he was talking about. It was John Gotti, the new Boss of the Gambino Family. What a fucking joke. I couldn't imagine Gotti going to this bullshit sit down. That would be like the Chin shedding his robe and getting dressed to attend this. Give me a fucking break. Not in a hundred years was Gotti gonna show up.

I didn't go to the sit down. I had other things to do, but the Indian and Lenny were there. I was thinking to myself that if Lenny had to go alone, it would be one big mess. I remember one time when Richard Carey came to our offices at World Wide, and he brought a friend of his with him. At the time, I didn't pay much attention to him, I was busy trading World Wide Stock, but in passing in the hall, he introduced me to his friend, Tommy Vastola. I shook the guy's hand, and that was the extent of our meeting.

Vastola was a Wise Guy. His nickname was "Corky." If Richard Carey had introduced him as Corky, I would have known who he was. He had somewhat of a reputation, and I knew the name. I never would have left Corky and Richard alone with George. Right before the collapse of World Wide, Corky sent word he wanted a meeting, and the Indian sent Lenny to see what he wanted.

"George promised me one million shares of World Wide stock," Corky told Lenny.

Lenny left the meeting and came right to me. When he told me what Corky said, I told Lenny that would never happen.

"George would never say anything like that," I said.

The next day, Lenny met with Corky again.

"George never said anything like that," Lenny said.

Corky was slick, and he was shrewd. Wise Guys have codes and rules, and one rule is you never call a made guy a liar.

"Is George your guy?" Corky asked Lenny.

"Yes, of course he's with us," Lenny said.

"Shame on you then. If you weren't there, who are you going to believe, that guy or me, your brother?"

Lenny got himself trapped. He couldn't call Corky a liar, because being his brother meant Corky was a made guy. Lenny lost the sit down.

I was really fucking pissed.

"I'm not going to give that motherfucker one share of stock," I told the Indian.

Joe agreed. He didn't like Corky, so we just kept putting Corky off every time he wanted to meet.

Lenny called me after the meeting at about 2:00 a.m.

"The pie is being split in so many pieces that I'll be surprised if there are any crumbs left to eat," Lenny said.

Tony called me the next day as well.

"I can't believe they sent that fucking asshole, Sammy the Bull," Tony said.

"He's your guy," I said.

Sammy was the Underboss, and I was actually surprised he was there. He must have been bored that night. Tony was telling me that he kept asking Sammy what his end was, and Sammy wouldn't answer.

"You know that fucking guy whacked every partner he ever had," Tony said.

"These guys deserve each other," I said, laughing. "I've been in meetings where we were cutting up hundreds of thousands of dollars, and seen Wise Guys fight over a ninety dollar phone bill."

I don't think that made Tony feel much better.

Marshall was playing two sides against the middle. He was trying to make a move with Vinny and Barbara. Laser Arms was getting a lot of attention from the SEC. My new boat was being delivered, and I couldn't wait for it to get to my Marina in Lake Hopatcong, New Jersey. I had phone lines installed at my boat slip, and I was going to work from my boat during the summer. Marshall did a big trade behind my back, thinking I would never find out. There were four hundred thousand dollars sitting at Bobby Bosse's firm, but the firm wouldn't release the funds until it had proof of ownership of the stock. There is a rule called "know your customer." The head of compliance for the firm wanted the customer to come in and show proof that he was who he said he was. Marshall fucked up. I was pissed at him, and I told him he was putting everyone in jeopardy.

Marshall wanted to buy a house from a couple on the lake where I kept my boat. Andy and Janice were very fucking weird people. They were players too, not only with money, but they also liked sharing sex. The wife loved fucking other guys, knowing her husband was close by or looking.

One day, we met at the Marina. We all got onto my boat and drove across the lake to the house that Marshall was buying. I docked the boat and stayed on board. I didn't feel like looking at the house again. I had already seen it twice before. I was waiting on the boat, listening to Alvin Lee's album, when Janice came back on board. She went down into the main cabin, and I joined her. I had the front hatch open, and I stood up to look out the hatch to see what Marshall and Andy were doing. Janice unzipped my pants and tried to give me a blowjob. So here I am, waving to Marshall and Andy while Andy's wife is trying to blow me.

The next day, I talked to Marshall on the phone.

"The things I do for you," I said.

He knew I was talking about Janice. We were both laughing.

"Yeah, Andy said, 'Look at the smile on his face. My wife is probably blowing Larry on the boat.'"

Marshall never bought the house on the lake, and he beat Andy for about one hundred thousand dollars. The shit was getting thick over the Chill Can deal, and I found out Marshall had beat me on other trades that he didn't tell me about. I confronted Marshall and gave him twenty-four hours to pay me.

My phones in my office were considered to be clean phones, meaning they weren't tapped. There is a law that states the Government has to use all other means before tapping someone's phones. As an example, all the business I did was stock related, which meant that there would always be a paper trail, so the Government wouldn't be allowed to tap my phones. They would need a better reason. Morris County, NJ, The United States of America, and the District of New Jersey found their better reason—Paul Genovese.

CHAPTER 30: THE TAKE DOWN

My case in Morris County was going really well, and I was confident that I would win. At a pretrial hearing, Jay Surgent made a motion for the case to be dismissed. The judge flatly denied it, saying that this case, in his eyes, was a defense attorney's dream. Well, it was a nightmare for me.

My problems with the U.S. Attorney in Newark, New Jersey were not going away. Morty arranged another meeting with them, and I agreed to plea out to the tax count and a money laundering count. I signed the plea agreement, and I was told I would have to appear in front of a judge to plead guilty at some future date. Robert Warren, the Chief Assistant U.S. Attorney, assured me that I wouldn't have to put up bail and that I would be released on my own bond. The probation department would then prepare a pre-sentence report for the sentencing judge. I wasn't going to take any chances with the federal pre-sentencing report. I had Jay hire a firm in Virginia that also prepared a pre-sentence report for the judge to compare. I think it cost me ten grand for their report. I was also doing volunteer work for the food bank in New Jersey. I had some crazy thought in my head that if I raised the food bank one million dollars, any judge would be hard pressed to put someone never convicted of a prior crime in jail. My goal was to stay out of jail.

I received a strange phone call from Dominick Feroreese. He told me he was hiding at a hotel, because the FBI contacted him and wanted him to cooperate. They offered him the witness protection program and told him that they had picked up, through a wire surveillance, that his life was in danger.

"What do you think I should do?" Dominick asked me.

"If you ever repeat what I say, I'll kill you myself," I said. "Fuck these Wise Guys. They all earned enough money from you. This is your chance to get out. Don't be a fool. Do it. Call the feds and go into the witness program."

I would have been killed if anyone ever knew I advised Dominick to go to the Feds. I heard talk that Dominick was going to be whacked, but I never paid much attention to it. Steve was there, building the studio. I purchased studio equipment, and had Guy Vaughn working the studio for me. I always knew Vinny was never going to help Guy. Lenny had just walked in almost as soon as I hung the phone up with Dominick. Lenny wanted to talk to me on the back deck with Steve and Tommy, so the four of us stepped outside.

"Word on the street is that Dominick went to the Feds, and they're holding him," Lenny said. "The Bosses are worried that they'll all get dragged into this fucking mess with Reifler and Dominick. If we find Dominick, we're going to whack him."

Dominick has to be the dumbest motherfucker in the world, I thought. I wonder how many people he called besides me, to tell them that the Feds wanted him to cooperate.

Everyone had reasons to be worried. I was glad I separated myself from that deal. The SEC had halted trading on Laser Arms, and Morty was working with Marshall to get it trading again. Morty called my office to talk to Marshall and me and give us some ideas on how we could get money out of accounts that the SEC froze. Morty suggested using Vinny and Barbara to say the money belonged to them. Morty planned the whole thing out with Marshall and me over the phone. We discussed holding a big press conference in New York City to give a demonstration that the can actually worked. We also talked about having a new president of the company at the press conference, since the President of Laser Arms was just a picture of an actor that Marshall took from a magazine. I had a brainstorm. I knew someone who would actually be big headed enough to want the spotlight—George "the Greek" Livieratos.

I couldn't wait to get off the phone with Morty and call George. I had not talked to George much since World Wide came to an end. I asked George to meet me at the marina where I kept my boat, and I told him I had something he would really be interested in. Prior to meeting with George, I had another idea. I called Amos Walls, the guy who invented the Safe-T-Scape. I told Amos that we were going to hold a press conference in New York, and I needed him to make me a soda can and fill it with Freon. I knew from when I worked on cars that Freon gets ice cold when exposed to air. I told Amos that I needed this can to get cold when the top pops. Amos assured me he could make it work.

The stage was set. Now all I needed to do was get George to become the President of Laser Arms. George arrived right on time.

"How much money can I get right now?" George asked Marshall and me.

George didn't care what we wanted him to do. He was happy to just be doing something again. If he could make some money, he would do it.

"The company would be yours to run, but you have to get it trading again," Marshall told him.

200

"You'll get a bunch of free trading stock, and we'll help you sell it," I added.

We decided that we would have the press conference at Windows of the World at the top of the World Trade Center. George was going to stand in front of all the cameras and pop the top of the can. I guaranteed him it would chill.

"Amos Walls is flying into town and bringing the cans with him," I told George.

"Those fucking Feds, I'm happy to fuck those motherfuckers," George said, laughing.

Marshall went out to the trunk of his car and took out some cash, and he gave George ten thousand dollars. The deal was done.

The morning of the press conference, Marshall and I sat in his new El Dorado in a parking lot near the World Trade Center. We were talking on the car speakerphone to Tommy Quinn, who was at a phone booth inside the press conference. He was on a three-way call through my office. Tommy was telling us that the place was crawling with Feds, and that George gave this crazy, fucked up speech and a demonstration of the Chill Can.

"When George popped that can, it got so cold from the Freon that George couldn't hold it. It almost stuck to his hand," Tommy told us.

Marshall and I were laughing our asses off.

"George was saying how the SEC fucks the small shareholders, and he was going to prove that this was just another scheme that the Feds and the SEC put together to hurt the small investors."

I had tears in my eyes listening to Tommy telling me what George was saying. The press conference ended, and Laser Arms, even with George Livieratos promising the world that the Chill Can really did work, never traded again.

It was shortly after this that Marshall Zolp disappeared, and left with a large amount of money he owed me and some bookies that I hooked him up with. I was going to kill Marshall, and I made it known to everyone around me. It didn't take me long to find out Marshall was hiding out at Vinny and Barbara's, and it was just a question of time when I was going to catch up to him. Robert Warren, the Assistant U.S. Attorney, called and said he needed me to come down to Newark to the Federal Court house and appear in front of the judge to put my plea on record and have the judge accept it. I was concerned why I had to do this now. Why couldn't it wait? The answer would soon be hitting me squarely in the face.

Judge Alfred Lechner was a new federal judge. I didn't get a good feeling from this guy at all, but Warren assured me that I would just plead guilty and walk out. I entered my guilty pleas to the two counts, and the judge did in fact accept the deal. He then set bail at two hundred thousand dollars. I looked at Warren.

"Your Honor, I request the court release Mr. Formato on his own bond," Warren said.

"I'll allow it," the prick of a judge said. "Mr. Formato must report to the federal probation department to prepare a pre-sentencing report. You're dismissed."

The federal probation officer was another prick. I didn't like this guy, not even a little bit. I didn't hide my feelings about him, and he let me know he thought I was a scumbag, as he clearly shook saying it. I think if I said, "Boo," he would have pissed himself.

"I'll need you to come back one more time for another interview, after I check out all my information," the probation officer said. "I'll call and let you know when to report."

I wasn't taking any of this seriously. I really felt I was getting probation for maybe two years, or at the absolute worst, I would wind up doing one year at some federal camp somewhere.

It was near the end of August, and I had planned a vacation with my family to go to Lake George. I had to have my attorney call to get permission from the U.S. Attorneys to let me go. I was having my boat taken up to Lake George, and I rented cabins for my wife's whole family. The vacation was a bust for me. I was too concerned about my stock deal that would soon be opening. I didn't like being gone at such a crucial time. I just had such a bad feeling something was wrong. Robin was furious with me because I wanted to go back home. I left anyway. I went home, and I left Robin there with the kids.

The stock deal that I was doing was going to open soon, and I had all my money tied up in it. I had gambled everything I had for my share on this deal that was going to make over one hundred and fifty million dollars. I purchased, through nominee names, the whole damn offering. I owned the box, meaning I had control of all the free trading stock. My relationship with Morty, Vinny, and Barbara had, for the most part, ended because of that scumbag Zolp. I had the biggest music deal on the street, and it was hot. Everyone wanted to get in on this stock deal. Even Joe the Indian was excited, and he agreed with me that this would be the last stock deal. I was going to make every one rich off this one deal. I was going to be doing what I always wanted to do all my life. I was going to be in the music business. There would be no more Wise Guys doing stock deals, or having to put up with assholes like Marshall Zolp, Lionel Reifler, Michael Rapp, or David Wellington. After this deal, I would be one of the biggest guys in the music industry in the country.

My sights were on the RCA record division, and I knew I could do a leveraged buy out of RCA. I had plenty of help with Freddy Heinz and Kuhn Suenfeld. My stock would be $21.00 per share at the opening, and I was going to sell all my warrants. My end of the deal would net me a cool fifty-five million dollars, and I would own the largest share of RCA Records. I would be unstoppable. I knew the world of the music business would soon belong to me.

Robin had come home from vacation, and she was so pissed off at me that she didn't talk to me for a week. Nothing was going to ever stop me from getting what I worked so hard for. I just had to handle my problem with the U.S. Attorney's Office in Newark, NJ.

Monday morning, September 7, 1986, I received a call from the federal probation department. This prick wanted me in his office at 9:00 a.m. the next day. That night, I stayed home. I watched the opening night of Monday Night Football, and I fell asleep on the couch downstairs.

Tuesday morning, September 8, 1986, I just took a quick shower and got dressed like a bum. I was only going to see that fucking probation officer, so I didn't give a shit what I looked like. I jumped in my white Jaguar and proceeded to the probation department. I got lost along the way and called my office for directions from my car phone. I parked my car and walked in the building. I walked past these two guys standing at the door. They looked at me kind of strange, but I kept walking right past them. I thought I knew what floor it was on, but when I got off the elevator, I didn't recognize where I was. I noticed that there were two guys up there too. I got back on the elevator and went down to the main lobby to look at the directory to see what floor I was supposed to go to. When I walked down the hall, one of the two guys called my name. I knew right then and there I was about to be busted for something. Michael Cahill identified himself as the FBI. The other Agent moved behind me and handcuffed me. They walked me to an unmarked car and put me in the back seat. There was a lot of chatter going on over their radios. Special Agent Cahill got in the back seat with me.

"We got you Larry," Special Agent Cahill said. "It's all over for you."

"You got nothing," I said. "I want to call my lawyer."

"Which one do you want to call?"

"Morty Burger."

"Nah, we got him."

I went down the list of my lawyers.

"Jay Surgent? Marc Bateman?" I said.

"Nope, we got them too," Special Agent Cahill said.

"Are there any of my lawyers you don't have?"

"I think we have them all. We got everyone, your whole crew, too: the Indian, Lenny, and Tommy. Oh, I forgot, we also got Freddy, Vinny, and Barbara."

"Fuck you."

"Did I mention George, and the brokers you had in your pocket? I didn't. Gee, sorry. Here's one you'll like—Marshall Zolp."

"Big fucking deal. You still have nothing."

"Oh, you're so wrong. I got this."

Cahill held up a cassette tape.

"It has your voice on it. We got you on tape," Cahill said.

"Big fucking deal. You got one fucking tape," I said.

Cahill smiled. He was baiting me the whole time.

"Oh, no. I got this tape, and four thousand, nine hundred, and ninety-nine more, filled with conversations of you and all your buddies," Cahill said. "Wire fraud carries five years per conversation. I'm sure out of five thousand tapes we're going to make a couple hundred years stick."

I was truly shocked. The car started driving away.

"You have from now until we get to Newark to decide if you're going to cooperate, or spend the next hundred years in jail," Cahill said.

I was quiet for most of the ride. I didn't say a word.

"They have indictments waiting for you in Florida, Denver, California, and New York," Cahill continued. "You're getting hit with RICOs in all those states."

I kept my mouth firmly shut.

"You know, the federal prison has this cool bus system," Cahill said. "You get to go for a ride, handcuffed, shackled, and chained, with your hands chained to your waist. You can't smoke or even scratch your nose. You're just sitting and riding."

He was really pushing hard now.

"In your case, they're going to put you on a bus and drive you to Denver," Cahill continued. "Then, they're going to drive you to New York. From New York, they might ride you to California, and from there, you're on your way to Florida. Finally, after what will probably take a good eighteen months, you'll go back to New Jersey, just in time for trial here. Oh, and that's not all. You'll be back on the road for all the other trials, no phones or contact with anyone. You are really fucked."

He looked at his watch.

"Time is running out," he said.

"Okay, what's the deal?" I asked.

As soon as I said that, he reached for his radio and called in to someone.

"Tell Bob to be ready," Cahill said into the radio.

They took me to the federal building in Newark, New Jersey. When I got out of the car, a team of photographers rushed towards us taking pictures. Once I was inside the building, they put me in a room with two chairs and a desk. Bob Warren, Chief of the Fraud Division, came in the room and was a real asshole to me.

"You're fucked unless you tell the truth right now," Warren said. "You have no time to think about it, if you're going to cooperate. Where are the guns?"

I looked at him as if he was crazy.

"I don't carry guns anymore," I said.

"Stop fucking with me and tell me where the shipment of guns are," Warren yelled.

I had no clue what the fuck he was talking about. The shouting continued for another fifteen minutes before I had enough.

"Hey, go fuck yourself," I said.

"Your phones in your office were tapped from May 1, 1986 through September 8, 1986," Cahill told me. "Vinny and Barbara's phones were tapped too. The Indian was never going to let you live after you finished the stock deal. You were getting too big and powerful."

I just listened and didn't say anything.

Warren wanted the codes and passwords for my safe at the Zurich Depository. The FBI raided it and couldn't get into my safe. They would have to blow the damn windows apart to gain access if I didn't give up my codes. They wanted me to give them Marshall's codes too, but I didn't know them. The Feds were able to gain access to the safe and take everything that was in it.

"I know you've been running guns in U-haul trucks from Florida to your office in New Jersey with Lenny," Cahill said.

"Are you fucking crazy?" I asked, shocked. "I don't run guns. I run stocks. Your information is fucking wrong. Whoever you got it from lied to you."

They raided my office and confiscated everything that was in there. They took it all out in trucks. Cahill told me they were also going to search my home. I felt bad for Robin, but I knew she would be okay. She had grown used to all this fucking bullshit over the years. I was still pretty much left in the dark as to exactly what was taking place. Running guns, were they fucking nuts? For that matter, I still didn't know what exactly it was that I was being arrested for. No one told me.

Warren entered in the room.

"They have everyone rounded up," Warren told Cahill. "The magistrate is ready."

Cahill walked me down a hall. Morty was coming out of a room a few doors down, also in handcuffs. They were lining us up and bringing us in to the federal magistrate's courtroom for arraignment. They started by reading the charges and setting bail for each defendant. They began with the defendants that were the least culpable. I was at the very end of the line, standing next to Marshall Zolp. It was pretty boring listening to the same thing being read over and over again. For the most part, everyone was being released on their own bond, but as they were moving towards me, I noticed the bail getting higher.

"You know, when we get out of here today, I'm going to kill you," I told Marshall.

"Just listen," he said, laughing.

"We request no bail for this defendant," the Assistant U.S. Attorney told the magistrate. "The Government believes he is a threat to society and we have proof that he conspired to kill a federal witness."

"Who the fuck are they talking about?" I asked Marshall.

"You," he said, still laughing. "They're talking about you."

I couldn't figure out what they were talking about. I was conspiring to kill a federal witness? On top of that, no bail? What a bunch of bullshit. Marshall was also denied bail because he was deemed to be a flight risk, and he was a fugitive.

After the arraignment, I was brought back to the U.S. Attorney's office and put in the same room as before. When Cahill came in, I was furious.

"What the fuck are you guys doing? I didn't conspire to kill any federal witness," I said.

"There is no way you're getting out of prison right now," Cahill said. "You should be kissing the bars tonight, because if you get released, I firmly believe you will be whacked."

To my relief, the Indian and Lenny were never arrested. Cahill was just playing me. Jay Surgent was never arrested either, and I'm pretty sure my rights were violated when I asked for my lawyer, Jay Surgent.

"I'll put you into witness protection if you cooperate with us," Cahill said. "You're going to the Manhattan Correctional Center. The U.S. Marshals will be coming soon to transport you and Zolp there. Be careful who you talk to, and watch what you say on the phones."

The Marshals arrived and chained Zolp and me together. I couldn't believe this happened to me the day before the biggest deal of my life.

CHAPTER 31: THE WAY OUT

The bus ride to Manhattan Correctional Center, for the most part, was quiet. I had Marshall Zolp sitting next to me, and he was trying to make peace.

"At this point, we're both fucked, so let's stick together," Zolp said.

He was right.

"Are you going to cooperate?" he asked.

"I'm thinking about it," I said.

When we arrived at MCC, we went through inmate processing. We were both put on the same floor, nine north. We both shared the same cell. I was actually happy at this point that I was bunking with Marshall rather than some stranger. The lines waiting for the phones were long, and the inmates were arguing over how long some guys were staying on the phone.

I finally got to make a call before the eleven o'clock lockdown. I called Robin. This was the first time I had a chance to talk to her since this all happened.

"I'm okay," Robin said. "Your arrest is all over the TV and the radio."

"Listen, Mike Cahill from the FBI might be calling you," I said. "Don't be scared. Just cooperate with him."

That was all the time I had to talk. I had to give someone else a turn. To my surprise, Marshall and I were woken up at 4:00 a.m., and we were told we had court, so we got up, took showers, and were taken to the holding pens on the first floor. It was like a Who's Who in the Wise Guy world while we were getting ready for court and waiting for court clothes. I mean, every Wise Guy I knew or heard of was in jail except for my crew, but I was really expecting to see them come through the doors at any time.

I was starting to feel like if you weren't in jail in 1986, then you were not a Wise Guy. The feds in 1986 had busted John Gotti, so they had his trial going on. Then, they had the pizza connection trial and the crime commission trial. They had two big trials in Jersey, The Lucchese drug trial that Jackie and Jerry the Jew were in, and they had my case.

Mike Cahill picked me up at the holding cell in Newark and took me to the U.S. Attorney's office to listen to a deal.

"If you agree to help us, we will do everything we can to help you," Cahill said. "You have serious problems. Bob Warren is working with the federal districts in New York, Florida, California, and Colorado to wrap all the charges from each state into the New Jersey case. This isn't just a slap on the wrist. You're facing twenty years in each state. Because you signed a plea agreement and violated it, the Government thinks you fucked them."

"Give me a fucking break," I said. "You fucking guys set me up with that bullshit agreement."

"I want you to talk to Bob."

Cahill stepped out of the room and returned shortly with Bob Warren. Bob shook my hand, and was a completely different guy than the prick I met the day before. He was really acting nice towards me.

"I talked with all the other states, and they will let me wrap all these cases into one, except for New York," Bob said.

"So what am I looking at?" I asked.

"We're not sure, and we can't make any promises. Depending on your cooperation, you could reduce your exposure quite a bit."

"So, I will be coming here almost every day for debriefing?"

After being there for an hour or so, Mike explained to me that I would be put into the witness protection program and that my family would be safe.

"There's no need to panic now about your family," Cahill said. "No one knows that you're cooperating."

There was a knock on the door.

"His wife is here," someone I couldn't see told Cahill.

That was a surprise to me, and I was really glad that I was going to get a chance to see Robin. They put me in a conference room and gave me some time with Robin to talk about my future cooperation as a government witness, as well as a way out of my life as a Wise Guy. Robin was with my son, Christian, who was only 17 months old, and he was a handful. It was hard to concentrate with Chris crying and running around. I thought Robin would be happy that I decided to cooperate and change my life, with a chance at a new start for us. I was so wrong

"Are you crazy?" Robin asked. "I can't leave my family. My mother is sick. You're crazy. What happened to you? And you told me you would always be a stand up guy."

You would always be a stand up guy. The words echoed in my head. Like a knife, her words went straight through my heart.

"I'm not doing this for me," I said. "I'm doing it for you and the kids."

Sonny, my oldest son at fourteen, also lived with Robin and me. I could see Robin was scared and confused. There was so much that had taken place in just the last twenty-four hours. Mike Cahill and Bob Warren were able to calm Robin down, and she finally agreed that cooperating was the right thing to do.

Mike and Bob were really good, and tried to answer all of Robin's questions. They told her a U.S. Federal Marshal from Washington would be meeting with us to explain the witness protection program, and that he would answer all our questions. Robin was clearly upset. I knew things wouldn't be easy on her.

The bus to Jersey, with Jackie, in the mornings was a lot of fun. He was really a funny guy. God forbid anyone on that bus ever suspected I was cooperating. I would never get off it alive. It was going to take about three months for me to get into the witness protection system in the Bureau of Prisons (BOP). I had to pass a lie detector test. They wanted to make sure applicants weren't just pretending to get into the program so they could hurt or kill someone.

Every day, except weekends, I would ride the bus with Marshall to Newark for debriefing. The first couple of months were rough on me. I really hated being in jail. My 35th birthday passed, and so did Christmas and New Year's. Some time in the early part of January, 1987, Cahill spoke to me after debriefing.

"You're not going back on the bus today," Cahill said. "The Marshals will bring you back."

My heart felt like it was going to come out of my chest. This was the time of reality. I was going to the third floor, where they keep all the "rats," or guys who were cooperating witnesses. I knew when that bus went back and I wasn't on it, everyone would know the Feds rolled me. I would be known from now on as a traitor, and worse, a rat.

"Marshall won't be coming with you," Cahill continued. "It didn't work out for him. Mike wouldn't tell me why. You're doing the right thing. Don't worry about Marshall. You're going to be okay."

I heard about the third floor from other guys who were in jail with me, but they didn't know any more about it than I did. Sometimes, a guard would tell stories about the third floor and how easy the guys there had it. I heard that they even had color TVs in their rooms. I was feeling happy to get to the third floor, and also, I was feeling bad that everyone who knew me and respected me would no longer have any respect for me at all. Now I was going to be known as what I said I would never become—a rat.

When a government witness is being moved in the prison, the prison actually has to lock down the entire prison population so that the witness never comes in contact with any inmates. I entered the third floor lockup through three metal doors. After being strip-searched, I was given a pair of khaki pants and a shirt to put on. I was put in lockdown until the unit manager cleared me to be free to join the general population.

The third floor held, at its maximum, twenty-four witnesses. The unit manager showed me pictures of the other witnesses, and if I had a problem with any one of them, I stayed in lockdown until they found a way to separate us. I had no problems with anyone, although I did recognize a few guys.

I was now cleared to join population on the third floor. I would never be called by my name, Larry Formato, ever again. I was now known only as LF, and that's how everyone on the third floor was addressed - by their initials. I was assigned a cell and a cellmate.

Everyone on the third floor was either a Wise Guy or a drug dealer. The notion that the rats had it better was way wrong. It was a walking hell in there. The guards, except for a few, didn't even like us. They were afraid that if they closed their eyes to take a nap, someone would rat them out. It was so fucking bad in there that the argument could be made that it was inhumane. There were no windows, no fresh air. All of the food was heated in a microwave oven. All rights, even as a prisoner, were taken away. It was the job of the BOP (Bureau of Prisons) to protect you, not to make you comfortable. That meant we didn't enjoy the activities that inmates in general population were granted. One of the things I especially liked was that, from time to time, there were only 12 to 15 guys on the third floor. It was unusual for it to get to 20 inmates.

There were two phones, and I could get on a phone and talk for hours without having to worry about someone needing a phone. I was one of the very few guys who could get a "patch call." When I made calls, I would call the FBI and they had my name listed as someone to make calls for, so I could make all my calls for free. The other guys had to make collect calls.

The days of going to see Mike Cahill were over. Now that I was in witness protection, I could only be moved by the U.S. Marshals, and only to a secret place in the Marshal's office where they held and transported government witnesses. I couldn't believe that George Livieratos was going to trial. In my wildest dreams, I couldn't believe he was that fucking dumb to go to trial and let me testify against him. Morty Berger was a fool, and he convinced Barbara Baker and Vinny Castalanno to go to trial too. My right hand man, Tommy Quinn, listened to me and pleaded out. He cooperated, although no one knew it at the time. I was really happy he did, because it saved him from doing any jail time. There were fourteen of us arrested, and of the fourteen, just five defendants were going to trial: George, Morty, Barbara, Vinny, and Bobby Bosse.

Mike Cahill had two big boxes of cassettes tapes delivered to the prison, and I was assigned a special room to sit in and listen to the tapes and identify voices. I explained what the people on the tapes were talking about. It took weeks and weeks to listen to the tapes. It was through listening to these tapes that I realized that I was a real asshole, and I didn't really like myself. I was no different than some of the Wise Guys I hated. In some of the conversations, I was worse. I decided that my life had to change. I needed to be a good guy, not an asshole with a big head.

The trial was coming soon, and I couldn't wait for it to start. I was told that I had to wait until after the trial was over before I could be sentenced. The reason for waiting was to be able to show to the judge the full nature and scope of my cooperation, giving the judge a good reason to give me a break. I thought that, because of my cooperation and the threat assessment on my life, that I was going to get time served. Mike Cahill had me convinced that I should be going home.

"You have been a great help," Cahill told me. "The judge will be made aware of your continuing cooperation."

I was convinced I would be getting time served.

I found out from Cahill how the FBI got the wiretaps on my phones: Paul Genovese, whose real last name was Weinberg -- Paul, or Big Pauly, got arrested in Morris County, NJ, and he tried to make a deal. He knew that Marshall Zolp was a fugitive, so he told the cops he could deliver Marshall Zolp to them. Morris County didn't know who Marshal Zolp was, and they really didn't care.

"Who else can you give us?" one of the cops asked him.

Paul said the magic words.

"Larry Formato," he said.

Paul made up the gunrunning story so that he could get off whatever trouble he had gotten himself into. Bells and whistles were going off after Paul said my name. The FBI was called in, and it was decided that, because they believed I was running guns from Florida to New Jersey, they would get a federal court order to tap my phones. From the time the wiretaps started in May, the FBI had surveillance on me twenty-four hours a day. Mike Cahill had some respect for me during this time. He knew from listening to the wiretaps that I passed a lie detector test about the charges in Morris County. He heard me turn down numerous offers to have my ex-wife whacked.

"I'm going to trial, and I'm beating these fucked up charges," I told everyone.

It would have been easy for me to make my ex-wife disappear, and the Feds knew it.

With the federal trial nearing, I needed to make sure I had a deal completed with Morris County. There was no way I could ever go to trial there. Not now, not being a convicted felon in the witness protection program. Bob Warren and Jay Surgent worked out a deal that I would plead guilty to some bullshit one-count charge, and that any sentence I received would be concurrent and coterminous with any federal sentence that I received. Whichever sentence ended first would also end the other. They would both end at the same time. I was happy with that deal, and the Morris County prosecutor signed the plea agreement.

The FBI made arrangements to move my wife and family to a safe house down at the Jersey Shore. They didn't want my family around when the federal trial started. I was still hoping that the defendants were going to make a deal and not go to trial. I didn't want to have to get on a witness stand and testify. I knew I was going to get hammered.

Marshall Zolp finally decided to plead guilty. The reason he didn't go with me in January onto the third floor was because the BOP had discovered that Zolp had planned an escape with the help of one of the correctional officers. They caught him and put him in twenty-three hour lock down. He figured his only choice now was to cooperate, or get at least twenty years if he was convicted. Marshall would soon join me on the third floor.

After months of being debriefed by the FBI, the trial finally started. They called my name to the witness stand by Assistant U.S. Attorney Jonathan Feld. He was trying the case along with Assistant U.S. Attorney Faith Hochburg. Jonathan started asking me questions, and I swear, from his questioning, it felt as though he was on the defense side. I was really getting upset with the questions. He was treating me like I was a piece of shit.

When we took a break, I talked to Mike Cahill.

"I'm not going back in the courtroom," I told him. "They can go fuck themselves."

I'm sure there would have been a mistrial if I didn't go back in there.

"Jonathan was hard on you because he wanted the jury to hear all the bad things you did in your life from you, not the defense lawyers," Cahill said. "They got to hear you admit what you did and see you're cooperating."

Back in the courtroom, Morty Burger stared me down and ran his finger across the front of his neck.

Then, one of the defense lawyers asked about money and where I had it hidden. They asked who owned the house my family lived in and where did the money come from to buy it. As a result of my testimony, my wife was sued, along with her mother, because I had put my house in my mother-in-law's name. My wife was forced to sell the house and give up all the money from the sale.

The newspapers destroyed and embarrassed me. I felt horrible for my family for what they were going through. I had to admit to my ties to organized crime, and how I manipulated the price of penny stocks. I could see that Judge Lechner hated my guts. He listened to my testimony and acted as if I had beaten him for some money. I made mention of this to Cahill during breaks.

"This is Judge Lechner's first trial as a federal judge, but that's just the way he is," Cahill said. "Everything will be fine."

When the defense started their cross examination of me, how bad I made his client sound depended on who the lawyer was and how he treated me. George's lawyer approached me and asked me to look at some papers he wanted me to identify. He threw them at me in disgust. I just let them fly and fall to the floor. I looked up at the judge from the witness stand and the judge never said a word. I knew this judge was going to fuck me. The U.S. Attorneys, I think, were in shock that the lawyer did this to me, and finally, Faith Hochberg stood up and objected to the treatment. After that, the defense lawyers weren't allowed to approach me.

There was nothing in my life that the defense didn't attack me on, and because Morty Burger was my lawyer for so many years and George Livieratos was my partner, there was practically nothing between the two of them that they didn't know about me. They dragged me through the gutter to bring out all the dirt on me. Wow, did they make me look dirty. I felt as though I was the one on trial and not them. I was asked about everything: murder, gambling, stock fraud, and even sex for money. The newspapers were eating it all up. I got beat up pretty bad on the witness stand, but I held my ground and kept my word with the Government. I completed my testimony. I told the truth about everything, no matter how damaging it was to me, and now I expected the Government to keep its word to me.

The trial came to an end, and Mike Cahill told me that the Judge did not even allow the defendants to go home after the trial. He revoked their bail when the guilty verdicts came in. I was happy, not that they were convicted, but that now, after one year in prison, I was going to be sentenced. I felt certain that I was going home. I was counting the days to my sentencing.

One week before I was scheduled to be sentenced, I got into a fight with another inmate over a card game. I was put in twenty-three hour lock down. We called it "the hole." I got no privileges, meaning I couldn't buy anything from the prison commissary, like cigarettes, food, or personal hygiene items. I wasn't allowed to make phone calls, except legal calls that had to be preapproved, and there had to be a time set for the call. I didn't care. I knew I was going home.

Fuck it. Lock me up. I'm outta here in a week anyway.

The day of my sentencing, October 30, 1987, I packed up my personal belongings, and I gave away everything else that I was allowed to keep in prison to some of the other inmates. I really didn't want anything from that place. I just wanted out of there. Federal Marshals took me to the Federal Building in Newark. I was taken to a holding room until it was time for me to go into Judge Alfred J. Lechner's courtroom. Mike Cahill popped his head in the door.

"Don't worry," he said. "Everything will be fine."

I was escorted into the courtroom. My whole family was there for my sentencing: Robin, Sonny, Christian, who was now two and a half years old, and even my sister, Patty, and her two daughters were there.

This will be my last day in Hell.

Robert Warren, the Chief of the Fraud Division for the U.S. Attorney's Office in Newark, New Jersey had written a letter to Judge Alfred J Lechner Jr., outlining the full nature and scope of my cooperation. He basically said I went above and beyond what was expected of me. I put my life at risk to cooperate and that I should, without actually saying it in writing, receive a sentence of time served.

The judge walked into the court, and we all stood. I was trying to read his expression, but his face was expressionless. I was sitting next to my lawyer, and the Government spoke first. Robert Warren told Judge Lechner all the cooperation I was able to give to help the Government. I felt great listening to him speak to the Judge about me. It looked as though the Government had kept their word. I was going home. My lawyer made a speech, but it wasn't as good as Bob Warrens. The Judge read my charges, and the sentences, one by one. I could feel the blood rushing to the top of my head, as he was throwing years at me like they were days. I looked over at Bob Warren, and I turned to look at Mike Cahill. They were expressionless. My whole family was in tears.

Judge Alfred J. Lechner Jr. gave me, Lorenzo Formato Jr., the witness for the Government, thirty years in prison, and imposed fines on me for millions of dollars. I could see the hate in this man's eyes as he was throwing all those years at me. Then he gave me a speech. He pretty much called me a scumbag, and he became outraged and he screamed at me.

"You, Mr. Formato, or someone you are very close to, has all this money," he yelled. "I want it. Do you understand me? I want it."

He started banging his gavel over and over again on his desk. I thought he was going to break it, from how hard he was slamming it.

"Get him out of my sight," Judge Lechner said, turning to the Marshals.

I could barely walk. I threw away my manhood, my respect, and I just got fucked by the Government.

Mike Cahill rushed into the room where I was being held while I was waiting to be transported back to prison for the next thirty years. I looked at him. He knew I was mad, and he knew I got fucked.

"Larry, I promise you, this sentence isn't going to stick," Cahill said. "We will get it changed. Don't give up. This judge is new. He doesn't know how the system is supposed to work. We'll talk to the judge."

"I don't believe anything you have to say to me," I said, still in shock. "I cooperated, and I got more time than all the defendants combined. What the fuck is that all about? How does the guy who cooperates get the most time?"

Cahill just stared at me, lost for words.

I was going back to hell, and worse, I was going back to the hole for sixty days. The other inmates were shocked to see me come back. I told everyone I was getting time served. My unit manager was even shocked. He thought I was being released.

I sat in total isolation, with nothing to do except think about how badly I got fucked by the Government. I was asked to trust them. I put my life in their hands, and they gave me back what would amount to be a life sentence. After a week, the unit manager of my floor couldn't stand to let me sit in the hole any longer. He must have thought that the sentence I received was far worse than sitting in the hole for sixty days, so he set aside the remaining days I had and let me out. I had nothing left. I gave away everything I had to the other guys before I left for court that morning, but the guys were cool. They returned my sneakers and some other items of mine. All I wanted to do was kill Bob Warren and Mike Cahill.

Cahill came to see me.

"I'm sorry, Larry," Cahill said. "This has never happened before to a government witness."

I glared at Cahill.

"There is a motion called a rule thirty-five, and I want you to have your attorney make it. It's a reduction of sentence based on many things, but mostly the of the person bringing the motion. You have a high profile case, and since it was the judge's first big case, he didn't want to send a message to the public that he was soft."

The newspapers all wrote about how the judge slammed me with thirty years, but the U.S. Attorney's office had a big problem. The other cases they had with government witnesses were falling apart. The witnesses saw how badly I got fucked by the Government and refused to testify. I think even some of the Wise Guys felt badly. The judge sent the wrong message, using me as his example. The Rule 35 would give the Judge a chance to resentence me without the newspapers knowing about it, and it would be done quietly, in the judge's chambers. No one would really know my sentence was reduced if my motion for a Rule 35 was successful.

"You really fucked me," I said. "How long will it take to do this rule thirty-five?"

"I don't know," Cahill said. "I only know you have to file it, not the Government."

My life is over, I thought. I'm a convicted felon sentenced to thirty years in jail, but worse than that, I'm now known as the "King Rat."

The Government was now working on the Federal Flushing Savings and Loan case. I was expected, as part of my plea agreement, to cooperate fully with the U.S. Attorney's office in the Eastern District of New York. I was told that, by cooperating, it would give the judge more of a reason to reduce my sentence in considering my Rule 35. Virginia Evans was the Assistant U.S. Attorney for the Eastern District of New York handling the Federal Flushing Case.

I developed a deep resentment for this woman, who I think should have been the one going to jail. She would come to debrief me for the case and actually try to get me to lie about things that other witnesses in the case had told her that weren't true. This fucking bitch insisted I lie to back them up. I told Virginia Evans on more than one occasion to go and fuck herself. I discussed this with Cahill, and he was going to have Bob Warren talk with her.

"Do not do anything to fuck this up," Cahill warned me as my motion neared. "Just keep cooperating and see what the judge will do."

On March 28, 1988, Judge Alfred J Lechner Jr. fucked me one more time. He reduced my sentence, but it wasn't reduced to time served, he gave me a total of six fucking years.

I had the big gun from the U.S. Attorney's office, Michael Chertoff,

2947P
RPW:mp

UNITED STATES DISTRICT COURT
DISTRICT OF NEW JERSEY

UNITED STATES OF AMERICA	:	Hon. Alfred J. Lechner, Jr. FILED
v.	:	Criminal No. 86-281
LORENZO FORMATO	:	86- -3 APR 18 1988
	:	87-390
	:	O R D E R At 8 h 3:00

This matter having been opened to the Court on March 28,
1988, on motion of the defendant Lorenzo Formato (Harvey J.
Michelman, Esq., appearing), for reduction of sentence imposed
pursuant to Fed. R. Crim. P. 35(b), in the presence of Samuel A.
Alito, Jr., United States Attorney (Michael Cherloff, Assistant
United States Attorney, appearing), and the Court having
considered the papers submitted in connection with the motion and
having heard the argument of counsel, and good cause having been
shown,

IT IS on this _____ day of April, 1988;

ORDERED that the sentence of defendant Lorenzo Formato
imposed by the Court on October 30, 1987 be and is hereby vacated
and the defendant is hereby sentenced as set forth below:

(1) As to the Indictment Criminal No. 86-281, the
defendant is committed to the custody of the Attorney General or
his authorized representative for imprisonment for the following
terms:

-2-

(a) As to Count 1, five years' imprisonment;

(b) As to Count 2, one year imprisonment, said
term of imprisonment to be consecutive to
the term of imprisonment provided for in
Count 1; and

(c) As to Count 3, five years' imprisonment, however, imposition of sentence is
suspended, the defendant is placed on
probation for five years, said term of
probation shall commence immediately upon
custodial release on Counts 1 and 2.

(2) As to the Indictment Criminal No. 86-299, the
defendant is committed to the custody of the Attorney General or
his authorized representative for imprisonment for a period of
five years, said term to be served concurrently with the sentence
imposed on Indictment Criminal No. 86-281.

(3) As to the Information Criminal No. 87-390, the
defendant is committed to the custody of the Attorney General or
his authorized representative for imprisonment for a period of
five years, said term to be served concurrently with the sentence
imposed on Indictment Criminal No. 86-281.

ALFRED J. LECHNER, JR., Judge
United States District Court

219

speak for me at the Rule 35 motion. I firmly believe that Virginia Evans was the reason I didn't get time served. Virginia Evans made it known that she believed that if I were released, I wouldn't testify at the Federal Flushing Bank trial.

I was getting sick and couldn't breathe. I was very short of breath. The BOP sent me for a chest x-ray, and the prison doctors told me I had a tumor on my lung about the size of a dime. I was going to have to be transferred to Springfield, Missouri to the Federal Prison Hospital. Nothing moves fast in the prison system. If you're a protected witness, things go even slower. I had written many requests to be transferred to the prison hospital. I knew that if I had lung cancer, it needed to be treated quickly if I had any chance to survive at all. The Government didn't care if I died. I would be one less person that they would have to take care of, or in their eyes, one less scumbag who would no longer be around anymore.

When I first got arrested, someone sent me a Bible. I would sit and read it in my cell. I spent much of my time after I was transferred to the "rat floor" reading the Bible. I took a much stronger interest in the Bible and religion. I had Robin buy me Harper's Bible Commentary and Harper's Bible Dictionary. I started a complete study of the Bible, line by line, using these two books as my learning guides. I also had the chance to meet with a Catholic priest. His name was Father Patrick Markey, and he became a good friend to me. One day, he gave me a prayer book. It was a devotion to Mother Mary. I studied every day, and I decided to do the devotional prayers. The priest would teach me and try to answer any questions I had. I was becoming more and more interested in the Catholic Religion.

After being on the rat floor for over a year now, praying every day and every night, I was now faced with the fact that I had a tumor on my lung, and I was probably going to die of lung cancer. Father Patrick Markey prayed with me and kept me strong in my faith, saying the Rosary and praying to Mother Mary.

Three months of mental suffering while waiting to get to a hospital, I was finally transferred to the Federal Hospital in Springfield, Stronghold 3. Stronghold 3 got its name because it was behind three doors that were like huge safe doors, just really big, heavy steel doors. The inside of Stronghold 3 was very small. A guard sat at the last of the three steel doors, and he watched over the inmates being held inside. No more than three inmates could be housed there at one time. That's how it was built—just three hospital rooms.

Thank God I wasn't in this place alone. In one of the rooms was George Harp. He was considered by the federal prison system to be one of the most, if not *the* most, dangerous prisoners in the BOP. George was responsible for the start up of the Arian Brotherhood, but unlike most other white supremacists, George didn't have a single tattoo on his body. George was about fifty years old, and he wasn't sick. He had a body better than Arnold Schwarzenegger, and he was being held in Stronghold 3 because the BOP had nowhere else to keep him where he couldn't hurt anyone. George killed a lot of people in federal prison, and all the guards had good reason to fear him. He was known to have killed or caused the deaths of a few prison guards.

"Can I make a phone call?" I asked the guard sitting in the hall, watching George.

The guard didn't answer me, so I asked him again, and again. I was getting really upset, and this went on for about an hour before the guard responded.

"Shut up, lunger," the guard shouted at me.

Fuck, I was literally in shock that he answered me that way, but not as shocked as I was with what took place next.

George got up and walked into the hall.

"Give that kid the phone before I kill you with it," George ordered.

The tough guard lost his bravado.

"Okay," the guard said. "I was just fucking with him."

George and I became friends after that.

"You have to stay strong in your mind and body," George told me one day. "Never give up. Keep fighting. Exercise every day. You'll beat this."

I believed him.

I was so amazed with George and all the stories he told me. The man spent most of his life in jail, and he was one of the smartest men I had ever known. George Harp knew it all. Why? Because he read books his whole life behind bars.

It was the end of May, 1988 when I arrived at Stronghold 3, and one of the things I loved most about being there was that it had windows. They could open, but not very high. I was able to smell fresh air. I remember it raining really hard, and I put my face to the small opening in the window and breathed really deep, smelling the beautiful fresh air. I was hearing birds sing for the first time since 1986.

I was scheduled for a CAT scan, and I can remember lying on the table of the CAT scan machine, praying.

Please let this thing be gone from me.

Over and over, I prayed as the scan was being done. Nothing changes in jail. Despite the scan being completed, it was two weeks before a doctor walked into my room.

"You're fine," the doctor said, nonchalant as can be. "There was nothing there."

"How can that be?" I asked him. "I looked at the x-rays myself. I saw it."

"It could have been a calcium deposit that just dissolved by itself."

I didn't think a calcium deposit would have dissolved that quickly. One of the first things the doctors did when I arrived at Stronghold 3 was take a chest x-ray. I still had the spot on my lung then.

I wasn't convinced. I didn't have a feeling of joy come over me that I was fine. It was a really weird feeling. I was happy, but cautious. To add to this all, not only did I have a Rule 35, but I also had my very first parole hearing right before I left for the hospital. The Parole Board didn't think I should be released early. I appealed their decision and hired a top gun to handle the appeal. I paid for him to fly to Springfield, Missouri to interview me and put together what he would be presenting to the Parole Board. He was shocked to learn about how I had been treated, about my living environment, and about the mental cruelty that I was put through.

"The chances of winning a parole appeal are less than three percent, but I feel I'm going to win this one for you," he said.

I remained at Stronghold 3 for three months, keeping George Harp company. I think the BOP would have left me there if Virginia Evans didn't request to have me brought back to MCC.

I was back in hell with no windows, no sound from the outside, and worst of all, no fresh air. I was glad to see Father Patrick Markey again, and I really believed that it was through the power of prayer that the spot on my lung disappeared.

I became a Minister of the Eucharist, and I was ordained through Saint Andrews in New York. I would hold mass every night for the inmates who wanted to come. I wasn't a "Bible thumper," but I was deeply moved by what I learned and how I felt about the Lord.

I won my appeal with the Parole Board, and I was given a date that I was going home. For the first time since September 8, 1986, I now had a real date when I would be going home. Virginia Evans wasn't happy with the news. I would be out of federal prison before the trial she was prosecuting was going to start. I was being paroled, and I would be out of this fucking hell forever. I would be a free man before Easter of 1989.

I called Robin and told her the good news.

"I'm so happy for you," Robin said. "I am, but I'm not going into the witness protection program with you. I just can't leave my family with my mother being this sick."

I was crushed. I changed my whole life so I could make a new start with Robin. After all I had been through, fighting with the Government almost every day to get the break I was promised, and all the mental pain and anguish, my wife decided to divorce me. I felt more betrayed by Robin than I did by the Government.

CHAPTER 32: THEY NEVER LET GO

When making the transition from a protected witness in the prison system to being in the witness protection program in society, the Government issues a series of psychological tests. They do this to make sure protected witnesses aren't going to go out and kill or rape their neighbors. Whenever these tests are given to an inmate, the rest of the inmates would know that person would soon be released. I couldn't wait to finish my testing and get the hell out of this place. This time it was real, no more disappointments. I was being released, and Sonny, my oldest son, would be the only person entering the witness protection program with me. As happy as I was to be getting out, my guts were wrenched thinking how Robin could do this to me.

I was now one of the lucky ones. My day had come to be released. As I did before, I gave everything I had away to some of the guys I had been living with in prison. The Federal Marshals came and took me to their holding rooms. All I needed to do was go to Morris County and appear before Judge Collister to be sentenced. My signed plea agreement had been in effect since 1986. What this meant was, even if the judge gave me ten years, it would be the equivalent of time served, because my plea agreement was coterminous and concurrent with any federal sentence I received.

I appeared in front of the judge, and he told me he could not, in good conscience, accept my plea agreement, and he ordered me to stand trial. This was far worse than what happened to me in 1987 at my first sentencing. With all the things I confessed to doing in my life, the judge broke the deal. He wouldn't accept the signed plea agreement. There are no words to describe what it feels like being locked up for so long, believing I was being freed, only to find out that I may never be free.

I felt so bad for my son, Sonny. This poor kid had been waiting for his dad to come back and be with him since 1986. Each time we thought I was getting out, he was let down.

Going back to MCC was like reliving a never-ending nightmare. Jay Surgent, whom I saved from being indicted by convincing the Feds the only thing he ever did wrong was having me for his client, came to my rescue. Jay wrote a great brief to try to persuade the court to accept the original plea deal.

Jay V. Surgent

We lost that court battle, but Jay managed to talk with the prosecutors. He was told the judge needed to be able to give me some jail time so he wouldn't be criticized. They worked out a new deal, and the judge accepted it. I didn't have to go to trial, but he ordered me to go to Avenel Correctional Facility in New Jersey for a psychiatric evaluation.

In New Jersey, if you are found to be repetitive and compulsive as a sex offender, they can keep you in jail for as long as they feel it is necessary.

"I don't trust the Government, and I don't trust the state," I told Jay. "How can we be sure that I'll be treated fairly and they don't rig the test?"

"Trust me, Larry, the state will play fair," Jay assured me.

I took the deal, and agreed to the testing. Virginia Evans, the bitch that she was, continued to pound me about my testimony at the Federal Flushing Savings and Loan fraud trial. I was convinced at this point, and so was Jay, that she must have called the Morris County judge to keep me in jail until after the trial was over.

The Federal Marshals took me to Avenel. I can't recall a time in my life that I ever felt so embarrassed or made to feel as dirty as I did when I went to Avenel for the testing.

"Whatever you do, make sure you tell the truth," Jay cautioned.

I was put through a series of written tests, followed by a direct examination by a female psychiatrist. I was never so glad to be done with anything as I was with this testing. It was going to be two weeks before the results came back. I was positive that if they didn't try to fuck with me, I would pass with flying colors.

While I was waiting for the results to come in, my ex-wife, Joan, wrote a letter to the judge. She basically said that if I gave her forty thousand dollars, she would drop the charges. The judge had to turn the letter over to my lawyer, and the judge wasn't happy. Basically, it showed the judge I was being extorted.

I now had a new decision to make. I had to decide whether to go to trial or to have my lawyer go through with the plea deal. I was in jail now for three years, and all I wanted to do was get out and go home, wherever home would be. I talked it over with my family and my lawyer.

"Take a deal," my lawyer advised. "You would have to do maybe one more year in jail, and that would be it."

As much as it disgusted me to do this deal, I decided that I would go forward with the plea bargain and not go to trial.

The wait for the test results were agonizing. When the results of the test came in, I passed with flying colors. I was so relieved, not that I passed, but because they didn't try to screw me. Virginia Evans was fit to be tied. There was no way she wanted me pleading guilty in Morris County until I testified at the trial. I agreed to hold off in Morris County on the plea bargain in exchange for a written letter from the U.S. Attorney's Office to the judge in Morris County. I wasn't taking any more chances with the Government. I had been screwed too many times in the past. I had learned my lesson with the Government. This time, it was going to be my way or no way.

The Federal Flushing Trial was something of a mix between Wise Guys and bankers. Jilly Rizzo, Tony DelVecchio, Marc Bateman, and Don Sheppard were there, along with Carl Cardascia, the President of Federal Flushing, and Ron Mortelli, the Vice President of the bank. The witnesses for the Government ranged from accountants and bank officers to Michael (Rapp) Hellerman and George Livieratos. George was ratting on everyone he could, and he viewed himself as someone just telling the truth as he testified against the defendants. To think he once called me a rat.

Mike Fusco lied his ass off for the Government so he would not be indicted, and it was his testimony that Virginia Evans wanted me to back up. She came right out and told me that if I didn't repeat the story Mike Fusco told on the stand, she would contact my Federal Parole Board and inform them that I broke my plea agreement and ask them to revoke my parole. This woman was obsessed with winning this case. She would stop at nothing to win. I heard from George Livieratos that she offered him sex to make up stories about the defendants. This was the Government of the United States and their representatives.

"I'm not going to lie for this fucking crazy bitch," I told Cahill over the phone. "She's trying to extort me for my testimony."

"Just get on the stand and tell the truth," Cahill said. "Don't worry about her anymore. She won't do anything to fuck you up."

I took the stand, and she asked me questions about transactions between Mike Fusco and some of the defendants.

"I have no knowledge of that," I said, loud and clear.

Her whole face turned beet red. Man, was she pissed.

When she had no more questions for me, the defense had their turn. Again, just to drive the point home that Mike Fusco had lied, they asked me again.

"Did these things happen?" the defense asked.

"No, sir, they never happened," I said.

My promise to cooperate at that trial was fulfilled, and, somehow, the bitch won her case. I still don't know how she did it with all lies everyone told. Now, I just wanted to get to Morris County, plead guilty, and finish my time in jail.

Jay Surgent saved my life, as far as I was concerned. He came to my rescue to help me in Morris County. Jay knew I was innocent. I passed a lie detector test, but the State had to have their pound of salt, even though they knew by now that my ex-wife, Joan, was only doing this to me for the money. I received five years in Morris County, which factored out to a little more than one year before parole.

I was finally at ease knowing this was my final sentence. I felt as good as I could, even though my wife, Robin, had betrayed me. There wasn't going to be any yellow ribbons waiting for me. Robin and my young boy, Christian, weren't coming with me to start a new life. I had provided for her the whole time I was in jail with the money I was making legally from the music business. I made enough money for Robin to build a new home in Pennsylvania. I gave her all my personal belongings, everything I had, so she could sell them. If I knew Robin wasn't coming with me, I never would have done it. She sold it all, including my motorcycle, my boat, my diamond bracelet, and my vintage guitar collection. I was angry and hurt, but I was getting out of jail. I was going to make it out, and there would be no more trials and no more testifying. The Government couldn't make me do anything ever again. I was doing my time and counting the days until I would be a free man.

Then, Mike Cahill came to see me at MCC.

CHAPTER 33: THE FINAL CURTAIN

I was surprised that Mike Cahill came to see me. I would talk to him every day, and sometimes he would talk to me for hours. He would listen to me scream, curse, cry, call him names, and still, he listened. I love Mike Cahill. He didn't have to put up with the shit I handed him, and he kept me going the whole time I was in jail. He was my strength when I had none left. This guy went out of his way for me.

Once, Robin's car broke down, her radiator blew, and Mike Cahill had Robin come to his house. He changed her radiator for her just so she wouldn't have to pay someone to do it. I'm talking about an FBI Agent who really cared and always kept his word with me. I had God first and Mike Cahill second.

"I'm going to ask you to do something, but you don't have to do it," Cahill told me. "This would be strictly something you would volunteer to do."

"What are you talking about?" I asked him.

"You're the only man who has enough knowledge of organized crime and the effect it has on penny stocks. You're the only one who could appear in Congress and give expert testimony to a congressional committee, and the only one who could explain how the Mafia has a hold on the penny stock market."

I stared at him in disbelief.

"Are you fucking crazy?" I asked.

"They need your experience and knowledge," Cahill said. "You would really be doing something that would be meaningful. You could make a big change in this country if you agree to go to Washington. I would arrange it so that no one would know it was you. They will alter the sound so your voice can't be recognized. They won't allow TV cameras to be pointed at you. Your name will be kept a secret."

"I'll let you know. I have to think about it."

I thought long and hard about going to Congress. My family told me not to do it. My lawyer told me I lost my mind, stating that I did enough for an ungrateful government. I had nothing to gain. I was going home, and this wouldn't take any time off of my jail sentence.

Why the hell on Earth would I want to go to Congress?

The answer came to me as I was looking at pictures of my sons in my jail cell.

"See, your dad tried," I thought of telling them someday. "I really did try to make up for some of the bad I did."

*   *   *

"So, your recommendation is that the laws be toughened?" Representative Markey asked.

"I have several recommendations," I said.

"Could you deliver them to us at this point?"

"Yes, I can."

EPILOGUE

Larry Formato, the King of the Penny Stock Market, was an innovator, whom many people have tried to copy (and only some have come close). He ruled the Penny Stock Market with money and power, unlike anyone before or after him.

They put a hood over his head as he was escorted into Congress to protect his identity. They altered his voice so it couldn't be recognized. They hid him from the TV cameras.

They also leaked his name to the press.

One more time, the Government screwed Larry.

On the evening of Formato's appearance in front of Congress, every TV and radio news station from coast to coast announced that Lorenzo Formato, convicted felon and self-proclaimed stock swindler with ties to organized crime, had appeared in Congress. He delivered what one Congressman called, "A blistering, scalding indictment of the entire penny stock market."

TV news stations across the country plastered pictures of Larry Formato. They showed his face when he was the President of World Wide Ventures, and also with a hood over his head. CNN was running his whole testimony, and the next day, Larry Formato was front-page news in almost every newspaper across the country.

Lorenzo (Larry) Formato will always be known as a convicted felon, but he is also the man who was responsible for the Penny Stock Reform Act of 1990.

Mr. Formato has received letters from Congress expressing the importance of his testimony. The Chairman of the Securities and Exchange Commission called the Securities Act of 1990 one of the most important securities acts passed since its inception. Mr. Formato suggested to Congress ideas that were ahead of their time, and they were adopted into law. His idea of what should be done with the pink sheets was nothing short of genius. He suggested doing away with the pink sheets, making them electronic, and giving pink sheet stocks a symbol similar to NASDAQ listed stocks. This idea was implemented, and we now know these stocks as Bulletin Board Stocks. Every suggestion that was made to Congress by Larry Formato was adopted into law.

Larry never asked for thanks or compensation for going to Congress. In his mind, and in the mind of many government officials, Larry Formato paid his debt to society.

Larry Formato walked out of the federal detention center, M.C.C., New York on February 1, 1991 a free man.

Larry with his mother after
his release from prison in 1991

"Rat"

That was the label put on me. Was I a rat? I have asked myself that question so many times since 1986. The Laser Arms trial never should have happened. George Livieratos and the other defendants never should have gone to trial. Morty Berger led them down the primrose path, and it cost them their freedom. The Government had them cold—ice cold. As far as I was concerned, I didn't testify against them. I testified about my involvement in the case and all the wrong things I had done in my life. I had to admit where all my money was and who was in control of my assets.

Rat? Maybe, if you consider telling on yourself ratting. I was taught to be a stand up guy, and I gave that title up when I cooperated with the Government. I never gave up the names of my associates in organized crime. No one can say I testified against a single Wise Guy. I never put any Wise Guys behind bars. Refusing to lie on the witness stand for the Government during the Federal Flushing trial was just another example of how I took the witness stand and told on myself. I never fucked anyone in my circle of associates who didn't fuck me first.

Was I a rat? You decide.

Larry Formato

Congressional Testimony

MR. RINALDO. You have not stigmatized an industry, you have indicted an entire industry, yet the testimony that you gave in the criminal trial of Marshall Zolp, according to materials that the subcommittee has received, had contradictory statements in it by yourself, and you yourself have admitted now that you engaged in various frauds.

Obviously, over the years, you have lied repeatedly time and time again. Is there any reason why we have to believe everything you say?

MR. FORMATO. No, you don't have to believe anything I say. I am here because I want to be here. I am not here because it is going to shorten the length of time that I stay in jail. I am here because I have, over the years that I have been in jail, had the opportunity to think back, to recollect, to recall everything I have done with my own personal life.

I am not here to wave a banner or a flag and say Larry Formato has redeemed himself. Larry Formato is a criminal. I know that, but I would like to be able to look my son in the eyes some day, and know that maybe, just maybe, I was able to do something to redeem myself a little bit.

PENNY STOCK MARKET FRAUD

HEARINGS

BEFORE THE

SUBCOMMITTEE ON
TELECOMMUNICATIONS AND FINANCE

OF THE

COMMITTEE ON
ENERGY AND COMMERCE
HOUSE OF REPRESENTATIVES

ONE HUNDRED FIRST CONGRESS

FIRST SESSION

AUGUST 21 AND SEPTEMBER 7, 1989

Serial No. 101–80

Printed for the use of the Committee on Energy and Commerce

U.S. GOVERNMENT PRINTING OFFICE

24060☆a   WASHINGTON : 1989

For sale by the Superintendent of Documents, Congressional Sales Office
U.S. Government Printing Office, Washington, DC 20402

COMMITTEE ON ENERGY AND COMMERCE

JOHN D. DINGELL, Michigan, *Chairman*

JAMES H. SCHEUER, New York
HENRY A. WAXMAN, California
PHILIP R. SHARP, Indiana
JAMES J. FLORIO, New Jersey
EDWARD J. MARKEY, Massachusetts
THOMAS A. LUKEN, Ohio
DOUG WALGREN, Pennsylvania
AL SWIFT, Washington
MICKEY LELAND, Texas
CARDISS COLLINS, Illinois
MIKE SYNAR, Oklahoma
W.J. "BILLY" TAUZIN, Louisiana
RON WYDEN, Oregon
RALPH M. HALL, Texas
DENNIS E. ECKART, Ohio
BILL RICHARDSON, New Mexico
JIM SLATTERY, Kansas
GERRY SIKORSKI, Minnesota
JOHN BRYANT, Texas
JIM BATES, California
RICK BOUCHER, Virginia
JIM COOPER, Tennessee
TERRY L. BRUCE, Illinois
J. ROY ROWLAND, Georgia
THOMAS J. MANTON, New York

NORMAN F. LENT, New York
EDWARD R. MADIGAN, Illinois
CARLOS J. MOORHEAD, California
MATTHEW J. RINALDO, New Jersey
WILLIAM E. DANNEMEYER, California
BOB WHITTAKER, Kansas
THOMAS J. TAUKE, Iowa
DON RITTER, Pennsylvania
THOMAS J. BLILEY, JR., Virginia
JACK FIELDS, Texas
MICHAEL G. OXLEY, Ohio
HOWARD C. NIELSON, Utah
MICHAEL BILIRAKIS, Florida
DAN SCHAEFER, Colorado
JOE BARTON, Texas
SONNY CALLAHAN, Alabama
ALEX McMILLAN, North Carolina

JOHN S. ORLANDO, *Chief of Staff*
JOHN M. CLOUGH, JR., *Staff Director*
MARGARET A. DURBIN, *Minority Chief Counsel/Staff Director*

SUBCOMMITTEE ON TELECOMMUNICATIONS AND FINANCE

EDWARD J. MARKEY, Massachusetts, *Chairman*

AL SWIFT, Washington
MICKEY LELAND, Texas
CARDISS COLLINS, Illinois
MIKE SYNAR, Oklahoma
W.J. "BILLY" TAUZIN, Louisiana
RALPH M. HALL, Texas
DENNIS E. ECKART, Ohio
BILL RICHARDSON, New Mexico
JIM SLATTERY, Kansas
JOHN BRYANT, Texas
RICK BOUCHER, Virginia
JIM COOPER, Tennessee
THOMAS J. MANTON, New York
RON WYDEN, Oregon
JOHN D. DINGELL, Michigan
   (Ex Officio)

MATTHEW J. RINALDO, New Jersey
EDWARD R. MADIGAN, Illinois
CARLOS J. MOORHEAD, California
THOMAS J. TAUKE, Iowa
DON RITTER, Pennsylvania
THOMAS J. BLILEY, JR., Virginia
JACK FIELDS, Texas
MICHAEL G. OXLEY, Ohio
DAN SCHAEFER, Colorado
NORMAN F. LENT, New York
   (Ex Officio)

LAWRENCE SIDMAN, *Chief Counsel/Staff Director*
HOWARD B. HOMONOFF, *Counsel*
KIRK JOHNSON, *Legislative Assistant*
STUART J. KASWELL, *Minority Counsel*

·II·

PENNY STOCK MARKET FRAUD
(Part 2)

HEARING

BEFORE THE

SUBCOMMITTEE ON
TELECOMMUNICATIONS AND FINANCE

OF THE

COMMITTEE ON
ENERGY AND COMMERCE
HOUSE OF REPRESENTATIVES

ONE HUNDRED FIRST CONGRESS

SECOND SESSION

ON

H.R. 4497

A BILL TO AMEND THE FEDERAL SECURITIES LAWS TO ELIMINATE ABUSES IN TRANSACTIONS IN PENNY STOCKS, AND FOR OTHER PURPOSES

APRIL 25, 1990

Serial No. 101–143

Printed for the use of the Committee on Energy and Commerce

❋

COMPLETED

U.S. GOVERNMENT PRINTING OFFICE

33-104±±   WASHINGTON : 1990

For sale by the Superintendent of Documents, Congressional Sales Office
U.S. Government Printing Office, Washington, DC 20402

CONTENTS

	Page
Hearings held on:	
August 21, 1989	1
September 7, 1989	95
Testimony of:	
Baldwin, John C., president, North American Securities Administrators Association	122
Benson, Larry L., investor, Gresham, OR	8
Birgfeld, Frank, director, District III, National Association of Securities Dealers	74
Finch, Foster D., Jr., vice president, Merrill Lynch, Pierce, Fenner and Smith	84
Formato, Lorenzo, convicted former broker and participant in the Federal Witness Protection Program	101
Gleaves, Curt B., chairman, Oregon State Bar, Securities Regulation Section	85
Goldstein, Joseph I., Associate Director, Division of Enforcement, Penny Stock Task Force, Securities and Exchange Commission	48
Howell, H. Wayne, Deputy Secretary of State, State of Georgia	245
Lynes, William and Lilly, investors, Powder Springs, Georgia	248
McDonald, G.W., assistant commissioner, Enforcement Division, California Department of Corporations, on behalf of North American Securities Administrators Association	66
Madison, Jack, investor, Independence, OR	37
Skillman, Laurie, securities administrator, Division of Finance and Corporate Securities, Oregon Department of Insurance and Finance	40
Wenstrom, Milton S., investor, Salem, OR	4
Material submitted for the record by the North American Securities Administrators Association: Report entitled "The NASAA Report on Fraud and Abuse in the Penny Stock Industry"	149

(III)

PENNY STOCK MARKET FRAUD
THURSDAY, SEPTEMBER 7, 1989

HOUSE OF REPRESENTATIVES,
COMMITTEE ON ENERGY AND COMMERCE,
SUBCOMMITTEE ON TELECOMMUNICATIONS AND FINANCE,
Washington, DC.

The subcommittee met, pursuant to notice, at 9:30 a.m., in room 2247, Rayburn House Office Building, Hon. Edward J. Markey (chairman) presiding.

MR. MARKEY. Good morning. Today's oversight hearing is intended to focus the congressional spotlight on the problem of rampant fraudulent activity in the market for low-price penny stocks. We will explore the means by which this fraud develops, the extent of the harm caused to individual small investors in the capital formation process, and the potential areas for future regulatory and legislative action to combat this black market on our securities markets.

This is the subcommittee's second hearing on this subject, the first being a Portland, Oregon, field hearing chaired by my colleague from Oregon, Mr. Wyden. I applaud his interest in this issue, and we all on the committee look forward to sharing with him some of the findings, which he was able to bring forward at that hearing in Portland.

The question we have to face today is whether there is a legitimate market for penny stocks; and, if so, how should it be regulated? According to the findings of the North American Securities Administration 50 States Survey, investors lose $2 billion or more each year due to fraud and abuse in the penny stock market, over one-fifth of the entire total of primary and secondary market activity in penny stocks. Incredibly enough, these losses linked to fraud come in addition to an estimated 70 percent probability that an investor in an unmanipulated penny stock will lose some or all of his investment, and all the likelihood of losing money in penny stocks runs at 90 percent. Comparing this market to a night at the casino seems an unfair slap at casino operators.

Penny stock fraud's harm to the capital formation process poses an even more sweeping economic threat to the Nation. According to the NASAA report, the $2 billion in investor losses equals two-thirds of the total of $3 billion raised by the U.S. capital venture industry in 1988.

Given that $25,000 is the average outside financing needed to start a new company, these rip-offs represent a loss of 80,00 potential new firms employing well over 150,000 new workers. These con artist schemes drive a stake right through the heart of our Nation's history of entrepreneurship and our future efforts to rebuild America's competitive edge in the world marketplace.

Perhaps the most frightening aspect of the penny stock marketplace is the pervasively corrupting influence of organized crime. Our first witness today, Mr. Lorenzo Formato, has seen first hand the danger, which that element injects into the operation of any legitimate enterprise. His willingness to come forward will help to illuminate the most common types of consumer fraud.

The NASAA report focuses on several major problem areas, all of which need serious congressional attention. First, the widespread use of blind pools, the securities industry's version of hide and seek, hard-sells of the stock in a company with no assets, no operating history and no business plan are fertile plans for easy rip-offs. Second, the incredible lack of information available to customers concerning the actual market value of the stocks they are purchasing and the previous illegal activities of many stock, penny stock brokers; and, third, the shady dealings of stock consultants and promoters who often possess long criminal records but who continue to move pervasively through the penny stock system just outside the reach of State and Federal regulators. I intend to work exhaustively in the coming months to address these concerns by seeking the most appropriate regulatory steps possible and by developing comprehensive legislation.

NASAA's report indicates greatly increased efforts by the SEC and State regulators in recent years, and this work is to be applauded. But Congress must step in aggressively in applying the full court pressure necessary to eradicate widespread fraud in the penny stock market.

That concludes the opening statement by the Chair, and now I will recognize the ranking minority member, the gentleman from New Jersey, Mr. Rinaldo, for an opening statement.

Mr. Rinaldo. Thank you very much, Mr. Chairman.

Mr. Chairman, I welcome today's hearing on penny stock fraud. The hearing will focus the subcommittee's attention on a frustrating and relentless opponent: the penny stock con man. These criminals prey on human frailties and weaknesses. Of course, these conmen exploit investors' greed and sing the siren song of the "get rich" scheme.

Other con men instigate ploys to higher motives, such as religion, and exploit investors with religious zeal. According to the Wall Street Journal, the victims of the scam include worshipers of all persuasions. But whatever the ploy, the conduct and injuries are reprehensible.

Today's hearing is particularly troubling to me because we are to hear testimony from a man who plied this despicable trade in New Jersey. Of course, I am angered and upset by such activity going on in my home State, but the harm is much greater than to any one State. I deplore the harm that such schemes cause to innocent investors whether they live in New Jersey or elsewhere.

The problem of penny stock fraud hurts more than just investors, however; it hurts and harms our entire Nation. Unless investors, legitimate investors, have access to funds, their ideas will never become realities, and without innovative new products, our country will fall behind our foreign competitors.

The penny stock con artist tries to appear to investors as the brilliant innovator with a revolutionary new product. By the time the scam is uncovered, he has skipped out on the investors and left them holding worthless stock. The criminal's legacy is that he deters the public from investing in legitimate new ventures.

The amount of damage that such schemes have caused to our Nation's competitiveness defy precise calculations, but the damage is large indeed. However, there are many reasons on the other side of the ledger to be heartened in the fight against penny stock fraud.

Very recently the SEC adopted Rule 15(c)26 which will complicate vastly the lives of con men. The rule attempts to protect the legitimate entrepreneurs while hamstringing the charlatans. I commend the SEC for this and other regulatory efforts in the battle against penny stock fraud.

Such initiatives justify this subcommittee's efforts to augment the SEC's budget in the coming fiscal years. In addition, the Department of Justice and the FBI have brought down many penny stock fraud perpetrators.

State Securities Administrators also are doing an excellent job. The NASD, the self-regulatory organization that polices over-the-counter markets, also has been a friend of investors. For example, in the last few years, the NASD has concluded or filed over 200 actions for penny stock violations, penalties range from expulsion of firms to fines of half a million dollars.

Finally, the securities industry itself deplores this fraudulent conduct. These coordinated and comprehensive enforcement efforts will put many of the con men out of business and into jail. Educational efforts also will diminish the likelihood of investors losing their life savings. These problems may never disappear entirely, but as the chairman of the subcommittee has appropriately said in his opening statement, and I repeat it or rephrase it because he echoed my sentiments exactly in this matter, we must take every reasonable regulatory and legislative action to protect both the integrity and viability of our markets.

Mr. Chairman, I intend to work with you in that regard because I feel that it is that important, as I mentioned earlier, not only to the individual investors but to all of the citizens and businesses of this great Nation of ours. I look forward to hearing the testimony of our witnesses, yield back the balance of my time, but before I relinquish my time, I would like to make a unanimous request consent the opening statement of Congressman Lent, the ranking minority member of the full committee, be included in the record at this point.

Mr. MARKEY. Without objection, it will be included in the record at the appropriate point.

Mr. RINALDO. Thank you.

Mr. MARKEY. The gentleman's time has expired.

I will recognize the gentleman from Oregon, Mr. Wyden, who has been especially vigorous in this area of penny stock fraud.

Mr. WYDEN. Thank you very much, and I just want to thank you for all your leadership on this issue, and in particular I look forward to working very closely under your leadership to addressing these matters, many of which I think we are going to hear today require legislation, and you have been extremely helpful in terms of assisting my constituents, and I look forward to working with you and also our colleague from New Jersey, Matt Rinaldo, who has worked always on these matters with such a bipartisan interest.

Mr. Chairman, what we heard in Oregon did not present a very pretty picture. These may be penny stocks, but it is quite clear that a lot of Americans are suffering big-buck losses; in particular it seems to me that this penny stock field is an ideal opportunity for rip-off artists. It has all the key elements where fraud and financial abuse can flourish. These operators set up a boiler room somewhere far from the investors, they use high-pressure phone tactics, they target inexperienced investors. The witnesses we heard in Oregon were people like retired citizens who were looking to plan for such things as financing long-term care.

I heard a very sad story, Mr. Chairman, about an individual from Salem, Oregon, who was taking his military savings. He was leaving the military, and he lost a good portion of his $40,000 nest egg, and it is clear that by targeting these inexperienced investors, using high pressure phone tactics, boiler rooms, and particularly stressing constantly the up side of the investment without ever talking at all about any of the risks, that this is a very fertile field for those who would like to fleece our citizens.

Now, I also share the view of you, Mr. Chairman, that these rip-offs really spell bad news for our capital markets, and I think it happens really two ways. One, we are draining off the dollars we need for investment when we see these rip-offs, but, second, it seems to me this is going to make it hard for the many legitimate small businesses in this country to raise funds. They get a bad name by seeing these kinds of financial abuses taking place in this field, and the head of the Oregon State Bar Committee on Small Business testified at our Oregon hearing that in particular he felt that this was going to make it much tougher for small businesses to raise the capital they need.

Now, just a couple other points I want to mention, Mr. Chairman. I too, like you and our friend from New Jersey, believe that the steps the Securities and Exchange Commission has taken are very helpful and certainly important at this point. But I would hope that we would go further and under the chairman's leadership and with our colleague, I would really like to pursue this. The Oregon Securities Commissioner, in addition to mentioning this blind pool matter, also talked about the problem of shell corporations where ineffective dummy corporations set up that, in effect, after a period of lying dormant are, in effect, revived to engage in these manipulative transactions.

We also heard in Oregon a great deal of concern about those who had been disbarred from work with the SEC somehow magically turn up as so-called penny stock consultants. It would seem to me this would be another area that we ought to be looking at.

Finally, a third suggestion we received in Oregon is that we ought to take steps to track the penny stocks financial performance. This idea came from one of the Securities Commissioners who said it would be helpful to have an analysis of penny stock IPO's to determine their financial track record over several years so we could really see which companies are prospering and address the chairman's question, and a very important one, about whether this market is essentially a crack and burn market where most of the investors are going to be fleeced.

So, again, I just want to thank the chairman. Oregon for some reason has seen more than our share of these rip-off artists gravitate to our State. Under the chairman's leadership, I very much look forward to working with him to try to clean up this cesspool, because I think it is long overdue, and I thank the chair.

[The opening statements of Mr. Wyden and Mr. Lent follow:]

OPENING STATEMENT OF HON. RON WYDEN

Mr. Chairman, I want to commend you for holding this hearing on penny stock fraud and the harm it does to individual investors and the integrity of the Nation's capital markets.

Penny stock abuse is growing by leaps and bounds. The North American Securities Administrators Association has called the problem the number one fraud threat facing typical investors.

At Chairman Markey's request, I chaired a field hearing of the Telecommunications and Finance Subcommittee in Portland, Oregon on August 21. The purpose was to investigate problems in the penny stock market and to lay the groundwork for additional hearings, like this one, in Washington.

The testimony at the Portland hearing painted an alarming picture. Joseph Goldstein, head of the Securities and Exchange Commission's Penny Stock Task Force, said penny stock complaints received by the SEC have jumped dramatically—from 1,510 in fiscal year 1988 to 2,462 in just the first half of 1989. Oregon Securities Administrator Laurie Skillman testified that her department has noted a similar increase in penny stock complaints this year.

But the most compelling testimony came from three Oregon investors who, all told, lost nearly $40,000 in the penny stock market.

Steve Wenstrom, an employee of the Oregon Public Utility Commission, explained how he lost much of his $41,000 investment with the Portland office of Blinder Robinson. Wenstrom, who saved the money during a 5-year stint in the Navy, said his investment objectives were income and security.

Wenstrom initially placed his $41,000 in a high-income mutual fund. However, his broker made a series of penny stock purchases without Wenstrom's approval—paying for them by transferring money from the mutual fund. As a result of these unauthorized transactions, Wenstrom lost about $33,000 of his initial $41,000 investment.

"I would recommend not getting involved with any type of penny stock," Wenstrom testified at the hearing. "It's a scam. All it does is cost you money, hard-earned money."

A second investor, Larry Benson, who lives in my Congressional District, told how he lost more than $4,200 in retirement savings through a penny stock investment with the now-defunct firm Power Securities.

A broker from Power's Fort Collins, Colorado office contacted Benson and his wife several times late last year. The broker told the Bensons they could increase their investment by 20 percent or more in just a few months by purchasing stock in a promising feedlot company.

The Bensons agreed to invest their Individual Retirement Account (IRA) savings in the company, and the broker purchased 60,000 shares of stock. Although the Bensons were seeking a safe investment for their retirement funds, their broker did not advise them of the risks involved in this particular transaction.

Today, the Benson's $4,200 investment is worth about $6. What's more, the couple has little possibility of recouping their investment because Power Securities shut its doors earlier this year—after being barred from doing business in New York State due to suspicious sales practices.

A third investor, Jack Madison, told how he lost $1,100 in a penny stock investment solicited by the Denver office of a firm called Marshall-Davis. Madison had inquired about one stock, but the salesman urged him to purchase another, saying it was a great opportunity for Madison to double or triple his money in a short time.

Two years later, the company Madison invested in has gone out of business, and his stock is worthless. However, that has not stopped the same broker from calling Madison again and urging him to invest in another penny stock—this time a "blind pool initial public offering."

These sad stories share much in common. In each case, the investors' objectives were income and security. Instead of being warned about the risks of the penny stock market, however, they were lured with promises of easy profits.

All three investors, reflecting on their experience, said they would never again invest in penny stocks and would recommend others to steer clear of these high-risk securities.

Mr. Chairman, as these examples demonstrate, penny stocks are at the very least highly speculative investments that are not appropriate for inexperienced investors. Hearings like this one play an important role in getting that word out to the investing public.

More ominously, however, there is evidence of serious fraud and criminal activity in the penny stock market. These problems call out for additional action by the SEC, by Federal law enforcement agencies, and by Congress.

Mr. Chairman, I pledge to work with you and other members of the subcommittee to address these serious problems

OPENING STATEMENT OF HON. NORMAN F. LENT

Mr. Chairman, I commend you for holding this hearing today on penny stock fraud. Penny stock fraud is a scourge on our economy and our capital markets. Capital markets are a central, driving force in our economy. They channel funds in an economically rational way from investor to industry. Capital markets make it possible for entrepreneurs to perfect and market new products, and for existing companies to modernize and expand.

The penny stock con artist is an economic terrorist. He exploits people's weaknesses, naiveté, and ignorance. He undermines investors' confidence in the market. And, he robs people of their life savings. But, perhaps worst of all, he sabotages the capital raising function as severely as if he used dynamite. He injures the operations of our markets—and that hurts all Americans. It can mean that capital costs are more for everyone—and that hurts all of our businesses and factories.

Fortunately, the penny stock con artist has encountered some very tough opponents. At the Federal level, the Securities and Exchange Commission and the Department of Justice have launched important enforcement actions and prosecutions. At the State level, securities administrators have moved with vigilance and vigor against the con men. And the NASD has taken a number of self-policing actions. For example, the NASD recently obtained SEC approval of a requirement to improve reporting requirements for "pink sheet" stocks. This regulation will help identify unusual stock movements and alert regulators.

Yet, in our zeal to attack the penny stock con artists, we must keep this problem in perspective. First, the penny stock operators constitute a tiny percentage of the securities market. Every year, billions of dollars of securities change hands in honest and proper circumstances. Underwriters bring new issues to investors with little fanfare. We cannot let the actions of an unscrupulous few traumatize all investors, and spread disproportionate harm.

Second, many new companies begin with little more than a gleam in a bright young man or woman's eye. Our efforts to prosecute penny stock schemes should not be so poorly focused as to damage legitimate new businesses.

Mr. Chairman, by combining our need for allowing legitimate new businesses to flourish, with the need for a strong, coordinated Federal and State enforcement program, we can ensure the continued strength of our economy while putting the stock con artist out of business. I think we are making important progress against penny stock fraud. I welcome today's hearing and look forward to the testimony.

Thank you.

Mr. Markey. I thank the gentleman very much. We have a plan for this morning. This is a hearing, which will break into two parts. First we will hear from Mr. Lorenzo Formato, who will give us an insider's account of how the penny stock market operates.   A n d then on the second panel, we will her from Mr. John Baldwin, who is the President of the North American Securities Administrators Association; Mr. H. Wayne Howell, who is the Deputy Secretary of State for the State of Georgia; and Mr. William and Lily Lynes, who are here to give us their insight as to how this marketplace operates and what needs to be done in order to correct deficiencies that exist in its regulation.

So now we are going to turn to our first witness. He is Mr. Lorenzo Formato. He is formerly a broker and promoter in penny stocks who has pled guilty to several Federal felonies in connection with his former activities. Mr. Formato is currently serving his sentence in connection with those offenses and is part of the Federal Witness Protection Program. His participation in that program is the cause for the extraordinary security measures in place for this hearing. Mr. Formato has agreed to testify here today concerning the broad scope of his former involvement in the penny stock market.

Despite the extensiveness of his previous illegal activities, we are grateful to Mr. Formato for now coming forward and helping us to shed light on a significant matter of public policy to the subcommittee.

Mr. Formato, if you could please begin with an overall reconstruction of how you entered the securities business and trace for us the development of the activities which eventually led to your apprehension by Federal authorities, that would be very helpful, and I would also ask that you try to keep this explanation initially somewhat brief so that members then would be able to ask questions of you, and I think in that manner, further elaborate or flesh out the areas members believe should in fact come to public light.

We thank you very much for your willingness to participate here today, and whenever you feel comfortable, we are prepared to accept your testimony

TESTIMONY OF LORENZO FORMATO,
CONVICTED FORMER BROKER AND PARTICIPANT
IN THE FEDERAL WITNESS PROTECTION PROGRAM

MR. FORMATO. I would like to point out first of all I have a high school education, and although I never graduated--

MR. MARKEY. If you could stop for just one brief moment, so I can explain to those who are in the room that the microphone has been modified by the security personnel in order to totally disguise Mr. Formato's voice. This is being done as part of the Federal Witness Protection Program. It guarantees to Mr. Formato, and although it will be somewhat difficult to grasp what it is that he is saying, I think with a little bit of extra attention within a very brief period of time it does become quite evident what it is that he will be saying. Just pay a little bit closer attention. I think you will be able to understand. Thank you.

MR. FORMATO. As I was saying, although I never graduated with my class, I did receive a high school diploma. I went into the auto body business and it was then a fellow classmate of mine came to my auto body shop to have his car repaired. It was a new car and I was kind of in shock he was driving such a new car. And I asked him how he was able to afford this car and he told me he was a stockbroker. I had no idea what a stockbroker was. I didn't know what stocks were.

MR. RINALDO. Mr. Formato—Mr. Chairman, I understand that the witness has to be protected, I understand he is under a Federal protection program, but I find it very difficult, and I think the press and the people who are attending this hearing find it very difficult to understand him. Perhaps there can be some modification made to this system so his voice can still be disguised but at least we can hear and understand what the gentleman is saying.

He is a key witness here this morning. The entire purpose of the hearing I think really goes down the drain if we can't understand and it becomes difficult to hear what he is saying. If there could be some way to adjust this system so that there is a little more clarity, it would be appreciated.

MR. MARKEY. I perhaps am having a little bit easier time just in the first minute or so in understanding what you are saying. I think I have heard every word. The gentleman from Oregon has been able to hear every word. If the gentleman from New Jersey is having some difficulty, then we will take a very, very brief recess. We will ask the security people if they could try to adjust the microphone slightly and hopefully it can be done in a way which will make your comments more audible, Mr. Formato, while still guaranteeing it is not possible to identify your voice. We will take a brief 2-minute recess. [Brief recess.]

MR. MARKEY. We will take another run at this. We will ask you, Mr. Formato, if you could perhaps start again at the top, and I would ask anyone who is on the staff if at any point they believe his voice is too unidentifiable, bring that to the attention of the Chair because that is of course a primary consideration and something which we have offered as a guarantee to Mr. Formato at this hearing.

I would want to make alterations at that point if it becomes necessary. If you could, please, Mr. Formato, begin your testimony.

MR. FORMATO. Let me just start over again. I have a high school education. I worked in the auto body business and I got into the stock business because a fellow high school mate came into my auto body shop with a new car and I was surprised he was driving a new car. I asked him how he got this new car and he told me he was a stockbroker. As I stated previously, I did not know what a stockbroker was, but I did ask him if he could take me to where he works, and I went with him that day in my work clothes to his office, which was Mayflower Securities in Hackensack, New Jersey, and I went into his office in my work clothe to his boss, knocked on his boss' door and said if this guy can do whatever he is doing to buy that car, I can do it better, and his boss gave me a job.

His boss' name was John Engle, who was then the manager of Mayflower Securities. He informed me I would have to take a test and pass it, and I got a little worried about that knowing that I didn't have the proper education, knowing that most of the time I spent in school I spent goofing off. So I was able to arrange to get a copy of tests that were given at that time. I believe there were three tests that were given and I had the answers to all three of those tests.

What I did, I took a job as a night guard, and I studied the questions and the answers and I memorized the answers to all the questions. And I went and took the exam to become a registered representative or what we know as a stockbroker, and I passed that exam. During the time that I was memorizing those questions I worked at Mayflower Securities using another registered representative's name and cold calling people from a phone booth.

What I did was I listened to some of the salesmen who were in the office and I formed my own cold call pitch by taking pieces of everyone else's statements, and I became quite good at it, and I used to call people from 8 a.m. until sometimes 11 p.m., 7 days a week. And the end result was that after 6 months I obtained more clients than anyone in the firm, and I became a one-man firm by having so many clients. I didn't know what the hell I was doing in the brokerage business but I had so many clients I could just pick up a telephone and sell anything I wanted to sell to these people.

Whatever my boss was telling me to sell these people and whatever I was making the most money at selling I was doing it. I was greedy and I was hungry and I wanted to make a lot of money. And I did. Because I had so many clients, I became the manager or co-manager of that office, still not knowing anything at all about the brokers' industry.

I didn't know what stocks meant, I didn't know what stocks were, all I knew was someone said this is the name of the company. If you sell 1,000 shares of this for $1, you are going to make $250. And that sounded good to me. I'd sell 10,000, 15,000 or 100,000 shares a day sometimes. Never knowing whether or not the stock was any good, whether or not the company had any profits, whether or not the company even existed.

It was shortly after that I went to First Jersey Securities. The president of First Jersey Securities was Bob Brennan. Bob Brennan knew how to treat his good salesmen well. Bob Brennan was, in my opinion, one of the smartest men that ever entered the over-the-counter brokers' industry as far as being able to manipulate stocks and manipulate people. He knew how to take care of his salesmen. He fed them very well Only his good salesmen.

I was a good salesman. I had trips to the Bahamas with my family paid by Bob Brennan. I met other top salesmen of First Jersey Securities that went on these trips and it was through meeting these other salesmen from other offices of First Jersey Securities that I was able to learn how to branch out not only with the skills that I had of being able to pick up the telephone and speak to someone and convince them to buy a dream, because that is what they are buying, they are buying a dream when they buy a penny stock. The dream of course turns into a nightmare.

But I was able to do this and I was able to do it well, and I made a lot of money. From First Jersey Securities I was moved out into another small over-the-counter brokerage firm called Excelius Securities. I did this with one of the top salesmen of First Jersey Securities. I stayed at Excelius Securities for a short time. We did one other item when I was there, called Level Computer. We bought it out at $4 a share, and it was shortly after that we completed the Level Computer underwriting that I left Excelius Securities and so did Bart Barrett, who is the gentleman I went to Excelius Securities with. Level Computer shortly thereafter went down from $4 a share to 5 cents.

I left the securities industry for a brief period of time and in 1977 I opened up a brokerage firm in New Jersey called A.L. Williamson and Company. I had a partner by the name of Don Messenger. Don Messenger and myself started A.L. Williamson and Company with a stock fraud. We started this company by taking shares out of a public company by the name of Boken Electronics, which to my knowledge was a legitimate company and is a legitimate company and the people that run that company, the president of that company, to my knowledge, is a legitimate businessman, but the stock manipulation that took place was nowhere's near legitimate. We manipulated the stock from 10 cents and through my buying power I had with my customers we were able to move this stock up to $3 a share. Don Messenger and myself successfully sold enough shares to give us the money to not only open up A.L. Williamson and Company but to meet the debt capital requirements and to hire the registered representatives and to have beautiful new luxurious offices in West Caldwell, New Jersey. We also did a secondary offering for Boken Electronics, and we did that at $3 a share. We raised that company $3 million. I sold my interest in A.L. Williamson at the end of 1978 to John Patman. John Patman and Don Messenger went on with A.L. Williamson and I went to a private consulting firm.

It was after that that I began with another friend of mine from First Jersey Securities who was then working at a brokerage firm in New York called Brook Hamburger. His name was Peter Ihoe. Peter Ihoe and myself decided that we would open a new brokerage firm and I would then take the salesmen that I knew and the salesmen that he knew and we would go and we would buy not an over-the-counter brokerage firm but a member firm, a firm that had a seat on the New York Stock Exchange.

We made a deal with a firm by the name of Ross Stephens. Peter, at that time, was sanctioned by the Securities Exchange Commission. I was not.

We financed Ross Stephens again similar to the way I financed A.L. Williamson and Company. We took a stock by the name of Revest Resources, which was supposed to be an oil stock out of Utah. We took this stock from $2 a share to $8 a share. It was my job to have this salesman retail this stock to the public knowing that I have his stock, my purchase price of this stock was $2. I knew that we could sell the stock at $8 and we did.

It was after we sold the stock at this average price of $8 that we walked away from this stock—I walked away from Ross Stephens because of an argument with Peter Ihoe I personally had with him. But Revest Resources went straight down. The people that bought the stock lost their money.

I then opened Royer Securities, which I owned on my own. Royer Securities was a brokerage firm I was going to style after Ross Stephens. I opened it in West Caldwell, NJ. I went back to Don Messenger and I bought from Don Messenger all his retail salesmen that he had, all his retail clients and I made a deal with him to take over the leases he had for his office space.

So in actuality what I actually did was I wound up with A.L. Williamson all over again and this was their retail outlet and their customers. While I was at Royer Securities I got involved with several stock manipulations, one of them being a company called Data Force International. Data Force International was a stock fraud that was started in the Cayman Islands. It was a company; the stock certificates were in bearer form. Anyone having the stock certificates could go to any brokerage firm on a given day they wanted to. They weren't in anyone's names.

They were in the name of the bearer. I never saw stock certificates like that before. David Wellington was the promoter of this. He had millions and millions and millions of these shares because he printed them. Data Force International was a bogus company. The shares were bogus, but when you looked at this company in the pink sheets, which is where it was listed on the over-the-counter market, there were approximately 22 market makers in Data Force International. These 22 market makers were all member firms, or the majority of them were. When I say member firms, I am talking about Merrill-Lynch, Oppenheimer, Bache, Shearson. I was amazed to see these people making a market in this stock.

I couldn't understand it. It wasn't until after I had met David Wellington personally I came to find out why he wasn't too pleased. He had gone to a gentleman by the name of Peter Loutine. And Peter Loutine working through David Wellington went to Oppenheimer and opened up an account at Oppenheimer and said to the people at Oppenheimer, I want to trade for my own account, I would like you to make a market in this stock forming. Then Peter Loutine called up all his friends at all these member firms and got them to take a market for him guaranteeing them that any stock they would buy, he would buy it from them.

Data Force International sold at approximately $1.25 a share. We traded millions of shares of Data Force International between New York, New Jersey, Salt Lake City, California, all over the country. And it was basically controlled by three people: Peter Loutine at Oppenheimer, Larry from Royer Securities and Bill Hirry in Salt Lake City, Utah.

Data Force was a major stock fraud. Royer Securities eventually went into business because of the Data Force stock fraud. It was after Royer Securities that I left the brokerage industry as a broker and became a promoter. I became involved as a promoter with another company by the name of Worldwide Ventures Corporation. Worldwide Ventures Corporation became a major stock fraud not only in the State of New Jersey, but all over the country.

There were times Worldwide Ventures Corporation was one of the most active stocks, over-the-counter stocks in the country.

Worldwide Ventures started at zero when I got involved, we had 55 million shares. I took that stock up as high as $9 a share. We, the people that were involved with me at Worldwide Ventures successfully sold all our shares.

It was after Worldwide Ventures Corporation I became involved in my own private consulting firm again. I want to point out during all of this time, from the time of A.L. Williamson to the time I came to jail I was involved with organized crime. I was involved with people at organized crime. The reason I was involved with those people in organized crime was so that when I would go and do one of these stock manipulations or one of these stock frauds or I wanted to successfully make a market in this stock without anyone else in the business getting involved and trying to undercut me or short one of my stocks, I needed the protection and I needed the strength of organized crime and they needed me. They needed me to wash money for them. They needed me to form companies for them. They needed me to be a money machine, and that is just what I was, and that is what I became; a money machine.

After Worldwide Ventures Corporation I became involved with other stock promoters and decided that it was time to try bigger and bigger stock deals. I didn't think there was anything that could slow me down or stop me. I did not fear the laws of the Securities and Exchange Commission. I knew that there was nothing that they could do to me criminally. They could only attack me on a civil basis and I have been attacked by the Securities Exchange Commission many times, I have been attacked by the Bureau of Securities of the State of New Jersey many times. They did not have anything that would scare me.

The only thing they could do to me was try to get me to sign an injunction barring me from possibly participating in any stock frauds again.

I used to laugh at the Securities and Exchange Commission. I used to laugh at the Bureau of Securities. I received a phone call from an attorney of mine, Mr. Martin Burger, who held out a client of his by the name of Marshall Zolp. Marshall Zolp was then down in Florida working with another stock promoter by the name of Lionel Reiffer, who I had previous experience with while I was at Worldwide Ventures.

We had a falling out. Marshall Zolp and I met once before in 1981, when Marshall Zolp, when he left Royer Securities after a visit,

left with some letterheads of Royer Securities, and Marshall Zolp
went out to Las Vegas and gave letters of intent from the securities;
received fees of $25,000 and up from these people.

I found myself getting phone calls from these people, saying
when are you going to take me public? I didn't know who they were.
I did find out afterwards that it was Marshall Zolp.

So, when Martin Berger asked me to help Marshall Zolp,
I almost had to laugh at him. So, my dislike was worse, and I had
Marshall Zolp fired from Florida to New Jersey to join forces with me.
Marshall Zolp took a company and named it Laser Arms Corporation.
This company was completely fictitious. The officers and principals
of Laser Arms was completely fictitious. There were no directors of
the company. The people that he used as directors of the company
were pictures of actors that he had taken. There were no financial
statements of his company.

There just simply was not a company. Marshall Zolp was able
to go ahead and have a brokerage firm file, what we know as a 15-
C-211, which is a shell company, and give that company a register
and enabled to trade. He successfully had a brokerage firm—and a
fictitious, totally bogus stock.

I helped Marshall Zolp sell that stock. The reason that I helped
him sell that stock was because he did not want anyone that he was
involved with, other than members of organized crime that he was
involved with, not the people I was involved with, but other families,
he didn't want them to know that he was trying to make a little more
money for himself.

He was also sharing these dollars with these people. So, I did
sell stock to him. I also agreed to cash checks for him, and I did. I got
a bank to cooperate. I paid the bank president off, and we were able
to successfully cash the dollars, the checks that Marshall Zolp had
obtained from selling shares in his bogus company, Laser Arms.

It was through the Laser Arms stock fraud that the FBI and
the District of New Jersey were able to obtain wiretaps on his phone.
It was through these wiretaps that the information they got was
acquired, and needed to go ahead and get an indictment against
myself, Mr. Zolp and 12 other individuals.

We were, in fact, indicted on Laser Arms stock fraud. I did, in
fact, go to jail on Laser Arms stock fraud. Laser Arms stock fraud is
just one fraud of thousands and thousands of frauds that are taking
place every single day. The over-the-counter market is controlled

by organized crime. The over-the-counter market is controlled by people like myself, stock promoters, stockbrokers who go out, raise millions and millions and millions of dollars for themselves and for organized crime to feed themselves.

It is virtually impossible for an individual who does have a legitimate company to go to a small, over-the-counter brokerage firm and take his company public without him having to give away half of his company, without him having to give away a big chunk of the money that is raised for his company.

If he wants to go public, he has to come and see a letter from Al, he has to go and make a deal or the door is slammed on him. And that is the way it is. That is the true facts of the over-the-counter industry. It is an industry that is controlled by a small circle of people, that, unless you have been sanctioned by the Securities and Exchange Commission, you have been in trouble with the NSAD, you have lost the brokerage firm.

You cannot become a successful stock promoter. You cannot give in to this circle, and this circle dominates by fear and by power. We not only tell stockbrokers what to sell, we tell them what price to sell the stocks for. We tell them whether to go up or whether to go down.

When I ran the company and I was chief executive also of that company, I had a machine in my office. I wasn't a brokerage firm. But I had a NASDAQ machine, and I was able to get it. And I could sit there, and I checked the price of my stock and the price of other stocks, and I could pick up a telephone from my office at Worldwide Ventures and tell my leading brokerage firms to move up a quarter, move up ahead a point, move down.

I would know if there was a blocked stock that was out there. I would tell them drop down half a buck and then move the market back up. These are the things that I was able to do, because I had the power and I wielded the fear of organized crime behind me.

Stockbrokers who were not knowledgeable about the over-the- counter industry, who are able to walk into an over-the-counter brokerage firm and make more money than they would if they were going to a Merrill Lynch or an Oppenheimer or a Shearson American Express, these people were new people. They were taught how to pick up the telephones. They were taught how to sell to unsophisticated investors, not just your moms and pops, but to your young people as well, young people who wanted a piece of this pie that was supposed to be so good.

It was not so good. And when they didn't do what they were told to do, they were scared into doing what they were told to do. If they wanted to sell a stock for their customers, if we didn't want them to sell, they weren't allowed to sell.

The only time they could sell is when we wanted them to sell. I could go on and say many more things. Maybe you might have some questions for me.

Mr. Markey. Thank you very much, Mr. Formato.

I will now turn to questions from the subcommittee, and the Chair will recognize itself first for a round of questions. What I would like to ask you is whether or not, in your mind, there is any legitimate market for penny stocks in the United States?

Mr. Formato. Well, I believe that there can be--

Mr. Markey. Is there today?

Mr. Formato. I don't believe so. I don't think so.

Mr. Markey. Well, that is a very important statement. Walk through for us, Mr. Formato, a typical case of how the Mafia injects itself into the life of a penny stock, and those people like yourself who would be responsible for marketing these stocks, and how they would derive their profit from this penny stock marketplace.

Mr. Formato. Well, there are people in the Mafia that are known as Easterners. These people are stock promoters, stock consultants, stockbrokers. What they would do is they would take into issue a shell, a blind pool. They would go ahead and give this stock to the close, inside people or nominees of the organized crime people that they work for.

If this particular stock was coming out at a penny, they would get it at a penny. They would then be taken out of that stock, the day the stock opened or the day after or very soon after, at two pennies, three pennies, four pennies, five pennies.

That is just the beginning. The other part of it would be if there were—if it was unit owned, where you would have one share of stock or one Shearson stock convertible to common stock.

They would take these units when they came out and they would strip the warrants. They would keep the warrants for themselves. Then, through the promotion of manipulation of these stocks, the stock would be successfully raised to a price exceeding the price of the warrants.

If the stock was raised to a dollar, for example, and the

warrants were convertible at 25 cents, these people would then go ahead, convert these warrants of 25 cents and make a 75-cent profit. That 75 cents doesn't sound like a lot, but when you have 10 million shares at 75 cents, it becomes a lot. This is the typical deal that is being done.

Mr. Markey. Why is this penny stock market so attractive to organized crime money?

Mr. Formato. Because it is an easy way to hide money and make a lot of money. It is also an easy way to get into the banking industry, because banks are corruptible as well.

Mr. Markey. What, sir?

Mr. Formato. Corruptible, banking people as well. And when you are dealing in large sums of money, banks want your business, and are willing to do things such as cash checks without reporting them to the IRS.

I have walked into a bank and walked out of a bank with a big green garbage bag full of $20 bills, which amounted to over $250,000. I did not fill out a tax form when I walked into that bank. I did not fill one out when I walked out, either. But I did come out with the money.

Mr. Markey. And that was in New Jersey?

Mr. Formato. Yes, it was.

Mr. Markey. When you said earlier that you laughed at the SEC and you laughed at the State regulators, that is a sentiment I would assume is shared by almost everyone who works in the penny stock marketplace?

Mr. Formato. That is a sentiment that is shared by almost everyone that has been in the business, I would say, over a year. You know, new people in the business are all afraid of State regulators and the Securities and Exchange Commission, but it doesn't take someone very long to realize that the Securities and Exchange Commission does not have the power or the funds to go after stock fraud experts, and they are only a civil arm of the justice system.

Criminal references must be made which are very rarely made, and if they are made, you must then have a criminal system, justice system that can go out and successfully indict and convict stock fraud experts, which is a very difficult thing to do.

Mr. Markey. So, your recommendation is that the laws be toughened?

Mr. Formato. I have several recommendations.

MR. MARKEY. Could you deliver them to us at this point?

MR. FORMATO. Yes, I can. As a matter of fact, I would be happy to. I am not saying that I—you know, some of these recommendations you may have already heard. I would like to start off with these recommendations, and if I may be permitted, I would like to finish with a written statement on my recommendations if I can. I feel the written statement is the first and most important one. But I want to use that one last.

One of the recommendations would be promoters or consultant should be licensed, much like a register representative or a stockbroker. They should have at least 5 years experience in the business before they can apply for a promoter's license.

Security violators should not be allowed to act as a promoter or a consultant. All over-the-counter brokerage firms should be required to have a minimum of $1 million bond, and each registered representative should be bonded.

I think that the net capital requirements for over-the-counter brokerage firms should be raised from $30,000 to $300,000. Over-the-counter firms should be required to send a financial statement of their firm and what experience the registered representative has before they can open up an account and make a trade for their customer.

The customer should have to fill out a suitability statement showing annual income and net worth. Based on that, a scale can be used to see how much money, if any, the customer can afford to lose. Pink stocks should be quoted much as NASDAQ stocks. There should be a system worked out for that.

This way, the individual customer does not have to call up the brokerage firm that he bought this particular stock from to get a quote on. He should be able to call any brokerage firm and get a call on his stocks. I think that is one of the biggest problems that customers have.

The only way they can get a quote on a stock that they own, these pink sheet stocks, is they have to go back to where they bought it from in order to get a quote. If you called up Merrill Lynch, they are not going to go and give you a quote unless you are a customer, and then it takes them all day long to get back to you.

So I think a pink sheet stock needs to be quoted like NASDAQ stocks. Blind pools should not be allowed to continue. Blind pools were set up for promoters and for owners of brokerage firms and for organized crime. A blind pool is the promoter's dream. All public companies should be required to do quarterly financial statements with audited annual statements in order to keep trading.

Each registered representative should keep his own diligence file. Any company he recommends should be able to explain why he is recommending this stock. I think you should raise the amount of shares they have to buy or sell before he can raise or lower the price of any stock under $5.

Those are some of the recommendations that I have. Now, if I can, I would like to say, the statement that I am about to read is based on my own personal experience and opinions. I am not saying these things because I want any particular agency to sound good, but because I believe it to be true, and I believe there is a real need to do something now, and I can't stress this enough.

I have traveled and conducted stock manipulations all over the United States. I am sure we are all aware of the headlines regarding insider trading. The Southern District of New York was given a budget and formed a task force, and everyone learned the name Ivan Boesky. Why?

Because through insider trading, he made millions of dollars, but small investors were not hurt by the Ivan Boeskys, they were hurt by people like myself. It is my opinion that the District of New Jersey is one of the few districts that seemed to have a handle on what is taking place across the country in the over-the-counter stock business.

They have successfully prosecuted difficult stock fraud cases like the Laser Arms case. The problem is in the other districts; they were not given a budget, not given the manpower. I myself am very frustrated that a Federal district that I know which has the expertise to not only investigate but also to indict and convict stock manipulators can only do so much because of a shortage of dollars and manpower.

You may be asking yourself why a stock con artist would be frustrated over this. Here is the answer. I have gone through extensive briefing with the FBI in Newark, New Jersey. After what would probably amount to hundreds of hours of telling my story to FBI agents and explaining it until he finally understood the workings of the over-the-counter stock market, he could see the tremendous impact stock manipulations have on thousands of small unsophisticated investors and the millions and millions of dollars being made by very sophisticated stock experts, he was removed from the case and not replaced because of a lack of manpower.

It was frustrating for him to be taken off the case, and even more frustrating for me to know that there would be a good chance that nothing would be done with all the information I had given him because of lack of manpower. It takes knowledgeable people to form a team of experts to stop the blatant out-and-out frauds that are being conducted on a daily basis, not against the sophisticated investors, but the average American citizen who thinks he is buying a piece of his dream, but what he doesn't know is that all he is buying is some promoter's trumped-up story, which brings me back to insider trading.

In the total scope of things, insider trading doesn't even scratch the surface of the thousands and thousands of investors being hurt by stock manipulators like myself. The most important tool needed to tear down their house of fraud and convict these people who committed these acts of fraud with complete disregard, not only to the investing public, but to the whole justice system, is dollars.

There are people I have met that are devoted to ending the long, lucrative careers these criminals have enjoyed. But without the proper funding, they cannot do it. I know they can't do it, and other stock manipulators know it, too.

The first step to ending corruption in the over-the-counter market is to provide the funds that are badly needed. Take away the name white-collar crime, because this is one of the dirtiest businesses there is. I know from a first-hand basis that behind the suits and ties are a lot of real nasty people.

Maybe if the jail sentence is longer, there will be a change in the over-the-counter stock business. Tougher laws is a big part of the answer, but without the right people to enforce the laws, you will never break the circle of criminals that make up such a big part of the over-the-counter stock market.

Mr. MARKEY. Mr. Formato, my time has expired for questions, but you this morning have leveled a blistering, scalding indictment of the entire penny stock market, and you have made the call, I think correctly, for a complete overhaul of the way in which this marketplace is regulated.

I think that you have now brought to the attention of this subcommittee and the country the need for us and for the United States to move in a way that will ensure the integrity of this marketplace and the protection of small investors is guaranteed. We must not rest until we have ensured that those kinds of laws are on the books, and that resources are made available to ensure that these thousands and thousands of people, who on a daily basis are exposed to these unscrupulous practices, are not left to the mercy of the types of operators you have described to us here this morning.

My time has expired. I will turn to recognize for a round of questions, the gentleman from New Jersey, Mr. Rinaldo.

MR. RINALDO. Thank you very much, Mr. Chairman.

Mr. Formato, you mentioned you are an auto mechanic, and then you said you went into the securities business.

MR. FORMATO. Yes.

MR. RINALDO. What year did you go into the securities business?

MR. FORMATO. 1973.

MR. RINALDO. How many years were you in the securities busi-

MR. FORMATO. From 1973 until I came to jail in 1986.

MR. RINALDO. Thirteen years?

MR. FORMATO. Yes, sir.

MR. RINALDO. How many different companies did you work for during that period of time?

MR. FORMATO. Approximately seven, eight.

MR. RINALDO. How many of those were you an owner of or a partner of?

MR. FORMATO. I was an owner in four of them.

MR. RINALDO. Were all those companies crooked?

MR. FORMATO. Yes.

MR. RINALDO. Did you know of any over-the-counter stock that was legitimately utilized in order to finance a legitimate, honest business that was starting out and needed this method of financing?

MR. FORMATO. Well, there are over-the-counter companies that are legitimate companies that start out with legitimate financing, but once the stock gets in the hands of the trader or the promoter or the stockbroker, it then becomes a manipulation. It can start out legitimate, but once it starts trading, it becomes manipulative.

MR. RINALDO. In other words, what you are saying is that every single stock on the over-the-counter market is manipulated?

MR. FORMATO. What I am saying is that every stock that I know of in the over-the-counter industry that is being traded today is being manipulated in one form or another.

MR. RINALDO. Every stock that you know of.

MR. FORMATO. That is correct.

MR. RINALDO. In the pink sheets?

MR. FORMATO. In the pink sheets and on NASDAQ.

MR. RINALDO. Then conceivably, there could be some stocks that are not being manipulated.

MR. FORMATO. Not that I know of.

MR. RINALDO. But there could be. You don't know of them all. Are you familiar with every stock and every pink sheet?

MR. FORMATO. No, I am not. I am not familiar with every stock, but I am familiar with the workings of the pink sheets and the over-the-counter industry, and I am familiar with the trading of these stocks and how these stocks are traded, and I consider myself to be an expert in that area.

MR. RINALDO. Are there any legitimate people in the over-the-counter market?

MR. FORMATO. Yes.

MR. RINALDO. You said you weren't afraid of the SEC, because they didn't have criminal prosecutorial powers in that regard. How about the Justice Department?

MR. FORMATO. I wasn't afraid of the Justice Department. I viewed the brokerage industry as white-collar crime, and if you did get in trouble or you did get indicted, in most cases you would be handed a light sentence, probation, maybe a year at some nice, fancy camp somewhere.

So, on a worst-hand basis, I never envisioned ever getting any major time for any of the crimes that I new I was committing.

MR. RINALDO. You explained to some extent your role with Laser Arms. Could you tell us how the scam worked? For example, how were the investors harmed? How was the test can faked?

MR. FORMATO. The investors were harmed because the company never existed. It wasn't even a corporation. It was in existence in someone's mind. He went out and had the stock certificates printed. He became the transfer agent for the company. He then got a brokerage firm to trade his stock. The stock was manipulated on an upward basis.

Advertisements were put out in newspapers to entice the public to buy this stock. There was a press conference, which was held. We showed the public at our press conference that there was in fact a can that chilled when popped. And how we did that, I got an inventor who I used on a previous stock fraud to make the can for me.

I told him to fill the can with Freon so that when he popped this can, it would chill. I knew from working on cars that Freon would turn cold as soon as it was exposed. So we filled this can with Freon and popped it in front of everyone and it got cold.

It got so cold no one could hold it.

MR. RINALDO. Everything you did so far you knew was in violation of law at that time?

MR. FORMATO. That is correct.

MR. RINALDO. I assume Laser Arms also had phony financials?

MR. FORMATO. That is correct.

MR. RINALDO. And the stock price was manipulated?

MR. FORMATO. Yes, it was.

MR. RINALDO. And you did this deliberately, knowing it was violative of the law?

MR. FORMATO. Yes, sir.

MR. RINALDO. And you did it because you felt the penalties weren't severe enough?

MR. FORMATO. I did it because I knew that if, in fact, I did get caught at this, I never thought that anything serious, as far as penalties of the law could affect me. I never believed for one moment that I would go to jail over any stock fraud that I committed.

MR. RINALDO. Your opinion has been changed, I assume?

MR. FORMATO. Yes, sir.

MR. RINALDO. What is Equities Processing and Clearing Corporation? You didn't mention that in any of your testimony.

MR. FORMATO. Equities Processing was a company again which was formed by Marshall Zolp, which was used to promote a book that he had written. Also, it was used for us to transfer dollars from the Laser Arms stock fraud into that company. We did transfer moneys from brokerage firms out in Denver and in Mexico to New Jersey, to a bank in New Jersey into Equities Processing and Clearing Corporation.

MR. RINALDO. How does it relate to an SEC order freeing assets at Reliance Savings and Loan in Rahway, New Jersey?

MR. FORMATO. It relates to that because the dollars that were in Equities Processing came from the Laser Arms stock fraud. And the SEC was able to make the connection and follow the trade of dollars leading from Laser Arms to Equities Processing and Clearing Corporation, even though we tried and we tried very, very hard to cover the trail, we fought the SEC, we invented principles of equities financing, we had people commit perjury to say that this money belonged to them and did not belong to Marshall Zolp or Larry Formato did not have anything to do with the transfer of those dollars. The SEC was able to prove that these dollars did account from Laser Arms stock fraud.

Mr. RINALDO. You have not stigmatized an industry, you have indicted an entire industry, yet the testimony that you gave in the criminal trial of Marshall Zolp, according to materials that the subcommittee has received, had contradictory statements in it by yourself, and you yourself have admitted now that you engaged in various frauds.

Obviously, over the years, you have lied repeatedly time and time again. Is there any reason why we have to believe everything you say?

Mr. FORMATO. No, you don't have to believe anything I say. I am here because I want to be here. I am not here because it is going to shorten the length of time that I stay in jail. I am here because I have, over the years that I have been in jail, had the opportunity to think back, to recollect, to recall everything I have done with my own personal life.

I am not here to wave a banner or a flag and say Larry Formato has redeemed himself. Larry Formato is a criminal. I know that, but I would like to be able to look my son in the eyes some day, and know that maybe, just maybe, I was able to do something to redeem myself a little bit.

Mr. RINALDO. What kind of legislation do you think is needed to prevent what has been described here today from ever happening again?

Mr. FORMATO. I think you need, as I stated earlier, tougher laws. It is not that no one is trying. They are trying. The SEC tries very hard. I gave a deposition to the SEC maybe a year ago regarding one of the stock frauds that I mentioned, which was Data Force International, which goes back to 1981, but yet, a year ago, I gave them a deposition.

You are talking 8 years later, the SEC is getting around to trying to do something about a stock fraud that took place 8 years prior. It is just not enough people working, not enough money to get the job done.

Mr. RINALDO. Do you think we need tougher penalties also?

Mr. FORMATO. You definitely need tougher penalties. I think

without a doubt, jail, not prison camps, jail is a deterrent. I have not spent my time in jail in a camp. I have not enjoyed a lucrative or pleasant jail life. I am not saying it to get sympathy here from anyone. I am just telling you that jail, in my opinion, is one of the biggest deterrents to end what is going on in the industry today.

MR. RINALDO. Is there any reason why you admitted, or omitted I should say, in your testimony so far, the boiler room operations involving Eve Computer?

MR. FORMATO. No, I have no problem in talking about that at all.

MR. RINALDO. Will you describe it to the committee?

MR. FORMATO. Sure.

Eve Computer Corporation is a subsidiary—was a subsidiary of another company called Computer Technology, which was an underwriting done by Royer Securities. Royer Securities, by the way, was the leader brokerage firm that I used in Worldwide Ventures.

What I did, I became a consultant to Computer Technology. It was through my dealings with Chuck Rothstein that I was able to take Eve Computer, merge it into a company which was a privately held company called International Trade and Management that I owned.

We then put together a product placement memorandum and hired an expert boiler room operation out in California. I believe we sold upwards to $300,000 worth of Eve Computer Corporation on a private placement basis.

This was not a public company. We sold this with the promise that Eve Computer Corporation would be merged into a public company or would be going public on its own.

MR. RINALDO. We are going to have to break in a moment, because we have a vote on. But let me ask you one question. Maybe you can give a quick answer to what I got lost on. You mentioned the role of organized crime and penny stock fraud. You said it is all-pervasive. That, in effect, there are no over-the-counter stocks sold or penny stocks sold without organized crime involvement. Could we explain that in greater detail? How they get involved in every single stock on the pink sheets?

MR. FORMATO. Well, they get involved through the promoters and through the owners of the brokerage firms or through the managers of the brokerage firms or through the traders that are trading these stocks. Some way or another, one form or another, organized crime has their hand on the shoulder of someone inside every over-the-counter brokerage firm that is making any kind of money in the industry.

MR. RINALDO. Thank you very much, Mr. Formato. I can only repeat what the chairman said. You have been very, very helpful to this subcommittee, and I can assure that you that we will do our best to come up with the kind of tough legislation needed so that people don't go to farms, but go to jail and serve long sentences, and the sentences are long enough that it will deter anyone else from engaging in the kind of tactics that you engaged in that fleeced innocent people, by your own testimony, of millions and millions of hard-earned dollars.

MR. MARKEY. The gentleman's time has expired. There is a roll call on the floor right now. Mr. Wyden has left a little bit early so he can come back and reassemble the hearing prior to my return, and that will probably be within the next 2 to 3 minutes.

So, let's take a brief 2- to 3-minute recess, and may I again just remind everyone, stay on this side of the protective curtain which is around the witness. Thank you. We will take a brief recess.

[Brief recess.]

MR. WYDEN [presiding]. The subcommittee will come to order.

Mr. Formato, the chairman will be right back. It will be a little bit of a juggling day. Let me ask you, if I might, you described that in the past you and others that worked in the field essentially laughed at the SEC and were not at all concerned that they could do anything at all to, in effect, deter your conduct or impose any punishment.

That was in the past, and after that conduct took place, as you know, the SEC approved a new regulation. It was a regulation dealing with cold calls essentially requiring brokers to obtain a written sales agreement with a buyer, an irregularity.

And as a result, this has been in effect heralded as a step that would make a difference. I have a Wall Street Journal article in August with the headline, "SEC Curbs Bad Penny Stock Sales."

My question to you is, do you think that the new regulation that the SEC has just adopted is really going to make a difference against the unlawful conduct that you have described here this morning?

MR. FORMATO. No, I am not really that familiar with that new regulation, but I am assuming, though, by what you are telling me that the prospective customer receives a form which he signs and states the information that he has received from the man.

I can tell you that on many occasions, private placements

that I have done there is often a suitability questionnaire, and the suitability of the customer, whether or not he can afford to invest in a private placement where there would be no liquidity for a period of 2 years or longer.

I can tell you that I told these prospective customers to sign it, don't worry about it, and they do just sign it and don't worry about it. It is also the same thing as when the SEC sends out questionnaires to customers when they are investing a stock, and they ask the customer who sold you this stock?

What was told to you about this stock? Were any promises made? And the customer gets this, and he is the average citizen who wants to do the right thing, but he is nervous. He calls up his stockbroker. I just got this in the mail, what does it mean?

He says, don't worry about it, throw it in the garbage, it doesn't mean anything. Don't even bother answering it, and they do throw it away. Not many of them answer it. These are the problems. I don't know whether or not this new law that the SEC has adopted will or will not work.

MR. WYDEN. I just listened to your testimony and then your comments in response to my question, and it is hard to see how this is actually going to curb, as the headline says, bad penny stock sales. We appreciate the answer. Tell me how you came to choose to be a stock promoter rather than a broker? Is it because you felt that this gave you more leeway and there was less oversight and less regulation?

Is this another loophole that we ought to be looking at?

MR. FORMATO. No. I became a stock promoter because when I was president of Royer Securities, Royer Securities had several violations from the Securities and Exchange Commission and the National Association of Security Dealers, and I entered into an agreement with the Securities and Exchange Commission that I did not admit guilt nor did I deny guilt, but that I would not own a brokerage firm again.

So, therefore, I became a stock promoter. However, I can tell you that I did own brokerage firms after Royer Securities. Maybe not in my name, but certainly I did.

MR. WYDEN. You made my point, though; you sort of came back into the business even though you agreed not to be a broker essentially through the promoter route, even though eventually you proceeded with these brokerage activities as well?

Mr. Formato. Yes.

Mr. Wyden. That is one of the things that we learned in our hearing in Oregon as well, that what happens is even if an action is taken, and they seem to be relatively rare, against a broker, people come back as the so-called consultant, people come back as the so-called promoter and that is helpful.

Let me ask you one other question about how you and others in the field looked at government on these issues, the SEC, prosecutors and others. Was it your sense that they really were very unlikely to address the small investor issue? Was there almost a sense that prosecutors, regulators and others felt that small investor cases were at the bottom of the list in terms of priority, and you had a pretty good chance to get away with it if you targeted small investors, retired people, inexperienced people?

Was that part of the thinking?

Mr. Formato. I think it was more or less that, not so much that prosecutors looked at it as though it was, you know, small investors. I think it was more than when you committed these frauds in most cases if you had a good securities criminal lawyer, the deal that you made with the Securities and Exchange Commission that they do not make a criminal reference, I think that is one of the most important things.

When you are outdoing the stock deal and you know the Securities and Exchange Commission is going to come down and eventually put an end to this, you know, I ought to point out to you that if the Securities and Exchange Commission suspects there is something wrong in the trading of a particular stock, they can halt the trading of that stock for 10 days.

Within that period of time, they look at the company; they review any financial statements that the company has. But if they want to get an injunction preventing that company from trading, again it can take them as long as a year or longer. After 10 days, there is nothing that they can do to stop that stock from trading again.

There is nothing they can do to stop me from opening up the market again at a higher price than what they shut it down at and dumping all of my shares and walking away and then telling my lawyer to go to the SEC and make a deal. Tell them that I won't get involved in that deal again.

Mr. Wyden. And this was perceived as something done fairly frequent. That you could make one of these deals, and that the likelihood of a criminal referral was not very high?

MR. FORMATO. That is correct.

MR. WYDEN. Let me ask you a couple of others, and I will recognize my colleague. Utah has gone to an approach where promoters of blank checks and blind pool offerings hold investor funds in escrow until they declare what business they would enter into.

Do you think something like that would make a difference if the Federal Government pursued it?

MR. FORMATO. No. As I stated earlier, I was involved with Laser Arms. I was also involved in a blind pool. At the same time, by the name of Oxford, I believe it was Oxford Financial. I don't recall really the exact title, but Oxford for sure.

In any event, Oxford was a blind pool, and we were raising $300,000 in Oxford, and there were warrants attached as well. When all was said and done, if we were successful in completing the conversion of the warrants, a total of about $5 million would be raised through this $300,000 public offering.

But the important thing that I want to mention to you is we controlled every share of that $300,000. The investing public did not get one share. We had the entire, what is referred to as the box, all the stock, myself and my partners.

MR. WYDEN. I read a recent article that indicated that a substantial percentage of those who had been involved in penny stock initial public offering were either people who had been felons or securities violators or in some way individuals who were targets of law enforcement actions.

Would you say that is essentially correct? Is it something like a half of the people who are involved in these initial offerings are those that have not exactly been interested in some of the niceties of the law?

MR. FORMATO. Well, I don't know what the numbers are, the percentages, but I know that in most cases, if a company is going public, as I stated before, the company could be legitimate, but one way or another, once that company starts trading, it stops being legitimate.

MR. WYDEN. One last question.

What do you think about the lack of disclosure between a bid and ask price and then the mark-ups that penny stocks can charge as a result? It has been said that if, for example, a customer is being

271

offered a stock for $3 a share, but knows he can only sell it for $1.50 a share, that perhaps not so many people would be ripped off in the penny stock market. Do you think that that is correct, and if so, do you think it would make sense to have more disclosure of business and ask prices as a way to deal with this?

MR. FORMATO. I don't think it makes any difference. I sold as a broker millions of shares of stock, and I always gave the bid and the ask price to my customers, and I always told them that it was not an issue that they were losing 50 percent of their dollars before he even got started, that that stock would also go higher.

So, it is not a question of disclosing where the bid and ask price of the stock is now, it is the dream you are selling the investor for tomorrow, not today.

MR. WYDEN. I want to recognize my colleague from New Mexico, but your testimony has been helpful. It has been very, very hard to get the small investor back in the market in many respects ever since the problems we saw, Black Monday and Black Tuesday. I think what we are learning about penny stocks is once again going to represent a very serious problem if it is not curtailed.

I think it will be another reason for some of those small investors to stay out of the market because they just don't want to get caught up in this kind of coast-to-coast field of rip-offs and frauds. You have been very helpful, and we are going to pursue your suggestions.

Let me recognize my colleague from New Mexico.

MR. RICHARDSON. Mr. Formato, because of your testimony to this committee today on penny stock fraud, do you fear for your life or safety from organized crime or mafia?

MR. FORMATO. I don't know that is so much my testimony today. I mean, I have been in the witness protection program now for 3 years. I think it is a combination of a lot of things, and, yes, I do think my life is in danger.

MR. RICHARDSON. You do?

MR. FORMATO. Yes.

MR. RICHARDSON. You have mentioned organized crime several times. Could you be more specific to this committee about names of alleged families, where they operate? Is that within the realm of what you might be able to tell this committee today? When you say organized crime, are you talking about mafia? Are you talking about drug entities that might not be mafia? Could you be more specific?

MR. FORMATO. I am talking about the mafia.

MR. RICHARDSON. Could you be more specific about names and where they operate and what--

MR. FORMATO. They operate all across the country, and I am not prepared at this point to mention any names of any particular organized crime members that I myself am associated with or was associated with, I should say, or any other groups. I can only tell you that organized crime as I know it, the mafia, reaches across this country and reaches and touches every securities brokerage firm through either a stock promoter, through a stock trader or a stock broker.

MR. RICHARDSON. In what percentage, in your judgment, of the penny stock transactions is there mafia involvement? Are you saying it is 100 percent, 80 percent?

MR. FORMATO. What I am saying to you is this, that a stock promoter, in order to be successful as a stock promoter, can never be connected to an organized crime family if he wants to survive.

MR. RICHARDSON. You have made a fairly comprehensive allegation that the entire penny stock business is fraudulent.

MR. FORMATO. It is.

MR. RICHARDSON. What percentage of the transactions, in your judgment, involves some kind of mafia involvement?

MR. FORMATO. Well, you know, again, I don't want you to get the wrong impression here. What I am trying to tell you is that I was in organized crime. If I am doing a stock deal and I am making money off that stock deal and organized crime is making money off that stock deal, if I go out and tell a market maker to make a market in a particular stock, then that market-maker, because he is doing business with me, is doing business with organized crime.

MR. RICHARDSON. To what extent does organized crime involve itself in penny stock operations as fronts for laundering drug profits?

MR. FORMATO. I don't know.

MR. RICHARDSON. Is there any laundering of drug profits through the penny stock fraud operations?

MR. FORMATO. I don't know anything about drug profits.

MR. RICHARDSON. The case in California, Mr. Minkow was alleged by the Chief of Police of Los Angeles, Mr. Gates, of basically operating the penny stock scam there as part of a drug laundering operations. Is there, to your knowledge, any connection between drugs and penny stock fraud?

MR. FORMATO. I do not know.

MR. RICHARDSON. Would you care to speculate? Is it likely or unlikely?

MR. FORMATO. I wouldn't even want to venture a guess. I have no idea.

MR. RICHARDSON. What is the main problem here? Are you saying that the SEC basically turns another ear to this problem? Is it lack of any kind of staff enforcement? Is it that they are just not doing their job? You have been fairly comprehensive in your indictment of any kind of oversight. Is there anything that in your judgment the SEC can do that would ameliorate this situation?

MR. FORMATO. Well, I gave you some ideas that I myself have of what they can do in the future. As far as what is being done in the present, I just don't know. I mean, if you wanted to get out of jail, when I get out of jail and go back into the brokerage industry disguise myself, use a different name, or even go back—I could. There isn't any Federal law barring me from being in the business of selling securities or being involved with public companies. I can be involved if I want to be. A Federal judge never barred me from being involved with a public company. I think there is something wrong. Somebody should say, "Wait a second. How come they never disbarred this guy from being involved with a public company?"

If I want to go out and start a public company tomorrow and disclose the fact I am in jail and disclose the fact I have committed security frauds in the past, as long as I make that disclosure, I am not breaking the law.

MR. RICHARDSON. I want to try to get a little more specific about the organized crime involvement. Are you saying that they are involved in every aspect of penny stocks? Are they involved, for instance, in the telemarketing, the hard sale to these poor defenseless people called 3 or 4 times? What is organized crime's involvement? You have given it a broad brush. I think if we are going to get anywhere, we need a few more specifics.

MR. FORMATO. I mean their involvement is in giving the support, their full support, to people like myself. That is their involvement. Their reward is in sharing the millions and millions of dollars that are made.

MR. RICHARDSON. My last questions is, in your specific case, the development of the self-chilling aluminum beer can, the public was ripped off for about $2 million worthless stock. What is the status of that case? Have those individuals who have lost their money been compensated, or have they lost that altogether?

Mr. Formato. I believe there was about $600,000 or $900,000 recovered from that particular stock fraud, and that was distributed to the investing public that have lost money, but I believe there is still at least $1 million lost by the public, $1.5 million.

Mr. Richardson. One last question. In your judgment, is the Justice Department, the enforcement Agency of this country that obviously you are working with now, are they pursuing this matter as aggressively as they should?

Mr. Formato. I think that if the funds were there, they would certainly pursue it. I think they are pursuing it as aggressively as they can. It is not that they don't want to. They want to.

Mr. Richardson. They are not doing it because of a lack of funds?

Mr. Formato. That is right. Funds create manpower. Without manpower obviously nothing can get done.

Mr. Richardson. And it is not a lack of political will or direction from anybody at the top?

Mr. Formato. Not that I know of, no.

Mr. Richardson. Thank you.

Mr. Markey. The gentleman's time has expired. The Chair recognizes the gentleman from Oregon once again.

Mr. Wyden. Thank you, Mr. Chairman.

Just a couple questions, and briefly. One of the things that concerns me is that you have suggested we put additional requirements on people going into the business, licensing and the like. What concerns me, though, is it doesn't seem to me, no matter how many requirements we impose, people go to jail, they get disbarred, and somehow they keep coming back in the business. They come back in the business as consultants; they come back in the business as promoters. What do you think really would be accomplished by just imposing more of these requirements?

Mr. Formato. Well, one of the requirements that I think should be imposed is that a stock promoter should not be allowed to be a stock promoter if he has security violations. A stock promoter should be registered like the stockbroker. So I think that would end probably 75 percent of the problem right there.

If you take away—it is much like the drug problem. If you take away the supplier, you don't have to worry about the guy that is dealing in the street. The stock promoter is the supplier; he is supplying the product to the brokerage firms.

Mr. WYDEN. Do you think sanctions should be considered since firms who hire people that have been disbarred or otherwise kicked out of the business?

Mr. FORMATO. Well, I think that if a brokerage firm hires someone who has been kicked out of the business, then I think they should be required to not only just monitor his actions but required to put up some sort of bond protecting the public from whatever this individual may do, because a securities violator will always be a securities violator unless he really knows the full wrath of the law.

Mr. WYDEN. I think that that kind of suggestion is where the rubber really hits the road, because, you know, just barring them from taking one title or another does seem to have done it in the past. We tell them they can't be a broker, then they are this. We tell them they can't be something else, and they come back somewhere else, and maybe that kind of monitoring arrangement plus some requirement that money actually be put up to cover what could be continued wrong-doing might be the way to proceed.

Thank you, Mr. Chairman.

Mr. MARKEY. The gentleman's time has expired.

Mr. FORMATO, what I would like to ask you to do is take a minute to tell us what you want this committee to remember, as we go through the next several months in deliberations on this penny stock issue.

Give us your summary of what you think we should keep in the back of our minds.

Mr. FORMATO. I think you should all remember that what you are hearing from me is something from someone who has had the experience and lived the day-to-day life from the time he wakes up until the time he goes to sleep of stock manipulations and working stock deals, and that unless you people do something to stop stock promoters, so-called consultants to public companies, traders that are allowed to move the price of a stock up or down just based on a whim, shorting stocks, you people must be able to get laws passed to stop, as I stated earlier, the blatant out and out frauds that are being conducted by brokerage firms, over-the-counter brokerage firms, that maybe—not because they want to, but because there is someone like Larry Formato who tells them you better make a market in the stock, you better move the prices of the stock up or you will pay.

That is what needs to be done. Cut out the Larry Formatos, get rid of the stock promoters, and then you can have a clean over-the-counter industry.

Mr. Markey. Mr. Formato, this has been an extraordinary piece of testimony, which has been delivered to our subcommittee. We thank you very much for having the courage to appear before us today, and as the weeks and months go by, as we continue to work on these issues, we are going to stay in close contact with you. I think that there is a ring of truth to what you are saying, and I don't think it is lost on those who serve on this committee.

You have provided an important public service here today, and we thank you.

We will take a 5-minute break so that we can adjust the witness table and so that Mr. Formato can be escorted from the room by security. So if we can just take a brief break right now.

[Brief recess.]

VISIONARY CRAIG MCCAW'S
TOUGHEST TEST

HOW THE MAFIA
MANIPULATES STOCKS

A GOLD-BACKED
RUBLE?

DECEMBER 25, 1989   THREE DOLLARS SEVENTY-FIVE CENTS

Forbes

THE GLOBAL WARMING PANIC

A CLASSIC CASE OF OVERREACTION

The names of the brokerages change, but the same people continue to play the same games with penny stocks. And behind the scenes, organized crime.

"Like a slaughter-house for hogs"

By Richard L. Stern
and Claire Poole

Lorenzo Formato is a car mechanic turned stock manipulator turned state's witness. He was once a broker at Robert Brennan's infamous First Jersey Securities (Forbes, July 16, 1984). In September, wearing a bag over his head, he appeared at a congressional hearing in Washington describing the major role played by the Mafia in the manipulation of low-priced stocks—so-called penny stocks, although they frequently sell for much more than a dollar.

Organized crime members have participated in "thousands of manipulations" of stocks, said Formato. Where are the Securities & Exchange Commission and the National Association of Securities Dealers? "I used to laugh at the sec," Formato testified. Fines? Suspensions! Merely the cost of doing business for the mob.

Formato is right. Forbes reporters have investigated the penny stock business and concluded that mob-controlled firms launder dirty money and steal millions from gullible investors through boiler-room-type sales operations that market and manipulate the stock of worthless public companies.

Mob activities even spill over into more conventional stocks. Forbes has learned of a major investigation by the Manhattan district attorney's office. Reportedly it is not only investigating penny stocks but also allegations that mob members and their friends made millions with insider information before Merv Griffin announced his bid for Resorts International.

So entrenched are organized crime figures in the low-priced stock business that the people in it have developed their own vocabulary. The stock technicians who front for the mob are known as "earners," or "easterners" because they generally work out of

A hooded Lorenzo Formato goes before a congressional subcommittee
"I needed the strength of organized crime . . . and they needed me to be a money machine."

FORBES, DECEMBER 25, 1989

279

DANGEROUS WAYS

Florida, New York and New Jersey.

At a federal trial in Brooklyn, N.Y. next year Formato may testify how World Wide Ventures, a company of which he was president, was used as part of a conspiracy to steal more than $8 million via loans from the busted Flushing Federal Savings & Loan. Some of the loans were collateralized by allegedly overpriced land in Pennsylvania's Pocono Mountains that was owned by World Wide, a public company of little value. Formato and friends also allegedly made out big by pushing the stock on gullible investors with rumors that the company was about to market a nifty new fire-escape ladder or build a fabulous Pocono resort. Among the defendants in the Flushing case: the bank president, Carl Cardascia, and Jilly Rizzo, long-time friend of Frank Sinatra.

Formato described to congressional investigators a symbiotic relationship between the mob and its promoters. "I needed the protection, and I needed the strength of organized crime, and they needed me to wash money for them. They needed me to form companies for them. They needed me to be a money machine, and that's what I became, a money machine." Brokers and traders—some of them at legitimate firms—who've gotten involved in the manipulation of mob-run stocks tell stories of death threats when they try to sell out or sell short while the mob is moving a stock up.

Pericles (Perry) Constantinou, a stock promoter under indictment in New York for stock manipulation in a company called Memory Metals, had refused to pay some brokers $400,000 for stock in a company called Keystone Medical. Federal documents say Bonanno family capo Frank Coppa, his associate Eric Wynn and other friends paid a visit to Constantinou and bashed him on the side of the head with a telephone.

Then there was Marshall Zolp (FORBES, June 2, 1986), who is serving six years for manipulating Laser Arms, a nonexistent public company that supposedly had a self-cooling soda can. Zolp got help from the Bonanno and the Pagano families. But when the "earner" stopped earning, he was kidnapped and beaten.

"The mob in the stock business is even better at squeezing out profits

Lorenzo Formato (right), working for World Wide Ventures.
Promoting a resort that never happened.

than a slaughterhouse for hogs," says Newark, N.J. assistant U.S. attorney Robert Warren. "They even use the oink."

A good example is F.D. Roberts. Started in 1985, it had over 200 boiler-room salesmen in New Jersey and Florida. The public lost upwards of $140 million in over a score of stock offerings before Roberts went out of business last February. The case is typical: By the time the barn door is locked, scores of horses are stolen.

One former Roberts president, Sheldon Kanoff, a former SEC official, recently pleaded guilty to stock fraud charges. He testified that cash was funneled from Roberts to organized crime figures who held an undisclosed interest in the brokerage. Albert Weiss, who was treasurer and later president, has admitted he arranged for fictitious salary and bonus increases to Kanoff and others at Roberts. Kanoff told the court he turned back part of his salary in the form of cash for distribution to the mob through Richard (Rick) Galiardo, brother of ex-Roberts chairman Fred Galiardo.

Enforcement officials estimate Roberts' annual gross profits at $60 million in 1987 and 1988. Where did all that cash go? U.S. law enforcement authorities reportedly have linked at least part of the Roberts operation to Joseph (Joe Butch) Corrao, whose son Vince worked for the firm. They identify Joe Butch as a capo in the Gambino crime family that is headed by John Gotti.

The mob has many faces. One difficulty the authorities have in dealing with stock manipulation crime is that almost as soon as they shut down one mob front, the same characters emerge under a new one. A firm

known as Southeast Securities of Florida, which actually was situated in Hoboken, N.J., was the apparent predecessor of Roberts. Southeast was shut down by the SEC for net capital violations in 1984. And even as pressure was building a year ago on Roberts, its principals were setting up two new firms—but this time unsuccessfully.

Although Southeast and Roberts show Gambino family ties, the firms also have lent a hand to the Colombos. One of Southeast's offerings was a stock called Big Apple Farms, which according to SEC documents had links to the now all but defunct Joe Colombo family. Federal officials note that families often work together.

Just how do the earners operate? An example was the Roberts firm's manipulation of Hughes Capital Corp.

One of the promoters was Lionel Reifler, who has served time for stock fraud and has been implicated but not indicted in the Flushing case. Reifler, who has pleaded guilty to manipulating Hughes stock, has testified that various organized crime figures and Roberts officials had "sitdowns" to plan the scam and divide up the spoils.

The Hughes manipulation started with what is known in the stock scam game as "stox in a box." In Hughes' case, that meant that Roberts, instead of widely distributing a public offering of 90,000 Hughes units at $each, actually placed them in 33 nominee accounts, mostly controlled by Reifler and Roberts Chairman Galiardo. From late August 1986 F.D. Roberts hucksters worked the telephones, selling Hughes to the public at higher and higher prices—$12 by early 1987. The sales pitch was as simple as it was false: Hughes was going to acquire other firms.

Meanwhile, the nominee accounts sold stock that had been part of the units at $2.25 and exercised hundreds of thousands of warrants at prices ranging from $2.50 to $4.50 a share. The stock converted from the warrants was sold back to Roberts at higher and higher prices. The SEC suspended trading in February 1987, and investors discovered the stock was worthless. Needless to say, the easterners got their previously agreed upon percentages.

For every such fraud uncovered,

dozens more go scot-free.

One that got caught was Renaissance Enterprises. It went public in 1984, raising $750,000, supposedly to get into the jewelry business. Instead, almost $700,000 went to promoters related to the Bonanno crime family. The company's books show receivables for bogus sales and debts for merchandise that the company never purchased. Where were the accountants? According to federal documents, some were cooking the books to conceal how money was being siphoned off to the mob.

Among the promoters were Wynn and Coppa, the boys who federal authorities say helped beat up Perry Constantinou. Documents show Wynn putting a $52,000 down payment on a house with funds that were filtered through a supplier. Wives of Wynn and Coppa received salaries from another supplier, allegedly to launder stolen money into IRS-reportable income.

Wynn, 30, is now serving a three-year prison term after pleading guilty to a tax charge. Court documents say he was taking orders from Coppa. The FBI has identified Coppa as a Mafia captain who in the 1970s trafficked in drugs and robbed banks. Coppa now runs a number of bus companies in New Jersey and allegedly controls a bus drivers' union local.

Investigators are also looking into an alleged partnership Wynn had with Barry Davis, formerly Barry Sutz, in a widely publicized, and still operating, 900-number telephone advisory service called Traders & Investors Alert. Davis, who has a long history of stock violations and is banned from the industry, allegedly recommended some of the mob's favorite stocks.

The brokerage firm that brought Renaissance public was New York City-based Monarch Funding, run since it was formed in 1965 by Leo Eisenberg. He has been the subject of numerous SEC stock manipulation investigations and NASD censures going back to 1971. In 1954 Eisenberg was criminally convicted for making a phony FHA application.

Over the years Monarch has been associated with a number of stock promoters who federal authorities say

have links to the underworld. Among them: Tommy Quinn, a disbarred former Genovese family lawyer. Although banned from the securities business, he found a home at Monarch as a stock promoter until 1983, when he reportedly got into a squabble with Genovese family capo Anthony (Fat Tony) Salerno.

Quinn, whose most recent address is a French jail, hightailed it to Europe and teamed up with stock swindler Arnold Kimmes to run overseas stock rackets that brought U.S. boiler rooms and apparently lots of Mafia-related stocks to the rest of the world (Forbes, Sept. 23, 1985; Jan. 9).

As for Monarch, after almost 20 years of namby-pamby civil complaints, the U.S. attorney's office in

Barry Davis (center) a.k.a. Barry Sutz
Pushing the mob's favorite stocks?

New Jersey in November filed criminal fraud charges involving at least six stocks against Eisenberg, stock promoter Richard O. Bertoli and former Wood Gundy research analyst Richard Cannistraro, who has done time for securities fraud. Bertoli, according to federal documents, was the accountant for Aniello Dellacroce, the late underboss of the Gambino family.

In Monarch, federal documents allege a complex game of shifting money and stocks between nominee accounts in the U.S. and the Cayman Islands. Besides swindling the public, these charges suggest they avoided income taxes and hid the stock scams' true benefactors.

Government documents allege, for instance, that stock analyst Cannistraro used a nominee account in 1983 to turn a $1,600 investment in a stock

called High Tech he helped manipulate into an $80,000 profit. To avoid paying taxes on the income—the government alleges—Cannistraro's nominee account paid $80,000 for warrants that were about to expire in a company called Cinematronics. The purported losses offset the gain on High Tech. The seller of the warrants? Allegedly a nominee account controlled by Cannistraro in the Cayman Islands. Presto chango. The warrants expire. Cannistraro can show an $80,000 loss against an $80,000 gain, and he travels to the Caymans to pick up his $80,000 in cash.

In this case, the authorities have likely uncovered a system used in thousands of instances of tax evasion and money laundering.

If the regular watchdogs of the securities industry—the SEC and NASD—have been relatively ineffective in fighting organized crime, some state and federal law enforcement officials are doing an excellent job, especially in New Jersey, traditionally a hotbed of organized crime. In Newark, N.J., Assistant U.S. Attorney Robert Warren has been tenacious, so much so that he recently received a backhanded compliment when he was described in open court by Bertoli as a "scoundrel." His counterpart on the state level is Richard Barry, head of New Jersey securities enforcement.

There are indications that FBI task forces in the East and in a number of cities around the country (Las Vegas, Denver, Salt Lake City, for instance) are now working with U.S. attorneys to bring criminal actions. They are looking into mob-connected relationships in recently defunct brokers such as Power Securities out of Denver and Las Vegas and Investors Center out of Long Island, which at their height operated boiler rooms with more than 1,600 salesmen.

Handicapped until recently because they had little knowledge of manipulation techniques, the law enforcement people have learned a lot in the past few years, in part from Forbes articles on the subject. They have learned, too, that there is political and media mileage to be gotten from prosecuting stock swindlers. ∎

CONGRESSIONAL WITNESS: WIELDS POWER IN OVER-THE-COUNTER STOCK MARKET

JOHN M. DOYLE, Associated Press

Sep. 7, 1989 12:13 PM ET

WASHINGTON (AP) _ A convicted penny stock swindler told a House subcommittee today that large segments of the nation's over- the-counter stock market are "controlled by organized crime."

Lorenzo Formato, a former penny stock broker and promoter now in the federal Witness Protection Program, testified that "organized crime has their hand on the shoulder of someone inside any (over-the-counter) brokerage that's making money."

He acknowledged, however, that while there are legitimate companies offering their stocks over-the-counter - that is, not listed on any stock exchange - they are often manipulated by brokers, promoters or salesmen.

Formato, who acknowledges ties to organized crime, entered the crowded hearing room surrounded by federal marshals and wearing a gray hood with holes for his mouth, nose and eyes. He testified from behind a screen with his voice altered deliberately to protect his identity.

According to a survey by state securities regulators, American investors have been cheated out of at least $2 billion a year by crooked schemes involving the low-cost, high-risk securities called penny stocks.

Formato, testifying before the House telecommunications and finance subcommittee, told of raising the prices of Utah-based oil stock from $2 per share to $8 per share and then taking their profits and abandoning the venture and investors.

"The people who bought the stocks lost their money," he said.

"Penny stock swindles are now the No. 1 threat of fraud and abuse facing small mom-and-pop investors in the United States," said Rep. Edward J. Markey, D-Mass., the subcommittee chairman, who called Formato's testimony "a blistering, scalding indictment of the entire penny stock market."

The subcommittee was also scheduled to hear testimony from a Powder Springs, Ga. couple who were victimized by penny stock scam artists and John Baldwin, director of the Utah Division of Securities.

Baldwin is also president of the North American Securities Administrators Association, a Washington-based organization of state securities regulators.

"The evidence is clear and convincing," Baldwin said in a statement to the subcommittee. "Penny stock fraud has evolved into a problem of truly national proportions."

Penny stocks - inexpensive but highly risky securities that usually aren't listed on stock exchanges - are legal, but they usually are issued by new companies with an untested or uneven earnings history.

While their price, a few cents up to a few dollars a share, makes them attractive to small investors with limited funds, they pose a risk because information about the issuing company often is hard to obtain and fraudulent claims are difficult to dispute.

Stocks that aren't traded on the nation's stock exchanges are said to be traded on the over-the-counter market. The largest and most stable over-the- counter stocks are listed with the National Association of Securities Dealers Automated Quotation Service, or NASDAQ, but smaller or newer companies - or those that don't trade frequently or only in a limited area - are quoted on the "pink sheets," or lists of stocks and their prices printed on pink paper. The pink sheets are distributed to brokers and investors can only get a price quote by calling a broker that deals in the company's shares.

In his statement, Baldwin noted that the penny stock market is not populated completely by crooks.

"When not abused, penny stock offerings may serve as an important source of capital for small and often innovative companies," he said. "Howwever, there is convincing and growing evidence that the non-NASDAQ over-the-counter market - the 13,000 stocks trading in the pink sheets - has been substantially overrun by unscupulous promoters pushing worthless or highly dubious stocks." A report on NASAA's 50-state survey of securities regulators noted that investors in legitimate penny stocks "are believed to lose all or some of their investment 70 percent of the time and the presence of fraud pushes up that figure to 90 percent."

While penny stock fraud is not new, it has grown from the phony mining stock scams confined mainly to the Far West in the 1940s and 1950s to widespread interstate schemes.

In Florida, only 5 percent of the registered brokers specialize in penny stocks but they accounted for 40 percent of investor complaints in fiscal year 1988-1989.

NASAA's survey also found that consumer complaints about penny stocks have risen from 1,767 in 1987 to 2,660 in 1988. "Several states have indicated that their offices have been swamped so far in 1989 with new penny stock investor complaints," according to the 98-page report. The Securities and Exchange Commission, which oversees the markets in stocks, bonds and other securities, said it received 1,510 penny stock complaints in all of fiscal 1988 and received 2,462 in the first half of this fiscal year. Last fall, the SEC created a Penny Stock Task Force linking federal and state agencies in a combined effort against fraud.

P.M. BRIEFING : 'Do Something' About Penny Stock, Convicted Stock Swindler Urges

September 07, 1989 | From Times Wire Services

WASHINGTON — A convicted stock swindler, wearing a hood to hide his features, urged Congress today to "do something now" to end what he called rampant fraud and organized crime control of the penny stock market, in which investors lose about $2 billion a year.

"The over-the-counter market is controlled by organized crime, the over-the-counter market is controlled by people like myself," Lorenzo Formato, the convicted stock manipulator, told a House Energy and Commerce subcommittee hearing on problems in the sale of cheaper penny stocks.

He admitted that during the years he promoted and sold penny stocks, "I was involved in organized crime." He said that organized crime gave him protection and that he helped crime figures launder their money.

"They needed me to be a money machine and that's just what I was--a money machine," said Formato, a former auto mechanic. He said he became a stockbroker in 1973 after passing a state test, the answers to which he obtained illegally and memorized beforehand even though "I didn't know what a stock was" at the time.

Investors lose $2 billion a year in penny stock swindles, two-thirds of all the money raised by venture capitalists in 1988, according to a report released by an organization of state securities regulators.

"This is one of the dirtiest businesses there is," Formato said. "Behind the suits and ties I know there are a lot of real nasty people."

Witness Tells of Mob Influence in Penny Stocks

September 08, 1989 | From Associated Press

WASHINGTON – An admitted penny stock scam artist, wearing a hood to conceal his identity, told a House subcommittee Thursday that penny stocks traded over the counter are often controlled by organized crime.

Lorenzo Formato, a former broker and promoter of the inexpensive but highly risky securities known as penny stocks, testified that "organized crime has their hand on the shoulder of someone inside any (over-the-counter) brokerage that's making money."
Formato is now in the federal Witness Protection Program.
He told the Energy and Commerce subcommittee on telecommunications and finance that although there are legitimate companies offering their stocks over the counter, the issues are often manipulated by brokers, promoters or salesmen.
Although their price--a few cents up to a few dollars a share--makes penny stocks attractive to small investors with limited funds, many are prone to abuse because information about the issuing company often is hard to obtain and fraudulent claims are difficult to dispute.
Small or young companies, or those that trade infrequently or in a limited area, are often listed only on so-called pink sheets rather than with larger and more stable companies. Brokers and investors must call a broker that deals in a specific company's shares to get a price quote.

Top Threat to Investors

According to a survey by state securities regulators, American investors have been cheated out of at least $2 billion a year by crooked schemes involving penny stocks.
The National Assn. of Securities Dealers, a self-regulating organization that oversees over-the-counter stock brokers, said any investigation of organized crime links to the industry was in government hands.
"We're cracking down hard on unscrupulous penny stock brokers, but we're not Elliott Ness," said Robert Ferri, a NASD spokesman.
"If an investigation has to go farther than our purview, the law enforcement agency we're dealing with will take it from there. And that's quite often the FBI or the Justice Department."
"Penny stock swindles are now the No. 1 threat of fraud and abuse

facing small mom-and-pop investors in the United States," said Rep. Edward J. Markey (D-Mass.), the subcommittee chairman. He called Formato's testimony "a blistering, scalding indictment of the entire penny stock market."

Formato entered the crowded congressional hearing room surrounded by federal marshals and wearing a gray hood with holes for his mouth, nose and eyes. He testified from behind a screen with his voice altered to protect his identity.

He said he got involved with the mob in his native New Jersey to prevent competitors from trying to undercut him.

"I needed the protection. I needed the strength of organized crime," he said.

But Formato, who is serving a six-year prison sentence, declined to say what organized crime family he was involved with.

Was Key Witness

He pleaded guilty in 1987 to charges of income tax evasion, mail fraud and interstate transportation of money taken in stock fraud, according to Robert Warren, a federal prosecutor in Newark, N.J.

Formato was the government's key witness at the trial of five people later convicted of participating in a penny stock fraud involving a bogus company, Laser Arms Corp., that purported to have developed a self-chilling beverage can.

Formato was described at the trial as one of the masterminds behind the scam. In addition to the five convicted at trial, nine other people pleaded guilty to charges involving Laser Arms.

Formato gave several recommendations for cleaning up the penny stock market, especially tougher penalties.

He said he used to laugh at the Securities and Exchange Commission, the watchdog of the stocks and bonds markets, because it did not have the authority to put him behind bars.

'Truly National Proportions'

"I did not fear the Securities and Exchange Commission," Formato said. "They could only attack me on a civil basis. The people who bought the stocks lost their money."

"There are thousands of people making millions of dollars doing what he did," said John Baldwin, director of the Utah Division of Securities.

Baldwin is also president of the North American Securities Administrators Assn., a Washington-based organization of state securities regulators.

"The evidence is clear and convincing: Penny stock fraud has evolved into a problem of truly national proportions," Baldwin said. A report on NASAA's 50-state survey of securities regulators noted that investors in legitimate penny stocks "are believed to lose all or some of their investment 70% of the time and the presence of fraud pushes up that figure to 90%."

The SEC has created a Penny Stock Task Force and has adopted rules that will make it tougher to sell penny stocks over the telephone.

www.ingramcontent.com/pod-product-compliance
Lightning Source LLC
Chambersburg PA
CBHW051714020426
42333CB00014B/976